Walking to Greenham

WALKING TO GREENHAM

by

Ann Pettitt

HONNO AUTOBIOGRAPHY

Published by Honno
'Ailsa Craig', Heol y Cawl, Dinas Powys
South Glamorgan, Wales, CF6 4AH

Reprinted November 2006

Published with the financial support of the Welsh Books Council

A catalogue record for this book is available from The British Library.

ISBN 1 870206 762

Cover design: G Preston
Cover image: Women for Life on Earth
Illustrations by Ann Pettit

Printed in Wales by Gomer

CONTENTS

Introduction 1

Part i: Walking to Greenham

Chapter 1: A tale of two fences 9

2: Red and blue 13

3: The city and the country 19

4: The anger and the spark 24

5: One - and a roomful of rubble 30

6: Women for Life on Earth 36

7: Walking To Greenham Common
Cardiff, August 26th 1981 48

Part ii: The Witness

Chapter 8: Solange's story 83

9: Zone Interdite, 1942-1943 92

10: The train 102

11: The news is new - January 1943 111

12: Colin 115

13: May 1937 - Eastwards from Berlin! 122

14: September 1981:'Camp one and camp two' . .131

15: Embrace the Base, December 12th 1981 142

Part iii: The Duck of Peace Flies East

Chapter 16: June 4th, 1982 in Maenclochog 157

17: June 4th, 1982, in Moscow 175

18: Welcome to the USSR 184

19: Welcome to the Moscow Group for Trust . . .196

20: Leningrad: Natasha's red gingham kitchen 214

21: Moscow - 1) Apparatchiks 229

22: The Tepid Tea Party .240

23: The red flag shivers and so do we 256

24: The bleak midwinter 272

25: January 1984, Greenham Common 283

26: How the Cold War ended 293

27: The dance - Tourcoing, October 1944 304

Postscript: Thunder and Lightning 309

Photographs 153

For Ben, Gus and Harri

Acknowledgements

I would like to say thank you to everyone at Honno, for offering to publish this book, and to my editor Caroline Oakley – a dab hand with the literary pruning shears – for helping me to put shape into my rag-bag of stories.

I am indebted to the archivist in Tourcoing, Mme Barthelemy, for her help with original testimonies about wartime France and the British soldiers who were hidden by French families; also to John Marshall for his detailed accounts of life with my father in the Communist Party before World War 2, and in Berlin at the end of it.

I am also deeply grateful to all those who read the draft manuscript and gave me helpful feedback, honest criticism and encouragement: Alf Hinkley, Tina Carr, AnneMarie Schone, Karmen Thomas, Mary Donaldson, Sioned-Mair Richards, Monica Pittendreigh, Barry Wade, Ben Pettitt-Wade, Barbara Ollet.

I am especially indebted to Caroline Westgate for her perceptive comments and suggestions about the structure of the book.

To my partner Barry I owe thanks for his constant encouragement and for all the dinners.

Introduction

*How the Peace-camp began and how the arms race
ended*

I love going on long walks. No, that's an understatement, I adore
going on long walks. I am just like an eager-beaver dog, wagging
its tail at the door, in this respect. This is one of the reasons why
I liked the idea of walking to Greenham Common in 1981. We
could have just driven down the motorway. It would have been
quicker and a lot easier, but had we done so, none of the things
that did happen, would have happened.

This book will not be a motorway journey, more the scenic
route. There may be times when you are taken to wartime France,
or perched next to a web-fronted radio in the corner of a front
room in northern England, circa 1940, that you will want to ask,
'Why can't we just get to the point?' Well, this is the reason…

There was a brief moment, the twinkling of an eye, the
proverbial flapping of a butterfly's wing, when it would have been
true to say, no me, no Greenham. No famous and notorious
Women's Peace Camp arousing horror in some and admiration
in others. No 'Greenham Women', in stripey leg-warmers and
woolly hats, living under sheets of plastic in a wood in southern
Britain in the declining days of the twentieth century, imagining
that by doing so they could stop the nuclear arms race between
the world's superpowers, Russia and America.

The fact is that I took a decision in the spring of 1981 and
thus began those particular – and often peculiar – events which

otherwise would not have happened. The decision I took was that I would organise a march to a place not many people had then heard of, the US base at Greenham Common, Berkshire. I wanted it to be a march of women, but to begin with I couldn't find anyone else to come on it, or share it with me, so I thought, 'If I have to, I'll do it on my own.' After that, after I made up my mind that I really would do it solo, if it came to it, I soon found other women to share the organising and thinking of it, and still others to come on it.

That was how I found out that if you have an idea and you want to make it happen, you have to take responsibility for it yourself. That moment really is tiny, vanishingly brief. Then with others, you can organise it, and with luck and goodwill it will grow, just like a baby, just like any living organism, and will learn to walk all by itself.

For many years I held on to this story, not writing it. It sat, maturing, in the compost-heap that is my life. Then one day I went on a walking holiday with a group of women I hadn't previously met. It was in the Howgill fells, the steep-sided round-topped mountains of Westmoreland in the north of England. When a group of open-minded women of different ages get together, they talk about all sorts of things. The talk ranges, often in one sentence, from really big ideas and current affairs, to the minutiae of their lives, from naming the plants around them to sharing their recipes for better health, their losses, their births, stillbirths and miscarriages, their ailments, their parents, their deaths.

'Is humanity heading for extinction? – oh look, a redstart, over there' ... 'Can armies be used to stop other armies committing atrocities against civilians? And who'd like a flap-jack?'

They joke a lot, and often wet their knickers laughing too much, or even, sober as judges, fall over. But when, in the evening, the talk on this occasion turned to their experiences of Greenham Common (it seemed they had all been involved in some way or other) and they asked me if I had ever been there, I said nothing. I didn't know where to begin, and anyway, it was late.

It all reminded me of an earlier time I had spent with groups of women. These were times spent in kitchens with coal fires, and toddlers playing with Lego while we perused articles and pamphlets about nuclear physics, about the three kinds of radiation, about warheads and delivery systems, and pencilled in dates on maps. Then there were times spent dancing down Tarmacadamed roads, or sitting dejected on garage forecourts, in meetings that were stuck, or meetings where everyone suddenly knew what we were going to do. There was a traffic-jam of coaches, buses and cars, all full of women, waving to each other, on a motorway. There were other times sitting with a tiny group under whispering poplar trees around a smoky fire, and times when the woods were full of fires, hundreds and hundreds of them, and women from all over the Western world, it seemed, sitting in the freezing December night, talking, singing, and waiting for the dawn.

The stories began to take on a life of their own and started lining up eagerly in formation, jostling for space and tumbling one on top of the other, peeling off in spirals and ramifications and sub-plots and before I knew it, it was light and I'd been talking all night in my head.

This, the story of that one hundred and ten mile walk and of what happened then, and of what happened when we went to Russia, is the story I wanted to tell those women. As to whether we did what we wanted, which was to stop the nuclear arms race, well we could argue about that for a long time. Most people think that the hoo-hah raised by the Women's Peace Camp could not possibly have made that much of a difference to the world, simply because nobody had heard of us, as individual people I mean, and everyone knows that to change really big things you have to be powerful and famous, like presidents and prime ministers, or kings and queens in the old days. But it was Mr Gorbachev, the leader of Russia, which was then called the Soviet Union, who took the first real step away from the nuclear arms race. He told the United Nations in a speech he made, that it was the people in the peace movement who had made him think about this, they had made him realise that somebody in power had to do something

3

different. He spoke of hardships that had been endured, sacrifices made, as evidence of how deep was their desire for a change. I know this because a friend of mine had just had a baby and she was in a hospital day-room watching the television when Gorbachev came on and said it; and she had been to Greenham when we all held hands around the base, and she thought, 'So we did make a difference then, after all, we made Gorbachev think.'

It was a long time ago, like all the stories in this book, and the baby is grown-up now, but it is still true because we can remember it and we are still alive to say these things. This is why this story begins somewhere in Wales, on the western side of the UK, and ends in the old USSR.

The secret of our success

If you'd rather skip the story and arrive instead at a neat conclusion, some sort of 'lesson to be drawn', turn to the back page. Myself, I always read the end first. Anyway, you already know the ending. What you don't know, is the beginning.

Part i
Walking to Greenham

Woman in pill-box hat and billowing cloak against a stormy sky, Greenham Common

Chapter 1

A tale of two fences

This is a story about two kinds of power and two ways of seeing the world. It is set in the last quarter of the twentieth century, when Europe was divided into two 'sides': a Communist East and a Capitalist West. Already the bones of this story sound so simple as to have a mythic, over-symmetrical quality. For the ruling powers of these two sides were in one fundamental respect identical: each believed the other was possessed by such insane malevolence as to be on the brink of armed invasion, an attack which could only be deterred by the possession of enormous quantities of unbelievably powerful nuclear weapons, enough to render the entire continents of Eurasia and North America burnt, radioactive, sterile deserts. Scientific studies concluded that in the case of war a 'nuclear winter' would occur (because the sun would be so obscured by all the dust, ensuring the mass extinction of higher life forms) and insects would inherit the earth.

This state of existence was called the Cold War, and it began right at the end of the last great 'hot' war, the Second World War. As atomic bombs were road-tested on Japanese enemy civilians by the Americans (who thought this weapon might come in handy should the Russians start getting ideas about expansion), so Stalin, who still ruled Russia, was deciding that this awesomely impressive weapon was also a must-have to forestall any ideas of invasion on the part of the US.

None of the successive rulers of West and East were able

to recognise themselves mirrored in the other. Instead, they created a deadly whirlpool of move and counter-move consisting of successive rounds of 'improvements' and 'modernisations' to their weapons systems, each one a 'response' to the other. The basis for this kind of power is an irrational fear of an enemy whose own powers must always be exaggerated. The modern psychological term for this state is 'paranoia'.

The Cold War was a truly vicious circle, a vortex fuelled by mutual mistrust which constantly re-created its own justification. No politician on either side could resist its suck and pull. To suggest, inside the Kremlin, that the West was too democratic and disparate to be intent on defeating the USSR by military means, would have been traitorous. In the US and Britain, to suggest that the place described by President Reagan as 'The Evil Empire' was run merely by a bunch of frightened, rigidly defensive old men, with no intention of launching all-out nuclear war, but who had convinced themselves that the other side might, was to be weak, unpatriotic and unelectable.

The worlds of East and West were certainly very different, although yet again those few who had intimate knowledge of both would see an ironic symmetry at work. For instance, had the free-market Capitalist West not been obliged, as a result of fifty years of political agitation by its working populations, to incorporate several key elements of socialism – the labour laws, the old age pensions, the health services for example, even extending in some countries to the state ownership of essential industries – the ensuing chaos and misery might well have brought about the demise of the whole winner-takes-all shebang. And similarly, the most casual brush with Soviet daily reality would reveal a thriving, illicit, black market in goods and services not supplied by the blundering, insensitive, inefficient state. Without this parallel system obeying the capitalist laws of supply and demand, run by small-time entrepreneurs whose 'economic crime' would have been heaped with rewards in the West, the entire country, from Minsk to Vladivostok, would have ground to a halt within days.

For the purposes of feeding the flames of the Cold War, for

maintaining a suitably supportive patriotic fervour on the part of the populations of East and West for such a clearly ludicrous form of defensive threat, the differences between East and West had to be exaggerated; the elements of the other within each system were viewed as Trojan horses, with appropriate suspicion. Yet those were the very elements, created by ordinary people in response to the hard facts of human need, which held each society together. Left-wing activists, trade unionists, Communists, made the welfare state, challenged the powerful and made democracy live; small-time crooks who peddled sweet peas and fishing-rods and fresh lettuce on the streets of Russian cities, made the harshness of life in the USSR bearable; people who braved prison to pass round faded carbon copies of dissenting literature, avoided death by boredom.

The boundary between these two over-armoured opposing giants of East and West, these blinded colossi, was given a metaphorical title by that linguistic genius Winston Churchill, who called it 'the Iron Curtain'. This metaphor was also perfectly real. It took the form of a fence running through the middle of Europe. For much of its length, it ran through forests of pine and birch. In cities such as Berlin, it turned into a high wall. The design prototype for all these fences of curved at the top concrete posts and barbed wire may be seen preserved intact at Auschwitz-Birkenau in southern Poland. It was meant to imprison. The fence thus embodied the kind of power which uses physical force, bullying, torture, intimidation, threat; the power of cruelty. It was both real and a symbol. Where people could get at it, in its wall incarnation, it became a huge canvas for graffiti, a riotous wall-newspaper, a glorious work of art, a monument to spiritual freedom.

Also during the Second World War, a patch of 'common' in southern England was fenced around. A common means a place belonging by historical right to the local people for grazing their animals, collecting firewood, picking berries, being out and about. It is a patch of land owned collectively, not individually. This common was taken by the Ministry of Defence to be used as an airbase, for sorties over Germany. Later, when the war had ended, instead of returning it to the local community, the Ministry gave the use of it to the Americans. Its boundary fence was nine miles long, much of it running through woodland. It enclosed a concrete runway, extensive woods and heathland, a few aircraft hangers, a few buildings. In 1979 the Americans, as part of the latest 'modernisation' of the Cold War weapons programme, decided to use the quiet, out-of-the-way airbase at Greenham Common as the site for new 'Cruise' missiles. By the 5th September 1981 this fence was a neat, simple affair – plastic-coated wire mesh surmounted by three strands of barbed wire supported on concrete posts. It became the setting for a new kind of confrontation between the two kinds of power. And like its Cold-War cousin, that other fence between East and West, between democracy and totalitarianism, it became a canvas, a potent, powerful work of art eight feet high, nine miles long.

As our story progresses, so does the pouring of more concrete as things called silos are built as houses for missiles intended to carry nuclear warheads. Inside the fence there will appear, as the months go by, rolls of razor wire and eventually watch-towers reminiscent of prison-camps. It will come to look more and more like that other fence. It too will have men in uniform, some armed, walking about the inside perimeter, nervously on patrol. Outside, there will be women, of varying shapes and ages, in motley colours and in numbers from less than a dozen to many thousands.

A friend of mine told me that the first time she saw the fence, she burst into tears at the sight of it, so clearly did its brute ugliness express the kind of mind that could develop and consider using the weapons it was there to protect.

This second shorter, but no less symbolic, fence snaked its way through an old, old English wood, and would, much later, be lit up along its length by arc-lights, as if it were indeed a stage setting for a play.

Chapter 2

Red and blue

I was born in Lancashire, on the edge of the Lake District, into the post-war new dawn, of ration-books and of the National Health Service, my cot shaded by a brand-new nuclear umbrella, my bones collecting their share of the radioactive strontium resulting from the fallout that came from the testing of the new weapons that would ensure peace.

My parents were not like those of my friends. My mother was a French ex-factory worker, my father was a teacher and a 'leftie'. She had left school to work in a textile mill at thirteen, he had forsaken the Greek and Latin of a minor English public school to teach himself French, German, Russian and electronics.

At around the age of four, I learnt to read by deciphering the speech-bubbles in the cartoon strip *Pif* that appeared in the Communist daily paper, the *Daily Worker*, which my father continued to receive long after he had stopped being an active member of the Communist Party. In the shrubberies and gardens of darkest Surrey, silver-haired couples held fundraising parties for the Party, and talked about the amazing advances in China. My primary school projects were enthusiastic cut-and-paste efforts drawn from back copies of *Soviet Weekly* and *China Reconstructs*, much to the bemusement of my teachers. One of my earliest memories is of my father listening to an orchestra playing on the old web-fronted radio set he had built, with tears running down his face. It made me cry too, seeing him. He was crying because

Stalin – whom I knew as Uncle Joe from the *Daily Worker* children's corner, had died. My father, who could understand Russian, was listening to the funeral broadcast from Moscow.

The only two colours then widely used in the Soviet Union to tint the black-and-white photographs of workers enjoying themselves at health spas and over-achieving their production targets in fields and factories – vermilion red, the colour of fresh flowing blood, and turquoise blue, the colour of clean sea water – became imprinted on my mind. There was often something slightly puzzling about the photographs, the way there is something puzzling, nowadays, about a perfect digitally-created picture. Some of them looked more like paintings than photographs. Visually, the new technology of photography claimed to present the whole truth, scientifically objective. Yet there was a softness about the faces, an agelessness that was odd. It was a look I would recognise when I saw it on Moscow billboards, thirty years later. By that time, I knew it as air-brushing.

Later on, when I was becoming a teenager, there were arguments all the time about Stalin and the USSR, but they were good-humoured because essentially my parents' friends were like-minded people. That meant they were concerned, they cared, they were unfashionably earnest about the world beyond their own suburban lives. The Russian revolution had given them one enormous thing which for years overrode all misgivings – a belief that ordinary little people could, if they got together and organised themselves, change things, alter their circumstances. This was the umbilical chord that connected them to those already distant events in October and November 1917, and along this umbilical cord flowed the best of human feelings – compassion for others, a desire to cooperate, trust in the human potential for good. They were too trusting, too eager, and had no idea that compassion itself had been all but extinguished in the Workers' State.

In those far-off, innocent days of Left and Right, Red and Blue, those who were active in right-wing politics had a different kind of motivation. They expected to direct events because they were born into that kind of family; they went to a fee-paying school with other children from families who kept horses in paddocks, and might become a judge, or a company director, or an MP. The new kid on this lazy-Tory block was of course Margaret Thatcher, who shared with the lefties an enthusiasm for ideology, for Big Idea canvasses across which the ant-like masses of the people moved; theirs in orderly procession towards perfect equality, peace and fairness, hers all scurrying hither and thither in pursuit of this or that individually tailored 'choice'.

Some of the friends who sat down with us at the brown 'utility' drop-leaved dining table to eat such novelty meals as spaghetti Bolognese, were refugees from Europe. Their families had been separated by the fences and watch-towers that now divided East from West, or else murdered behind the fences of the Nazi death-camps. Two very close friends had been sent to England, as children, on the *kinder-transport* at the last moment before the Second World War broke out. They had been put on a train, alone, by a mother they would never see again. It was many years before I listened to their extraordinary stories of escape, but I heard and knew enough even then to guess at the horrors that lay behind them. I grew up knowing perhaps too much, for an impressionable child, of the truth of the holocaust.

My parents were wonderfully loving and I had a very happy, sheltered, safe childhood, but I was often in the room when grown-ups were talking. I had no brothers or sisters with whom I could be grouped and sent outside to play and from an early age I could read and how did I read! So I grew up knowing that unspeakably awful things really can happen to people like us; that the reassurance of everyday life can be utterly shattered and turned into a living nightmare. In my bright, newly built primary school, we were taught that barbaric cruelty belonged firmly to the long-gone, medieval times from which we had progressed into a modern enlightened age. Somehow, the most shocking thing of all, was and still is, that barbaric cruelty takes place in the midst of a modernism from whose comfortable trappings – telephones, toilets, trainers – we still expect some form of protection.

All this made me feel a bit odd, an only child growing up in

Surrey, in the peaceful, increasingly prosperous, and quite delightful suburbs. My friends and I would pick young hawthorn leaves to eat from the hedges on our way to primary school (we all walked then) which we called 'bread and cheese', and I would tell them about something awful I had read in the *Daily Worker*, such as the fact that there were still slaves in Saudi Arabia. It used to drive me to tears the way they shrugged off these terrible things and preferred skipping games. Now I realise I felt so upset by the carefully selective accounts of injustice in the Capitalist world-zone that constituted my daily reading, because the atmosphere of my home assumed that people could change things. That meant that if people didn't bother to stop bad things happening, they were nearly as responsible as the active perpetrators. I hadn't yet heard that memorable quotation 'for evil to prosper, it is only necessary for good people to do nothing...' but something very similar was indelibly printed through my young, fervently moral mind like the writing in a stick of rock. Perhaps if I and my ten-year-old friends wrote to the Saudi Government, they would ban slavery. I did manage to persuade our little girls' gang to send a long congratulatory letter to the first cosmonaut, the Russian Yuri Gagarin. We sent it to the Russian Embassy and asked to be liberated from the oppressive conditions of our state school. I was a bit disappointed when we received no reply.

Then I became a teenager in the Sixties. I was going to write 'a normal teenager' and then I asked myself was there such a thing, before the late Fifties, before Eddie Cochran, before Elvis, before rock and roll? I became a teenager and bunked off school with my mates to cram into the padded-cell-like booth of my local record-shop, listening to a young Bob Dylan croaking, 'Don't think twice, it's all right...' and sending our souls on long journeys with his sad harmonica. Something happened to me that shattered the normality. I was in a car accident.

It was the night of the midwinter solstice, the 21st December, and I was being driven home from a dance by the friend of the spotty, gawky youth who was my 'boyfriend' for that one and only evening. The lad had not long passed his test and had taken – with neither permission nor insurance, it would later turn out – his father's dinky little yellow sports car. He drove at a break-neck speed sufficient, he must have thought, to impress us (me and the boy, crammed into the bucket seat beside him) with his driving skills. The road was icy, he hit a patch on a bend (the speedometer, I remember, was registering 75 mph) and then spun into two cars coming the other way. The thing had a cloth roof. We were all shot out centrifugally into the road. I came to, still spinning. I was warm and wet and could feel nothing at all of my body. I was lying on my back looking at a group of trees against the deep blue-black sky and I saw the frosty stars. It was the first time I had really seen them. I was looking at a constellation I later identified as Orion. I had never seen anything so beautiful in my life. I thought 'I must be alive, because I can see these stars.' I wondered if the rest of me was there, because all I could feel was an eerie numbness and all I could hear was a muffled confusion of sounds. I raised my left arm – it appeared to be present, so with my left hand I felt for my chest – it was there also. Patting my body I continued downwards, past my stomach as far as my legs. The thick duffle coat and mohair skirt I'd been wearing seemed to have disappeared. I raised my left leg and looked at it, and then did the same with the right. They were covered in blood, but definitely there and working, feet included. It was when I raised my right arm that I understood the reason for the odd feeling I had that something was radically wrong. Rivulets of blood, black in the starlight, ran down my arm from my hand, from which, attached by the merest thread of skin, a severed thumb hung uselessly, almost comically.

I passed very quickly from pain to acceptance. I was no longer perfect, no longer whole. I was no longer like most people. I did not have ten fingers and ten toes. I would have to cope with other people's embarrassment for the rest of my life. There would be things I couldn't be, like a concert pianist, an acrobat, or a right-handed tiddly-winks champion. Later, I would find tennis a pain, since on forehand shots the racket would fly out of my hand. I had just begun, the previous summer, to get the hang of tennis, too.

By the time my anguished father arrived to see me having my

shredded tights removed with tweezers, from badly burned legs, in the local casualty unit, I had decided that the loss of a thumb was a small price to pay for having been introduced to something immeasurably bigger – a sense of what it means to be simply alive. I was filled with overwhelming gratitude to the whole universe. I was ridiculously cheerful, to the extent that the nurses thought I was very drunk, and would not be convinced of my complete sobriety until they saw the pumped-out contents of my stomach, which contained only a few peanuts and the remains of a half of bitter consumed hours earlier.

My minor disability became a sort of teacher, helping me to realise that nobody's life is ideal, that all lives are flawed to one degree or another. The important thing is to appreciate the fact of being alive, and not be too fussy about the conditions under which our life is given to us in this place and at this time. Shakespeare, for instance, could, given hindsight, have bemoaned the lack of electricity, or the absence of antibiotics that would have saved the life of his son who died in his teens. Instead, he wrote plays.

It made me bolder, impervious to embarrassment, and more inclined to ask questions that are so obvious they don't get asked by people afraid of looking like an idiot. In the bed next to me in the hospital where I spent quite some time, having skin grafts and what-not, was a girl with cerebral palsy. She had little control over her movements but her mind was razor-sharp and so was her tongue. She spoke with a loud cockney accent and would give the patronising, well-meaning occupational therapist who would try to get her making pink plastic lamp-shades, such a mouthful of abuse that I was left speechless with admiration. In some situations, she taught me, there is simply no point in being polite.

Many years later my absent digit would play its tiny part in the story of Greenham Common, starring in a memorable appearance at Newbury Magistrates' Court.

Chapter 3

The city and the country

I had started reading when I was very young, and by the age of fourteen had devoured much of Dickens, sitting for hours in our homely toilet where there was a bookshelf. His nervous energy, delight in human character, and passionate conviction that injustices can be righted, bursts from every page and I admired him then and still do. I read so much that writing essays and hence getting good marks in exams seemed absurdly easy.

I went to Bristol University to study English literature, but it was 1965 and the world seemed to be turning itself inside-out. The years 1965 to 1968 were not especially conducive to sitting in a library quietly making notes on plot construction in Henry James' novels. No one seemed very interested in a writer of such preposterously obvious appeal and old-fashioned readability as Dickens, either. A drier literary gruel, stopping well short of the twentieth century, was preferred. The result of half-heartedly going through the motions of doing a degree, whilst inhabiting a fantasy world of revolution and barricades, was that I left university utterly confused about what to do next. Expecting, as we all do, the capital to provide me with a purpose to my life, I moved to London, and trained as a teacher.

I moved into the semi-communal world of squatting. It took me too long to admit how boring I found smoking dope and sitting in a roomful of silenced, comatose people. It also took me far too long to admit how utterly bored I was listening to left-wing men talking, at length, about how things should be run. Since I had been a Stalinist at ten, a Trotskyist at fourteen and an anarchist at sixteen, by the time I was twenty I had literally heard it all before and I was already allergic to ists and isms of every variety, including even feminism. Hour upon hour was spent in a smoky basement long past our bedtimes, with nobody plucking up the courage to say the simple words 'Goodbye, I'm going now.'

I worked as an English teacher in a comprehensive school by day, returning every evening to my 'radical activist' world where, at one point, I even allowed my teacher's income to be distributed in an 'income-sharing scheme' between my house-mates – two men, self-styled 'community activists', too lazy even to claim unemployment benefit – and me. A close friend of my father's – a 'leftie' of course, remarked drily when I shamefacedly revealed this situation: 'There's a word for that, kid – it's called exploitation'. At the next 'house meeting', I said, in a tiny voice, that I didn't want to do income sharing any more. I didn't dare shout, 'You exploiting, lazy hypocritical bastards,' though.

In the end I decided that I just wanted a simple, realistic goal for my own life: I would walk the opposite way to that of most of mankind, intent on urban riches, or urban revolution. I would move from city to country, I would cultivate my patch and do the best I could for my children (whilst depriving them of metropolitan museums, well-stocked libraries, and gang warfare) by giving them fresh air and home-grown food. I wanted to do practical things and have dirty hands. This is still the anchor of my life and I am, above all else, a woman who grows her own vegetables. Having an edible garden kept me sane and my family healthy for the next twenty-five years.

In 1978 I moved to west Wales to live with my partner Barry and our first baby boy in a dilapidated farmhouse, which we had managed to buy because it was so cheap. Even so, we still couldn't afford to buy it, just the two of us, and shared the cost with two other people, buying them out ten years later. It is a tribute to the friendship and bold informality of those times, that we were able to act on trust between friends to that extent.

I moved to the country for cheap thrills – real fires, real stars, hooting owls and barking foxes, real food grown without chemicals. I wanted to see if it was possible to lead a fulfilling life outside of a city.

Over the next two years, we would slowly get to meet other people like us. We were, basically, the sort Stalin called 'rootless cosmopolitans', trying to make a go out of living in the semi-ruined, very cheap farmhouses abandoned by a generation of Welsh, depressed by rural poverty, who had moved into towns. Often the houses were left to rot because they were isolated to the point of near inaccessibilty, tucked away down miles of muddy track. It was common to sneer at us as 'romantics'. Of course we were romantic – we had chosen to plunge ourselves into lives of physical hardship. The vision that inspired the Romantic poets, fuelled us through the muddy grimness. This was the notion that people can draw strength and spiritual sustenance from living in surroundings of natural beauty; that actually feeling the weather, uncomfortable though it may be, gives you a sense of being alive, and can even make you feel good.

By 1980 I had two young children, boys aged two and four, a partner trying to scratch a living as a builder (like every other English immigrant family to Wales at that time) and a vast vegetable garden and small field full of unruly animals we were meant to be eating. I was incredibly busy. Every minute of my time was accounted for. My whole life seemed to be spent in the service of my own and others' alimentary canals – growing the food, boiling up the nappies on the stove and then hanging them out. I got huge aesthetic pleasure from my line of flapping white nappies under a pine tree, summer nappies against the viridian grass, winter nappies against the pinky-mauve sky. It was all cooking the food, feeding animals, making cheese and making sausages, feeding the pig, making compost, cooking, changing nappies, feeding again. I'm not saying I was having a terrible time and you should feel sorry for me – I wasn't, but I was lonely. My parents had gone to live in France – a bad decision in which I had blithely encouraged them – so I had no family nearby to help or turn to in a crisis. The one or two other mothers with young children I was just beginning to get to know were all a carride away, and I was only a learner driver. And when you do have little children, it's very hard to be close to people who don't, because your life is so much not your own.

I used to feel so frustrated with how much of my time was spent picking up toys with fiddly tiny parts. I kept trying to read the paper, because suddenly the news and the letters page seemed desperately important. I felt compelled, I really mean compelled, to give these things my attention.

War

Why did we begin to be so frightened, in 1980, that there might be a war? Why were some people more frightened than others? Why did some people think they could do something to stop a war happening, and others feel that nothing they might do could possibly influence what we know as history, to that staggeringly enormous, that really decisive extent? For some reason that eludes me, accepting the idea that there might be a nuclear war, and that this could be unavoidable, was identified as the sensible, realistic view.

My neighbour wasn't worried. 'There won't be a nuclear war,' she said, 'because nobody who's in charge of these things would be that stupid.' I wanted to agree, the more so as I didn't want to live in fear and terror, and I didn't want to put myself out by going on protest marches that would probably be futile. I was busy anyway. I had toddlers to wash, dress and feed. I had a life to lead. But there was a nagging doubt in my head.

What percentage of risk for nuclear war is acceptable? One per cent? Point nought-one per cent? Less than that? Or as much as two per cent? In 1980 the facts of the arms race, and the Cold War, seemed so utterly stable and grounded in irrefutable reality that all protest was reduced to laughable futility. No majority of any Western population was ever going to vote for a government that would advocate removing its own nuclear weapons from a precariously symmetrical equation. The Eastern population had no choice, but anyone within their leadership who seriously advocated arms reduction would simply have been relegated from Polit-bureau member, enjoying a luxury flat in Moscow with country home nearby, with access to shops stocked with proper food and consumables, to night-watchman at a widget factory in Tomsk, overnight, and nobody would be any the wiser. That was the point about the Old Soviet Union: anything, absolutely anything, could happen, and nobody would know.

That, incidentally, was what made negotiating treaties with them difficult – how could you know they were sticking to them, when you couldn't find anything out? I remember looking at my two children, bright-eyed and muddy, and trying to think about the future – it was like looking at a solid wall, with no chink of light, no windows or doors. I began to aim punches at the wall.

Chapter 4

The anger and the spark

Light bounced off tree trunks and filtered through young branches of newly-planted apple trees. The fields were drying out after the long winter of cold and wet. The smell was intoxicating. The young ashes, a lurid green, were unfurling like a green felt roll of cutlery. I felt driven to sink a fork into the crumbly soil, to rake it, to sow into it the first radishes of the year, the first Webbs lettuce. I dressed the two little boys and took them with me down the muddy hill to the vegetable patch. I was thinking all the time about nuclear war.

The emotion that drove me was not so much fear as anger. Childbirth is never easy, and it wasn't for me. It was ridiculously painful, long, and at moments I felt well aware that a tiny percentage of women, even in our Western hi-tech hospitals, just die. With the birth of my babies, emotions new to me in their ferocity were also born. I, like most Seventies feminists, used to disbelieve utterly the notion of maternal instinct. In fact, so uninterested did I know myself to be in babies and children – at least the few I had so far come anywhere near – that I felt very worried, when pregnant for the first time, about whether I would be able to love my child at all.

They took the newborn boy off somewhere and tucked me firmly into the hospital bed. My labour had lasted more than twenty-four hours, finishing, after I had reached a state of clinical exhaustion, with a gruelling four hours of induction on a syntocinon drip, producing remorselessly fierce contractions.

Out of a teeth-gritted determination to protect this nascent being from any adverse effects of drugs, I had of course refused all pain relief, much to the open scorn of my medical minders. But now, in this high bed, deep in post-traumatic shock and saturated with my own adrenalin, I knew only one thing, I had to find the baby. It was dawn, the place seemed empty. I could faintly hear babies crying somewhere.

It took all my strength to lift the sheets and lower my feet to the floor. The skin of my abdomen immediately flopped downwards, like a large deflated balloon. Clutching the folds of my newly vacated belly with one hand, and the furniture and walls with the other, I set off down the hospital corridor in search. The one kind nurse I had seen since entering the place was wheeling something towards me. 'Go back to bed before dey see you,' she hissed in her Jamaican accent, 'I am bringing you de baby.' She had seen the look on my face when I had asked, 'When can I see the baby?' and the sister had just said, 'Later,' pulling the sheets across me like ropes. Now I am not a particularly brave person, physically – I mean, I chicken out of scary rides at fun fairs, I'm scared of heights, spiders, needles and frisky herds of cows, I'm a fairly nervous sort of person – but if anyone had got in my way at that moment I would have knocked them down. The baby, alert, calm, and waving all his arms and legs at me, was the most beautiful thing I had ever seen. His strong suck began to heal me from the trauma.

This is about the anger. In the following weeks, months and years, I realised, that I had made myself inescapably vulnerable. That if any harm came to my children, then I would feel anguish even greater than that I would feel over the death of my parents. I would feel an inconsolable kind of pain. Giving birth had taught me a literally painful lesson – it had taught me, about the value of life. Not my life this time, but that of the miraculous creature just emerged from between my legs. I couldn't help thinking about all the young men who get killed in wars. I couldn't help thinking about their mothers. I was reading in the paper about nuclear power, and how radiation affects the youngest most, starting with the embryo in a living creature's womb, because their cells are dividing the fastest, and I was reading about the cover-ups of leaks and how easy it is to flannel the public about something you can't see, smell or hear and whose damage is long-term anyway, and one day, not long after my second baby was born in a hospital in Wales, I sort of blew a fuse.

This was the spark that landed on me

'How can we stand by and do nothing to prevent the destruction of our world?' I wrote out some quotes such as this one, from a speech given by Lord Mountbatten, of all people. I'd read it in the paper, I couldn't ignore it − a brilliant speech about the dangers of nuclear power and the nuclear arsenal. I wrote some bits of in large letters on some rolls of old wallpaper, took them in to the local wholefood shop, and the owner − another ex-city invader of west Wales − said, 'I agree,' and called a meeting. That's how we got started, in 1980, here in Carmarthen in west Wales.

Other people were also blowing fuses, other people were starting groups. No one told them to. A lot of them thought they were the only ones for miles around. They just did it.

A year later I was trying to help write a leaflet in someone's house in Kidwelly, about nuclear-free zones. I was feeling bored and stuck generally with the way we seemed to be creating a re-run of the CND campaigns of the Sixties. We stuck to the same script, the usual suspects doing the usual thing in greater or lesser numbers. We were another item of conventional furnishing in the political room − what was the point of your local town declaring itself a 'nuclear-free zone' when what we were facing was the possibility of a nuclear war 'limited' to Europe? My eye caught an item in a *Peace News* magazine that was lying open on the floor, about a group of women walking from Copenhagen to Paris to protest about this threat. I no longer felt bored or stuck, I felt terribly excited.

Dolly the cow – her role in history

That moment, the moment when a small paragraph in a tiny-circulation magazine caught my casually wandering eye and sparklers, Roman candles, Catherine wheels, bangers and rockets all began going off in my poor head was in the spring of 1981. We had a Guernsey cow to milk. We called her Dolly, after 'Hello Dolly' by Louis Armstrong.

Every morning I would go across the field and get the cow – who wasn't always cooperative, sometimes she would see me and simply turn round and run, yes run, through the deep muddy ditch bit right on into the next field, and the next. I would have to use psychology – never my forte – and try and pretend I didn't care, I could milk her anytime (instead of this precious window of opportunity before I had to dress the kids and take them down to playgroup, and I had a head full of lists for the precious time-slot when they were in the playgroup), at which point, seeing me turn round and walk back she would, for all the world like a spurned boyfriend, slowly turn full around, orient her huge fringed eyes and massive soft velvety ears towards me, and ever so slowly start to trundle, with long gaps and pauses, towards me and the collapsing wooden gate. The gate was by the old well, the well that we couldn't use because when we came to the farm it was full up with whisky bottles and other rubbish. And walking the cow across the field towards the gate, I would try to wrestle away this idea, of lots of women, walking down the road, carrying their message and spreading it. I could see it. I could see the road even. It was a road I knew well, it was the old A4 from Bristol to London. Whilst at University in Bristol, I used to hitchhike up it a lot, going to see my parents in Surrey or my schoolfriend Lizzie in Oxford, when you'd turn off it at the Newbury roundabout.

We women would have to go to Newbury, because early in 1981 Nato had announced they would be putting 'Cruise' missiles there.

This decision about 'Cruise' had begun to raise a bit of a flurry of public alarm about escalation and so on. So, to reassure us all, the Government (you may remember, if you were alive then, we were into the long years of Torydom) gave out a leaflet called *Protect and Survive*, which gave all sorts of practical suggestions about what to do and how to behave if the worst came to the worst and there was, unfortunately, a nuclear war (or 'exchange' as it was called). Things like, 'get under the table or into the understairs cupboard' and 'don't go out of doors for a bit' because there might be radiation, and 'be sure not to look at a nuclear weapon going off anywhere near you' or it might be the last thing you'd ever see. Was it sensible for us to prepare a little 'nuclear shelter' stocked with tins of tuna, a radio and first-aid kit – or was it utterly lunatic?

It seems so hard to believe now, but people, civil servants with working brains, spent time in offices writing this sort of thing, and a lot of money was spent ensuring the mass distribution of these leaflets, so that we'd all feel a lot safer.

The historian E.P. Thompson, God rest his soul – because he's dead now – wrote a reply to this piece of terrifying lunacy called *Protest and Survive*. This was one of the most stirring pieces of polemic ever written in the English language. People rang each other up and said 'have you read it?' and passed it from one to the other. It described precisely how the 'Cruise' deployment would inevitably bring us right onto the brink of a possible nuclear war, simply as a result of the inertial forces in the situation, and the appalling paranoia resulting from ignorance about the other of both sides in the Cold War. His simple message was: this can't go on any longer.

'Cruise', remember, was a small nuclear warhead, only a few times bigger than the Hiroshima one, mounted on a cleverly guided missile that was meant to be put onto lorries and trundled around the leafy lanes, ready to be fired, 'at times of international tension'. What would the Soviets make of the sight of 'Cruise' being distributed in readiness – because see it they would, with their spy satellites – would they wait and see? Or would they too be under pressures we could only guess at, pressures which would cause them to fire in case they were about to be fired at?

Now it was May 1981, and my visions of women walking down a road had taken on a life of their own. I would dig my head into the cow's tummy while I milked, willing her not to lift her big cow's foot and plonk it into the bucket of frothy milk. 'I haven't got time' I would say out loud, but in my head I had already written the leaflets and put up the posters – in between feeding the pigs and hanging out the nappies and putting up parties of London school children, who were coming down to see what the country looked like, and plastering walls and weeding, weeding, weeding and digging and digging – in my head, I was explaining to a phalanx of eager reporters, notebooks at the ready, why we were walking to Greenham Common.

I know that if I had been living in another place, as one piece in a kaleidoscope cannot shift without changing the whole, everything else would have been different. I would not have decided to walk to Greenham Common. The cow-patted fields of Gwastod Bach, and even Dolly the cow, play as integral a part of this history as do the dark-suited decision-makers who inhabit wood-panelled rooms and enter conference chambers through classical porticos kept clean by the humble low-paid.

Chapter 5

One – and a roomful of rubble

My mother, whom I loved dearly, died, aged fifty-six, eighteen months after we moved to Wales. I was then three months pregnant with our second child, and the first was still only a year old. My heart-broken father, after a failed suicide attempt whilst staying in our house shortly after her death, had declined from deep depression into Parkinson's disease. He was living in the southeast in a Quaker-run home. As an only child, I felt overwhelmed with responsibility for my father; there seemed to be nothing I could do that would console him or assuage his anguish. I was devastated by the death of my mother, and felt that I would never be able to smile or laugh again. My spirits cheered with the birth or our second boy. There was no real time for mourning, life was simply too pell-mell.

So, I wasn't somebody with time on her hands or particularly well positioned to run a campaign. For a start, I couldn't drive. The telephone was positioned in a room that was full of builders' rubble – we had taken the old plaster off the walls and things had got abandoned for other more pressing priorities. The window-ledge in that room was the only clear surface, and much of the organisation of the march was carried out from there.

I kept trying to find another woman who would take this march idea on, and off me, or who even responded to my mention of it with more than casual interest. Planting out the young broccoli, I decided that I would have to organise it, even if it meant doing it all by myself.

Four and a kitchen table

We have never married, but 'partner' seems a dreadfully cold word for someone with whom you have shared a bed and a life for thirty years. Oh well, it's the best we have I suppose. My other half, my spouse, my lover, my non-legal husband, Barry, knew my dilemma because it kept me awake and so he didn't sleep properly either.

The local anti-nuclear groups had proliferated and begun to generate their own structure (under the weight of which most campaigns, run as they are by voluntary campaigners, eventually stagger and die, suffocated beneath an avalanche of newsletters) Barry had been going to the west Wales CND meetings and one day in early May 1981 he said he had met a woman called Karmen Cutler who seemed sensible and energetic. He suggested I try contacting her.

'That's a good idea,' she said when I rang. 'Come over and we'll talk about how to do it.' That's Karmen, she's very direct and straight-talking; at times she can be downright rude especially to pompous people, men or women. There are quite a number of people in positions of power in west Wales who have egos bruised from encounters with Karmen in some meeting or other. This straightforward, encouraging response was exactly what I needed. Although I was thinking, all right then, I'll do it all by myself, I knew I couldn't and was trying to persuade myself to give up on the idea. Shortly after that, I spoke at a meeting in the small town of Newcastle Emlyn and afterwards two other women said they'd help, Lynne Whittemore and Liney Seward. They came over to my house and we got a road map of south Wales and southern Britain out on the table. We looked at the map. They agreed that because of 'Cruise' missiles, the march should go to Greenham Common, and we had little time. We would have to go for that summer, even though it was now May, which left us barely three months for organising.

Karmen

Karmen didn't drive, Lynne had a driving licence but no roadworthy car, I was a learner driver needing to be accompanied, so Lynne and I drove to Karmen's house. It took about forty-five minutes to get there. The route lay up the Towy valley. At the other end lie bigger mountains, like bald heads rearing up, and long strings of drab-looking, grey little villages with a sprinkling of Spar shops, video shops, and pubs. These are the communities that grew up around the coal seams that run through the limestone hills. These are the mining villages of south Wales. At that time, they were fairly cheerful places with men in work in the mines. Ten years later, with the work gone, they would be starting to disintegrate, becoming hot-spots for heroin abuse, child abuse, wife abuse and car abuse, creating new jobs for an army of social workers and managers of things called 'projects' and 'schemes'.

A young, slim, woman with short dark hair opened the door of a small terraced house in Bettws and we went and sat in the kitchen. We settled my two children and her two down with Lego. Immediately we began to sort out those decisions that needed to be made quickly – when to do this thing, the route, how long it would take, how to get other women to come with us – and decisions that could be left to later. There was no time for talking about our recent life histories; we just focused on the march idea.

Working with Karmen was like changing over to stainless steel in the kitchen – it worked and things didn't stick, because she always says what she means and vice versa. Her clothes always look freshly ironed and her house freshly cleaned, which is odd because she doesn't spend oodles of time on either. I think she just has economy of energy.

The second time the others couldn't come. I had just passed my driving test, and it was just Karmen and myself. I was looking around at the room all the time and eventually I said to her, 'I feel like I've been here before. There's something very familiar about this room, the furniture or atmosphere or something'.

I remember the room looked as if it had been freshly swept out, and there was a newly lit coal and wood fire flickering in the open hearth. Karmen said that was impossible because they hadn't brought any of their old furniture with them when they moved into this house from Lancashire where they'd been living before. Then I remembered something, I remembered being in another room that felt the same.

I asked where they'd lived before that, and then how old the little boy outside was and I began to realise that we had in fact already met, in London. I told Karmen, who was wide-eyed with incredulity, a story about how the birth of that little boy outside had begun in the bath in a neighbour's flat.

Madge

Before moving to Wales I lived in a little terraced house in a drab area of the East End, right behind the London Hospital. It was a squat, as were about half the houses on the street. Round the corner was a big Victorian red-brick block of flats with Dickensian features such as dark archways and open drains and something always dripping somewhere. This was Fieldgate mansions, and most of the flats had fallen empty at some point and so were squats too. This all sounds very squalid and dangerous, but in fact it was one of the safest places to live because a lot of people knew each other, by sight at least, and men and women walked around at all hours of day and night, quite nonchalantly, without awful things happening to them.

The area looked poor and was poor, and was rapidly being colonised by Asian immigrants, who also all knew each other because they all came from neighbouring villages in Bangladesh. The overlap of generations of immigrants lent a special eclecticism to the dingy setting; it was far from supermarkets and so corner shops still flourished and I could buy chopped herring – out of a barrel straight from the Baltic – and bagels from Barney Levi's on one corner, a bottle of Cypress red wine and some sesame bread, olives, a big bunch of flat parsley and baklava on the opposite corner, and fresh ginger, turmeric, and coriander in the Asian grocers' round the next corner. This is what I still miss about not living in a city.

My first baby was due in February 1977 and I had a midwife who visited me at home. She was a tall very black woman from Grenada called Madge. Her mother was also a midwife and she used to send Madge all sorts of potions and substances highly esteemed in Grenada, which she thought would be equally welcomed by Madge's clients in London. Of course, the only women to whom Madge dared to proffer any of these things, which I recall included a hand-grenade-like wodge of sticky black, incredibly bitter raw cocoa beans, were myself and another expectant mother, living round the corner. She told me that this woman, like me, had no family nearby to support her, and also had plants and – she gestured round my room – things like yours. But I didn't make the effort to go and see this like-minded mother-to-be. Then one nasty, sleety February day Madge came round and told me this other woman had just had her baby, and I had better get round and see her, 'C'mon now Ann, you is going to see her right now, I am not having any excuses.' She must have thought I would feel a kind of kinship in non-conformist maternity with this woman, a stranger to me. So I girded my by then massive loins – I was full-term pregnant myself – and went round there, to a squatted flat in Fieldgate Mansions.

The room looked as if it had just been swept out, and there was a freshly-lit wood and coal fire burning in the hearth. There was a young woman with long dark hair shading her face, which was turned to the tiny newborn she was breast-feeding. Maybe I didn't remember her face because I never actually saw it. She had only just come home from the hospital, and there was an atmosphere of intense fragility and intimacy.

She told me about how her contractions had begun while she was having a bath in a friend's flat opposite – real bathrooms were a rarity hereabouts – and how her labour was so swift she'd begun pushing while being rushed through the columnar entrance of the London Hospital in a wheelchair. She and her partner were students at the London College of Furniture down the road, but they were planning on moving up to Lancashire to live in the shadow of Pendle Hill, as soon as they could. We were planning on moving to west Wales in the spring, so I left feeling a bit sorry that there didn't seem any point to trying to pursue the relationship.

I never did ask the baby's name, but when I realised this Karmen person was the same woman, when I started putting the jigsaw together in an oddly familiar room in Bettws, it turned out we had given our firstborns the same name, Ben. Karmen remembered Madge talking about me – that there was a woman living round the corner who had the same things on her kitchen shelves, the beans and lentils and wholefood stuff. She had nagged her to go and see me, but then Karmen was overtaken by her own labour. Neither of us had recognised the other when we had met again, nearly four years later, in Wales.

It seemed quite a coincidence that we had shared a midwife, who had moreover recognised that we had a lot in common, and had made repeated attempts to connect us, apparently failing, but, through the intervention of sheer chance, ultimately succeeding. We didn't say much about this to each other, but I think it made us feel that things lay ahead of us of which we had little inkling, that our meeting had a purpose, that we were on a path, albeit blind-folded. It made us feel very, very determined, for now we were motivated not only by fear and anger but also by the far more enjoyable emotion of curiosity.

Chapter 6

Women for Life on Earth

Putting the big blue book down on the rubble-strewn window-ledge, I turn the telephone dial. The book is where I keep all the phone numbers I've been given. The rubble is lumps of plaster made with materials such as lime from Pendine and sand from Pembrokeshire, minerals which have no man-made radioactive isotopes in them because they were removed from the ground and crushed before nuclear bombs were tested in the atmosphere, spreading a thin film, microns deep, of fission materials over the entire northern hemisphere. It takes ages, pushing your finger in the holes in the dial, pulling it back, letting go. I dial a Bristol number. It is a young man in the Labour party in a village, a suburb of Bristol really, and I want him to do something, but he doesn't know me. I've been given his name as a keen left-wing activist and CND person. I hate doing this sort of thing, asking people to put themselves out, but I'm getting better at it.

'Oh! Hello!' I say. 'My name is Ann Pettitt and I'm organising a march by a group of women to the US base at Greenham Common, where they're going to put the 'Cruise' missiles, you know?' Silence, so I carry on, 'And I wonder if you could find enough people to do us a lunch on the day we shall be coming through where you are. Probably about fifty we'll be...'

'Who are you?' A reasonable question, but I have told him. 'I gave you my name, we're just four women, we're acting on our own initiative and we're organising this event to protest against

'Cruise' and the Arms Race. We're going to start in Cardiff and—'

'Yes I know all that, you sent me the stuff remember, but who are you really?'

Now this is difficult – who are we really? Are we still 'ordinary', or aren't we any more? I haven't got time to hang around philosophising about identity, any minute now a cry from upstairs will announce the awakening of a toddler from his afternoon nap and then that's it...

'Look, I've told you my name, that's who I am, that's who we are – what is the problem?'

'Because this thing you're talking about, this march thing, is too big to be just ordinary women, like you say you are, doing it. There must be some organisation behind you – I just don't believe you're acting on your own, that's not possible.'

'Well, you're just going to have to find out aren't you? Just tell me one thing – are you going to organise lunch for us or am I going to have to find someone else?'

'Oh all right then. What do you call yourselves?'

'Women for Life on Earth. Thank you. I'll be in touch.' Good, I thought, that's another lunch-stop sorted.

So— who are you really?

Between the four of us, me, Karmen, Liney and Lynne, we had six below-school-age children, creatures belonging to the category described by that literal English word, 'toddler'. We met mostly in Karmen's house in Bettws, where her husband Paul fed cheese on toast to the children while we got on with our plotting and wrote leaflets and pored over maps.

Lynne lived on her own in a railway carriage in a field in a remote valley, where she grew her own vegetables. She owned the field and the wooden carriage, which was dark, candle-lit and cosy, with a stove in it, but was in constant anticipation of receiving a bi-lingual Welsh/English letter:

'We understand you occupy a structure as your permanent dwelling which is sited within a field outside the nearest development zone. This structure does not fall within the parameters of those permitted on such a site as a temporary measure i.e. is not a caravan or mobile home. We therefore give you notice that this structure falls outside the strictures regulating development within the rural sector and you will be required to remove it immediately. It has also been brought to our attention that the lack of sanitary facilities constitutes a health hazard to yourself, and that the structure you occupy is unfit within the meaning of the Act. Failure to comply with a closure order will result in prosecution. Should you wish to appeal against this ruling, please use the form provided.'

Liney lived in a wooden 'A' frame house tucked away down a long track, in a fold of the hills, with her husband – another in-and-out of work builder – and their two young children. They had bought the little plot from a neighbouring farmer, and the house was light, warm and well-built, but they too were in constant fear of receiving a letter (see above). The house had no planning permission and the neighbour thought they were dirty hippies and wanted them out. The only one of us whose dwelling had not been officially described as 'uninhabitable', was Karmen.

That is who we were: four young women who were ordinary in the sense that they – we – were poor, had no powerful connections, were burdened by the care of very young children in rural isolation; young mothers with no family nearby to back us up and support us. But we were not 'ordinary' in most senses. We were outsiders, immigrants into remote rural communities with a distinct culture and language, communities that had been suffering decline and depopulation, but whose reaction to people like us – universally identified as English hippies – was very mixed. Some, like my own Welsh farming neighbours, welcomed us with genuine warmth and real friendship. Others didn't.

The rural Welsh have for centuries fought a long hard battle, with hooks and scythes and tractors and sheep, and latterly with chainsaws and concrete and weedkiller, against nature's rampaging summer growth, which threatens to engulf all in brambles, saplings and grass, and against winter's ghastly mud. The prevailing values that result are encapsulated in the special meaning given to the word 'tidy', which is a universal and general term of approval. It was hardly surprising that many of the indigenous Welsh would look askance upon this motley jetsam of romantic, goat-keeping country-lovers flung upon their hillsides by the great retreating wave of the Sixties.

However, if we were not typical, neither were we unskilled, nor ignorant. It soon turned out that I was not the only one who had been involved in squatting. Liney as well as Karmen had been part of this 'direct action' movement, both to solve our own need for housing and to help others. This had meant enduring many meetings, some fascinating and many appalling, learning the tolerance necessary to live with horribly difficult others, writing leaflets, demonstrating, living with uncertainty, taking risks and initiatives, putting your case across to the public and to local authorities, and getting the right kind of press coverage – all the things people now go on management and team-building courses to learn. It also provided a ringside view of the way people with certain fixed leftist ideological agendas could wreck a good organisation with practical aims likely to be of benefit to poor and homeless people.

After working as a teacher, I had worked for a solicitor, and spent two years sitting in courts listening to people in curly white wigs trying to construct convincing arguments. Between the four of us we had read most of what was in print about the development of the nuclear power reactor, about nuclear weapons, about the three types of radiation and its effects on the living organism, and the likely outcomes of a nuclear war. We were probably better informed on the subject than was the Secretary of State for defence and most of his staff of civil servants. I had attended several formal and intensive weekend seminars on nuclear physics given by an eminent scientist, Don Arnott. This pioneering former employee of the nuclear industry had changed from being an advocate of nuclear power to an ardent opponent and was determined to arm people like me with as many facts as he could cram into us.

Lynne had a very cool, calm, slightly humorous approach to everything. She weighed decisions up and thought carefully about things. She had been involved with the anti-nuclear campaign in Carmarthen for the previous year, and was well-informed. Liney looked so much like an elf, you would not have been surprised to find her at the bottom of your garden (if you had a garden that is). She liked bold moves, and it was Liney and Lynne who would later come up with the idea that catapulted a finite event with fixed time-limits, into the realm of infinite possibilities. Lynne and I got Liney and Karmen over for a meeting in my house. In true Seventies fashion, we had knocked down internal walls, making a bigger lighter kitchen where, in Gareth, our predecessor's, time, had been the dark 'gegin' (the kitchen) and the gloomy front parlour. Now the sun flooding in made me itchy to be outside, planting things.

'Why should it be only women?' said Liney, 'I mean, we live with men, three of us have got boys – bombs drop on them too.' We thought about this, humming and haa'ing, standing round my big kitchen table with the oilcloth on it. I was absolutely convinced it had to be a march by women, but why? When I tried to explain, I found I was trying to articulate feelings so profound and elusive it felt like I was hauling them up from inside me in a flimsy bucket, my words a thread liable to snap. Maybe, it occured to me, it was just that, a feeling, and the reasons didn't yet fully exist... this decision was absolutely crucial and I knew it, but it was no good if the others didn't think so too. We all had to be committed to the idea, or it wouldn't have a hope.

We were worried we might be giving off mixed messages, and alienating not only men, but also women who might associate us with the simplistic, anti-men style of feminism that so obscured and distorted the facts of women's inequalities. But we felt that women felt differently about war and violence than did men, and that these feelings – that life could never be seen as cheap – came from the fact that so many of us were mothers and carers for others. Of course this is not universally true, and the then new Prime Minister, Mrs Thatcher, was to challenge the notion that women in power would be any more compassionate than men.

Of one thing we were certain – women were far more concerned about nuclear weapons than were most men, and this concern was both a gut instinct about a weapon that goes on killing silently and invisibly, through generations as yet unborn, and a robust common sense about a weapon too utterly horrific ever to be any use in legitimate warfare. In fact, women in general seemed to just be less easily blinded than men by visions of technological advance, by the pseudo-scientific nonsense that masked the playground posturing of the Cold War. In the growing anti-Cold-War movement, if women did have a distinct voice saying new things in our unique, female, way, that voice was not being heard.

The big-brush facts were these: men, overwhelmingly, made the decisions about wars, how to fight them, and what weapons to own and use to threaten real or illusory enemies. Civilians, overwhelmingly, suffered the consequences, and of those civilians, women and children would always be predominant and would, if they were to survive a nuclear war, be the ones to give birth to the deformed babies.

These facts are as true today as they were then. Twenty-five years later, men make the wars and women and children do the suffering and dying.

We decided the march would be women-led. We had no wish to be too rigid in our definition of this event. We would need the cooperation of friendly groups along the route to find us accommodation and, of course, food. These groups would have men all inconveniently mixed up with their women. Moreover, we wanted people to accompany us along our route out of the towns, to show their support. We decided that the marchers themselves would be women and the pre-publicity would make that clear, but that men as well as women would be welcome to show support by walking with us for part of the day as long as they accepted that was the way it was – a women's march, women in front, literally, women as spokespersons, women taking the decisions.

It was a practical, sensible approach that ensured us the goodwill our group, a fragile organism like all new-born things, needed along the way. But our cheery tolerance would cause problems later, and the ambiguities over what constituted a 'women's' event would not be cleared up until the day, many months later, that the men were finally asked to leave the 'Women's Peace-camp'.

The other three shared my frustration with the low impact the CND revival seemed to be having on our national life. Part of this seemed to be to do with the way the spokesmen handled the rare media opportunities they were granted. Some avuncular, bearded scientific type would appear on the screen and bend over backwards to sound reasonable, calm and full of know-how and nobody would ever remember a word they had said. The main point – that the whole arms race was approaching a truly lunatic level of obvious danger to everyone – would get lost in the minutae of this or that weapon system and arcane calculations of 'balance'.

We felt that a little screaming, a little shouting, would not, in the circumstances, go amiss. The arguments against MAD (Mutual Assured Destruction) were so easy and obvious that a bright ten year-old could have put them to a Cabinet Minister. When you train as a teacher, you are warned never to make a threat you are not, ultimately, prepared to carry out. However, nobody was going to invite the likes of us to comment on the sense or otherwise of deterrence theory.

So, the first aim of the march was this: to gatecrash the closed world of the media debate on defence issues. It was to use the media to wake up the public to what was happening. 'We are going to make this place, Greenham Common, a household word.'

Then we had to give the thing a name, so we called it 'Women for Life on Earth', because we felt that nothing less than the future of the entire planet was at stake here, and this just about summed it up. In case this title might be mistaken for some kind of anti-abortion, religious right-to-life outfit, we threw in for good measure the explanatory sub-title: 'Women's Action for Disarmament'.

We made a banner in Lynne's field out of an old sheet dyed pink. We painted the world and a tree on it, like an upside-down CND symbol, with the prongs as branches. Later we had to cut holes in it so the wind didn't turn it into a sail when we carried it along. We made a starkly simple leaflet explaining what we were doing and why. Instead of the usual two sides of densely-packed A4 in small print, this piece of paper merely asked the question: WHY ARE WOMEN WALKING 120 MILES ACROSS BRITAIN, FROM A NUCLEAR WEAPONS FACTORY TO A BASE FOR CRUISE MISSILES?

The 'factory' reference was because parts for nuclear warheads were – and as far as I know still are – made at Llanishen, in Cardiff. On the other side was a horrible picture of a baby deformed by radiation from the Hiroshima bomb, 'THIS IS WHY' it said, giving one sentence of information about the effects of nuclear weapons. At the bottom of the page it said, 'STOPPING NUCLEAR WEAPONS STARTS WITH YOU.'

Inspiration

Inspiration is not born inside an individual. It is a chain, a relay; if it's not passed on it dies. It is like a virus. I caught it from several sources and passed it on, and because the time was right for it a chain reaction happened, a bit like an atomic reaction. This happens sometimes if the time is right and something is needed in the world. I was vital, those three other women who organised the march with me were vital, every individual on that march was vital, the hundreds who kept the Peace-camp alive were vital and so were all the thousands upon thousands who in the end made an incalculable difference to our history. The thousands, the few, and the one – we were all absolutely necessary to each other and to this story. But it is in our fragile beginnings that the absence of just one would have sent events off in a different direction entirely.

Oh, and we had no money.

The money

We needed money for phone calls, printing leaflets and posters, sending letters. Not a lot, but we couldn't spare anything ourselves. We were all living on very small incomes. To be precise, three of us were living on bits that our partners earned from doing building jobs, bolstered by Family Credit, which was called FIS then, and Lynne, I think, was a student at the art college. CND were handing out grants and loans to groups, so we asked them for a loan of £250. What is hard to get across is how difficult it was to get anybody to take us seriously, because we had no recognisable label. I mean, we weren't walking around with badges saying, 'Hey! Pay very careful attention to what I have to say, because in six months' time we are going to be really big and important!'.

So, basically, CND said, 'You must be joking, who are you lot anyway? Do we know you?' when I asked them on the phone about the possibility of a small loan. Fair enough, I thought, they're overworked and overwhelmed with the problems of sudden growth, so I'd better talk face to face with somebody and convince them of the merits of the idea. So I went up to London, to see a woman in the office at Goodwin Street. Whoever it was I was speaking to was apparently organising the entire Glastonbury pop festival on the telephone at that precise moment, and every time I got further than three words into a sentence she'd get another call from some incredibly famous pop star who wanted to give all his money to CND and play the festival for free. I left empty-handed and rang up John Cox, who was one of the few people who had responded really positively to the women's march idea from the first mention.

I forget exactly what position John held at that time in the CND organisation – chair, vice-chair secretary or what, but it's irrelevant – John was a canny player, and wherever he was, it was never far from the purse-strings. He was a Communist but not a Stalinist (to a non-lefty these distinctions may seem fussy, until you remember some of the things 'Uncle Joe' did) and had stuck faithfully with CND right through its doldrum days, after the first Aldermaston marches, and when all the protests at the atmospheric testing had died down, and people protested about other things while governments just quietly got on with the accumulation of vast hoards of nuclear weapons. Whilst lousy on television, he was a very good speaker for a local group, because he was brilliantly well-informed and could explain the science, the politics and the statistics of mega-death in a quiet, deadly calm way. He never exaggerated or dealt in unverifiable, dodgy facts.

He knew Karmen and me because he had come down to speak at our local meetings when we'd got our groups together and shown the film *The War Game* (which showed the likely effects on Britain of a small nuclear attack), and he knew we were serious, determined and good organisers.

He'd persuaded me to make my first speech in public, at a demonstration at RAF Brawdy, out on the wild cliffs of Pembrokeshire, which was another base used by the Americans. I hadn't written anything down, and halfway through found myself choked by my own words, which were about the men who make the decisions and what little they know of life; then afterwards people kept saying to me, 'You made me cry.' I made lots of speeches after that, none as good probably, but I never wrote anything down. I thought about what I wanted to say, and said it, memorising the beginning and the end and leaving the middle to whatever came into my head. I told John of our little problem and pretty soon there was a cheque in the post, so we could really begin.

Getting money wasn't the only problem. We needed contacts in every town en route to organise a meal, rally supporters and find us somewhere to sleep. This had to be done in advance, when of course we had no idea how many we'd get to come on the march; so we made a guesstimate, plucked from the air and on the basis of no information whatsoever, at fifty. Bristol was the biggest place we'd go through, and had the largest CND group and also lots of active feminists, so, 'no problem there', we thought. I was given the name of a woman who'd be sure to be interested and had good contacts so I drove down to Bristol to meet her, and someone else from Newbury, to talk about arranging something.

I had just passed my driving test and this was the first time I had driven on my own, ever. I even pulled over on the motorway to ring Him Indoors from one of those phones they have, to tell him there was a funny noise. I described the noise. 'That's the engine,' he said. So when I got to the right house in Bristol, after a few U-turns along the Gloucester road, I felt pretty pleased with myself. The sensation did not last long. My anti-nuclear feminist contact did not like the idea of a march, thought we should all hold local 'peace picnics' in our nearest parks, or preferably in the privacy of our own back gardens instead, and expressed serious doubts as to whether women would be capable of walking the average twelve miles per day, without rigorous and lengthy pre-training. Five miles was the maximum that could be expected without life-threatening blisters, and, basically, the whole idea was unfair to women, just another burden I was dumping on already overworked shoulders. Furthermore, she was horrified that the march was not clearly defined as 'women-only' and thought that our 'women-led' concept was an invitation to be taken over by men.

I reported back to Karmen in despondent mode. Her reaction was more robust. 'With attitudes like that, who needs these people? She can fuck off,' she said. 'We must be able to find someone else in Bristol.' We tried the CND group, but they didn't want to get involved because they were too scared of being criticised by the feminists if they did, and the feminists, who had their own 'WONT' (Women Opposed to the Nuclear Threat) group, didn't want to know because we weren't strictly 'women-only', and they had been warned about us and our bad attitude.

This kind of suspicious reaction, I remember, was fairly typical of the women's movement of the time, whose agendas seemed dominated by discussion of the concerns of women who wanted to live their lives completely separate from men and by theories that were rapidly losing any contact with the reality of most women's lives – which involved men and children. Lots of meeting time was spent 'confronting prejudice'... Afterwards those unfortunate or foolhardy enough to have become mothers would collect their whimpering infants from the crèche and take them home, worrying about whether they were harbouring inner heterosexist prejudice so cunningly concealed that they didn't even know about it themselves. There seemed to be precious little thought or concern, or even sympathy, given to the women who swelled up into a ridiculous shape, gave birth and often, as a consequence, really were suffering ordinary, deeply embedded, age-old, institutionalised, practical disadvantage and prejudice in just about every way you can think of.

Consequently, we found it difficult to organise anything in Bristol – somewhere to sleep, someone to offer food. Eventually we were offered a church hall floor for the night, thanks to my old university friend Mary, who lived outside Bristol, a woman whose common sense had miraculously survived higher education intact and whose brain function was unimpeded by labels and preconceptions, a woman who just laughed and said, 'Fine, I'll see what I can do,' when I rang her to ask if she could organise somewhere central for maybe 50 women to sleep for free.

Chapter 7

Walking to Greenham Common
Cardiff, August 26ᵗʰ, 1981

The four of us got the train up to Cardiff, to sleep on the floor of the Friends' Meeting House, so that we could be up early for interviews on local radio in the morning, and then ready to set off. We were meeting the other women that night. There were just over forty of them, recruited by various means: word of mouth, notices in CND newletters and the like, and – for we wanted to cast our net wide – small mentions in *Cosmopolitan* and one or two other women's magazines.

We had entertainers and speakers and information videos organised for every evening; we had lunches and church halls and floors for the nights, often thanks to the Quaker groups in the stop-over towns. We had a beautiful scarf as our motif, created by a woman from Bromsgrove who had drawn an image of herself, naked and with raised clenched fist, and had screen-printed one hundred scarves in the suffragette colours of purple and green on white. In the days to come we would wear these, and little else, as turbans, tops and mini-skirts in the steady heat.

We had a hired van to carry our luggage, and one of the women, Ev Silver from Loughborough, had an HGV licence so was able to drive it. We had a back-up car belonging to Margery, our oldest participant, who was then sixty-five and lived in Cardiff, and who had thought we were probably some sort of weird religious group but had decided to give us a try. We had lots of lemonade and biscuits and Elastoplast and sun-block.

On the warm evening of August 26th we sat around in an upstairs room in the Quaker meeting house in Cardiff, waiting for more women to arrive. I remember feeling sick with anxiety. Some women were bringing young children, and the night before I had woken in the midst of a nightmare in which these children were being run over on the road, and it was all my fault. In fact, Karmen had taken on the job of organising a police escort for us for the entire distance, liaising and negotiating with each different county constabulary, to ensure the safety of ourselves and motorists. There didn't seem very many of us. We were all ages, and our various accents proclaimed our origins in different parts of the British Isles. We all felt uncomfortable and apprehensive, not knowing each other. We had managed to disabuse Margery of her misconceptions about our motives, and convince her that there were indeed no great shadowy organisations behind us (that 'who are you really?' question again), but what about all the others? What were they thinking?

The meeting began. I introduced the four of us and explained the arrangements for the night and the following day, when we would walk the twelve miles to Newport.

A white-haired woman, who I guessed to be in her early sixties with a sharp, enquiring face, looked around us rather severely and said in the ringing tones of the Welsh valleys, 'There must be somebody here who is an expert in these matters, who can explain to us why we are all here – well, I know why I'm here, but...'

Oh dear, I thought, feeling suddenly very inadequate. There was a short silence, and then we all started laughing. 'That's the point,' somebody said. 'It's listening to the experts that's got us into this mess in the first place.'

So then we began to tell each other why we were there. Eunice, the white-haired woman who had started this off, said she was here because her grandson had begun to ask her if there was going to be a nuclear war. As she reassured him that no, *bach*, of course there won't be a nuclear war, she had suddenly

49

realised that she could give him no such reassurance... She had heard about the march and decided to come on it. We had all experienced the same emotions – concern, anger, fear, frustration, building up to the point where they simply shut everything else out, erupting into nightmares at night and waking dreams by day. Each woman described that little, 'Yes! That's it!' feeling, when first they read about or heard about our march, which was just what I had felt when I had read about the women walking from Copenhagen to Paris.

Apart from these feelings, you really couldn't say we had much in common. We really did seem to be a very mixed bag. There were nurses, a midwife, a probation officer, social workers, students, young girls, single mothers, married mothers, grandmothers, women with a history of political activism and feminism and women – the majority – for whom this was their first protest of any kind. One woman said she came because 'interesting things can happen when women get together'. What can she mean? I thought.

Walking to Newport, August 27, 1981

The next day we gathered in the park in front of the City Hall in Cardiff and set off, supported by about fifty people from the CND groups locally. It was scorching hot as we got out of the city and onto the old A48 road to Newport. Despite my stern pre-march mailed instructions about sensible footwear, some women wore flimsy sandals and one was even in flip-flops. I feared the worst. We would all succumb to blisters by the end of the day and would have to complete the journey by coach, looking ridiculous. We stopped in a lay-by for our first break for drinks and biscuits. A woman called Helen, who had a child in a pushchair, said, 'I trained as a nurse. I'll inspect everyone's feet and nip any blisters in the bud, how about that?' I knew she was the best person to do this because she was quite capable of chivvying everyone to take off their shoes and succumb to twice-daily foot inspections.

I knew this because I had met Helen before, when she had asked me to come and speak at a meeting where she lived, the deathly quiet, innocent little town of Llanwrtyd Wells. Above the single Victorian main street loom the Eppynt mountain ranges, an upland area so sodden, gloomy and generally nasty that they are used as a training ground for extreme conditions by the British Army. Helen had called a meeting on the basis of a rumour that 'Cruise' missiles would be stationed there. The rumour was entirely false, but Helen took the opportunity to instruct the assembled citizens fully as to their duty to resist the forthcoming American invasion of our soil. With Helen John in charge of everyone's feet, no blister would dare peep above the parapet and my mind was put to rest.

By lunchtime a kind of irrepressible mirth had set in, and by the time we reached Newport, in a golden evening haze, to a wonderfully thoughtful reception by people who had provided us with a paddling pool for our weary feet, and a feast of fresh home-cooked food for our tummies, the four of us felt things were going better than we had dared hope.

Walking to Bristol – How small we felt

It was in Newport that we were ambushed by our own ambiguities. The two young men who had walked with us from Cardiff begged that evening to stay and do the rest of the route. They had been along to Cardiff CND, they said, but evidently the experience had been bewildering. 'Nobody seemed to want to talk to us, all they did was argue among themselves, and you'd no idea what they was arguin' about...' They painted a familiar picture of the good cause overwhelmed by old leftist agendas, whilst unnoticed, a couple of genuine working class youths sat there at the back wondering what the hell was going on. 'You people are what we've been looking for, you're doing something that makes sense – we'll babysit while you have meetings, we'll stay at the back, we'll do anything – please can we stay?' We put it to the meeting that evening. They stayed. We were a soft-hearted lot.

The sun shone hot. We made friends, we made banners – a woman called Thalia Campbell had brought her daughter Lucy and big felt pens and banner-making things – and someone had even thought to make our own postcard, showing the route of the march. We hadn't asked them to do this – they had just done it. We were whipping up an infectious, mad-cap spirit of optimism. Over the Severn Bridge we walked while a juggernaut, thumping into a passing pigeon, scattered us all with little symbolic, bloody, feathers. The Labour Party man who had asked me on the phone, 'Who are you really?' and had told me, 'You can't just be ordinary women, this is too big an idea,' was there eating his words along with the quiches at our lunch-stop and down we went into Bristol.

I had always envisaged the march as coming down a hill in the north of the city called Blackboy Hill (a reference to how the city got its wealth). Although you have by then come through several miles of suburbs, this approach connects the higher green parkland known as the Downs, bordering the dramatic tree-lined Avon Gorge, with the busy built-up area of the University and its cafés and Georgian squares, which then connects in turn, still moving downhill, with the modern shops and strange elongated roundabouts known as the City Centre, somewhere near which was our overnight accomodation. In other words, it is a geography which works, psychologically, as a way of entering a city because it feels as though you are coming straight in from the country into the city centre in about two miles of busy, shop-lined, people-packed pavements. What's more, those particular people couldn't be more ideal recipients for our leaflets. I had even had a dream, weeks earlier, about walking down Blackboy Hill with a group of women marchers, and it didn't even occur to me to question that this was what we would do.

However that was not what the police who were accompanying us had in mind. We assembled somewhere north of the Downs and were presented with our route – long, dreary and circuitous, mostly through suburbs which at that time of day, mid-afternoon, would be deserted. I protested and was told that our proposed route was not possible because of the disruption it would cause to traffic. I really can't remember what I or any of us did then – I probably sulked.

I remember nothing more until we were approaching the point at which we would have to turn off on our long afternoon ramble round the nether regions. We were stopped while the police talked into their radios. Some sort of traffic problem had occurred on the route they had chosen for us – we'd have to go down Blackboy Hill instead!

But despite this happy turnaround, Bristol was to be the low-point of the march. On our arrival in the centre of town, a sort of sunken roundabout was the only place we could find to gather. It was a dispiriting experience. Although we knew the CND-minded feminists and the feminist-minded CND people were having difficulties working out whether they were 'allowed' to show any support for us, we had sort of secretly hoped they might have sorted it out by now. The arrival of our little march had been well publicised by our beautiful, graphic poster which my friend Mary and a few other women from the village of Pill, who claimed distinction neither as 'leftists' nor as 'feminists', had put up all over the place. Here, besides our tired selves, three bemused punks, and the handful of significantly older CND members (presumably past caring about correctness) who came to greet us, we listened to excellent, well-informed and inspiring speeches by Dorothy Thompson, wife of E P, and the medical campaigner Dr Lynne Jones. It was a sad indictment of Sixties' town planning and of post-Sixties' leftist feminism. Our spirits were rallied that evening, however, by a fantastic black woman soul singer who sang her heart out for us in a club – organised again by my ex-Bristol University friend Mary.

Walking to Bath – How our spirits were revived and we became goddesses going nowhere

But the next day it seemed hard to shake Bristol off our shoes and out of our minds. The bald fact was that only about a dozen people in this city of vast networks of progressive, liberal-minded, anti-nuclear citizens, boasting MPs such as the likes of Anthony Wedgwood Benn, had bothered to greet us. We felt this to be a sobering foretaste of uphill struggles to come. In Newport a local councillor, Paul Flynn, later to become the MP, had enthusiastically led us through town in a radio car, until we had tactfully pointed out that it sounded a bit odd to hear a male tenor voice booming out to shoppers, 'This is the women's march against nuclear weapons...' But what the hell, it was better than being shunned altogether. In Chepstow too we had been met by a large, encouraging group of local enthusiasts, some of whom walked with us the next day, but now we were reduced to uncharacteristic silence, plodding glumly along through the traffic past the endless puddingy red sandstone, semi-detached landscape of the Bristol suburbs, lost in our thoughts on the Bath road. Even the sun had disappeared and a somnolent thundery greyness had replaced our jovial heat-wave. We stopped for the toilet and drinks halfway to Bath, at a garage lay-by, squatting tired and dejected on the low kerb-stones and I began to feel it had maybe all been a big mistake. I wanted to go home. There were so few of us, really, we knew we looked ridiculous – what kind of delusions had made us think we could have any impact on anything other than the clutch-plates of the accompanying police cars obliged to drive at three miles an hour?

A big van pulled in, stopped and the back doors opened. About half a dozen people got out in bright, feathery, clownish apparel. They produced musical instruments and the sun, which had started to shine again, flashed glamorously off saxophones, a trombone, trumpets, a drum, an accordion and immediately, there and then, on the garage forecourt, they started playing, singing, and dancing. The van drove off, leaving them behind with us.

The Fall-out Marching band had come from Bath, where they were playing in a festival that weekend. They had heard about us and had come to accompany us into the city. Some of them would end up walking with us the whole way to Greenham Common.

With the aid of the Bath summer festival and the wonderful silly danceable tunes of the marching band, we recovered our morale and from that moment, mood-wise, there was No Turning Back. Furthermore, we were growing in number, although you couldn't yet describe this as exponential growth. Thirty-six had set off from Cardiff and now we were over forty. But we were getting bigger in ourselves, I mean. On the way to Batheaston for lunch we ransacked the hedgerows for wild hops and arrived covered in green garlands. 'When you walked in,' someone told me afterwards, 'you looked liked goddesses.' He noticed! We had indeed become goddesses. Each one of us had grown at least three or four inches taller (though not in girth) and we were all wearing not flip-flops or dusty Clarks walking shoes, but proper seven-league boots as worn by other, older, legendary giants.

Our route, the old A4 road, makes a big meander round Silbury hill on the Wiltshire downs. We didn't plan this or, at the time of deciding the route, know anything about Silbury Hill, other than that the road has a big kind of meander in it, which tells you that it was there when the Romans came swinging along in their little skirts and their sandals, with their little swords and their little crucifixions for people who upset their plans. This hill was there when they (or others under their direction) built the road. This mysterious, ancient, man-made structure, a perfectly round hill, a great big grassy bump, has its place, so one theory goes (as expounded by Ev Silver from Loughborough), as the womb of the Great Mother herself. So up we romped – we thought we might as well – to invoke Her blessing on us. Indeed more than just the sun seemed to be shining upon us, for as individuals, we had each become special, more extraordinary, our qualities and talents more uniquely appropriate to our new job as planet-savers. Wit abounded and we often staggered along bent double with laughter, crossing our legs. Absence of toilets out on the open road ensured an abundance of farce. Long serious conversations also took place because we were all very interesting people with fascinating lives. The 'march' had become 'us' and yet we seemed more than the sum of our parts.

Our behaviour reflected this. Whenever we approached a town or village we would wait for everybody to catch up, then stride up the middle of the road, singing at the tops of our voices. 'Take the toys from the boys... and No plutonium', which began, 'I like the flowas, I like the vegetables,' and carried on to fit the words, 'and I want to live in a nuclear free societeeee,' somehow into the rhythm. One of the oldest and most eccentric of us, Effie, ran up and down the pavements thrusting our leaflet into the hands of the Wiltshire townsfolk who were staring at her luminous green sun-shield. We were wonderful, we walked on air not Tarmac, we could do anything, and *we were getting absolutely nowhere.*

Walking to Melksham –
Liney and Lynne have an idea

Oh, we were big in East Germany – they turned up to film us every day, and Karmen and I had got into a car at one point with a bunch of very strange men allegedly to film an interview for Moscow television. We also appeared on the local news programmes, for about twenty seconds – just a picture of us walking over the brow of a hill, say, or a flash of Janet or Sue or Helen pushing a baby in a buggy – no interviews about *why* we were doing this. Every morning I would find a phone somewhere, either in someone's house or, if not, a payphone, and ring up the papers, an exercise in frustration that seemed designed to humiliate, as if I was ringing the news desk of daily papers trying to sell them double glazed plastic windows. Yes, they knew about it. No, they had no plans to do a story or a feature on our action. Peace, they said (this isn't peace, I would say, this is protest, but to no avail), peace, they would patiently repeat, has been done already and was last year's story. After several days of this I ended up losing my temper with somebody or other and shouting, 'Look, we may not be black and white and furry and possibly pregnant, but we are walking a hundred and twenty miles because we don't want a nuclear war and we are not going to go away or stop banging on about this until you do take some notice of what we are saying.' The black and white bit was a reference to the really big story of the moment, which was about a silly panda in the zoo. At that point I decided to give up on the gentlemen of the press and enjoy the march for its own sake. But for the four of us who had poured the last three months of our lives into this thing, the frustration was building up.

That evening we stayed in Melksham. The golden evening light stole in upon the quiet stone façades of the old houses around the central square. We had entertainment laid on for us in one of those buildings. In an upstairs room in the town hall, that venerable folk couple Ewen McColl and Peggy Seeger were singing.

It was so hot. I knew I was meant to be enjoying it, but I wasn't, perhaps because of all the moral authority that is invested in these innocent, catchy ballads, which were really meant to be sung by people as they go about their daily business, cutting wood, shearing sheep, binding sheaves, shovelling shit, getting plastered on yeasty hoppy beer and rough cider, getting worn out after walking to and from work like everybody used to, not listened to in reverent silence by people who clapped politely at the end of each slightly sanctimonious recital. Outside, only the screams of swifts disturbed the balmy evening, whose light and cooling air proved irresistible. I crept out stealthily, feeling naughty.

To discover I was not alone – there sitting on a bench in the deserted square below (the faint wails of Ewan McColl could still be heard from the upstairs windows) were Liney and Lynne. They were sharing a small joint of west Wales home-grown marijuana. 'Listen,' they said surreptitiously beckoning me over and passing me the tiny one-paper cylinder in an underhand fashion, 'We've been wanting to talk to you. We've thought of an idea'.

What sort of an idea?
Liney and Lynne conspire in a period setting

Liney was looking more brown and elfin-like with every passing day. Later she would give up on the wild inhospitable climate and grim, 'proper' culture of west Wales, and return to the semi-nomadic world of travellers' buses and city squats whence she had so bravely and boldly sprung. She would part from the father of the two children she had then, at the time she sat on this bench in the town square of Melksham, and have a third baby with another man. By this time she would be living in a squat with some very feminist-minded friends, but would suffer severe post-natal depression, partly, she said, much later, when she had got better, because she felt surrounded by an atmosphere of disapproval for such a reactionary, unliberated thing as having another baby.

It seemed to me that traditional, rural, Welsh culture, with its tendency towards primness, was the very antithesis of London lefty liberalism, but over the years I came to appreciate the value of many of the traditional attitudes that used to irritate me. At least here when you have a baby the neighbours all come round to view the new human being and cross its tiny palm with silver. Fair play, *chwarae teg*, they do know what to do about a baby. Clucking, approving, giving cards, showering with surplus gifts and tiny babygrows and pink and blue rattles, doing funny faces, making gurgly noises, inspecting minute crinkly hands and feet, asking to hold the baby, getting sicked on by the baby – none of this, (as I used to think, in my single London life) is silly or in any way superfluous behaviour. It's a vitally important part of adjusting to the onslaught that is motherhood. A new mother is suffering post-traumatic shock. She needs all the help and cuddles she can get. If she has no mother of her own and her partner is busy working to keep the money coming in, she needs her friends to be her mummy, and cook and clean for her – but I digress, again.

'We're not getting anywhere are we?' they said. I agreed. 'So, we need to do something else. We thought just marching was enough – it isn't. I mean, we're all having a great time,' said Liney, 'but really, we didn't get all this together just so's we could come all the way to Melksham and hear this lot tell us how wonderful we are, 'cause they're not the people who matter. We're not getting across to anybody. We'll have a lovely time and go home and it'll all have been a complete waste of our time, basically.'

'Yes.'

'We certainly aimed to achieve a lot more coverage than just a ten-second glimpse on *Network South-East*, didn't we? I mean, you've been on to the papers every day and they just don't want to know do they?' said Lynne in her measured, calm, slightly gravelly voice.

Lynne, was looking at me with grey eyes, arms in her lap, our purple, green and white scarf draped elegantly round her neck against the freshening evening air and a sky behind her turning from aqua to rose to violet.

'No they don't.'

Scream, scream, go the swifts on their third round since I stepped outside...

'So, look. Remember when we were squatting?' This was Liney again, in denim dungarees, who had begun to wave her thin brown arms about. 'The council wouldn't listen when we said they should put all the homeless families in all the houses they had empty – so we had to demonstrate, go to their meetings. Look at the suffragettes, the vote and all that, no one now thinks that's some kind of outrageous thing, like women shouldn't have the vote. It's about the most basic reasonable thing you could ask for, and they were regarded as nutters, and ignored, so they chained themselves to parliament didn't they? They began with marches and petitions, they got nowhere, so they had to up the ante – that's what we'll have to do.'

We were all a little vague about our suffragette sisters – but yes, we all knew they had resorted to several pretty extreme forms of demonstration, including hunger srtikes and throwing themselves in front of horses, to get their simple, basic, obviously just and right, demand taken seriously.

'So,' they concluded brightly, 'that's what we should do – chain ourselves up to the place when we get there. There's bound to be one of those fences – we'll find something to hook up to. I mean, if they couldn't open the gates because we were chained up to them... What do you think?'

What did I think? I wasn't thinking; my brain had seized up. I felt as though I had inadvertantly stepped on top of a small drain-hole and now my entire forseeable future was pouring down it. The innocent harmless-looking bit of paving that I had stepped on, in the Georgian centre of a quiet Wessex market town turned out to be a concealed trap-door and already I was falling, like Alice down the rabbit hole, into another world. You see, I knew they were right, 100 per cent. This idea had the hallmark of the absolutely obvious and inevitable next step stamped all over it. But all I could feel, as the pins and needles coursed up and down my arms and legs, was dismay, because all I could think was, 'So – when do we get to go home then?' and, 'Oh my God,' and, 'I thought this business had a beginning a middle and an ending, how silly of me.'

I had my firstborn starting school in a month's time (they grab them before four in west Wales). I had leeks to transplant, celery to earth up, broccoli and sprouts to go in where the early potatoes had been cleared, rocket and lambs' lettuce to sow for our winter salads. By now the butterflies would have laid their caterpillars and the caterpillars would be making lace of the sprout and cabbage leaves in my garden. All of these things should have been done a lot earlier, but there just hadn't been time before leaving. Now I was counting on getting back, while there was still some fine weather, before the awful wet set in again. You think none of this should have mattered? Well I'm sorry, but there we have it – these things did matter, to me. Everybody else had everyday things that mattered to them desperately, secret little projects with targets and production quotas only they knew about, must-do and can't-miss lists, let alone plain ordinary money-earning work, so why would I be any different?

Oh, it sounds mild and innocent enough, I know, a little chain-ourselves-to-the-fence-for-a-few-hours, or a few what – days? So why all the tingling, why the slightly jelly knees, why the 'Oh-oh, here we go!' little voice? Up to this point, we could have gone home, melted back into our local CND groups, told a few stories, argued for holding a demonstration of some sort at

Greenham Common, held a reunion or two, got on with our lives, or not, history depending. But from this point on we would give ourselves no choice but to make a success of what we had begun, for support would be crucial. Walking a long way is a minor martyrdom, highly ignorable unless it attracts a rolling snowball of public support. But chaining yourself up is a bit like going on hunger strike: it is a kind of hostage situation, with your body as the hostage. The authorities, you hope, will feel forced to notice you and react. People in chains are awkward; they obstruct and have to be cleared out of the way.

These two looked very determined. I could see that by the way Lynne had folded her arms and the way Liney was looking at me. That meant that my job was to get everybody else to agree.

Why did everybody have to agree? Because disunity, at this point, would destroy not only what we had done so far, but also what we might do in the future. Whatever shared spirit we had conjured up had to be gathered up and poured, every droplet, into any new action any of us undertook. I felt this was absolutely necessary if a step further was going to have any chance of success. Everybody had agreed to the original action; they had not agreed to any escalation. It was something for which no one had bargained or budgeted for in time, or commitment, by any measure.

'You must be joking,' I said. Then, 'Trouble is, you're right. If you want to do it, we've all got to back you up or it'll be a shambles. Or maybe we all do it.'

Then Karmen, having noticed our absence, appeared. The idea was laid before her. She was at once enthusiastic, immediately got practical and began adding up the days we had left for planning; the places with shops where we might purchase the required hardware and so on. We were all staying in different people's houses that night, so we agreed to think about it and make the suggestion at the meeting the following night, when we'd be in a hall in Devizes.

The sun still shone out of a cloudless sky and the roads were long, shadeless and bounded by chalky banksides. Powder-blue scabious nodded and waved. Larks sang along. Saxophones and flutes tootled. Thalia performed cartwheels, at which she was exceptionally good. The police car with us broke down on a lonely stretch across the Wiltshire downs, so the women at the front held the banner with one hand while pushing the car along with the other. Oncoming motorists saw a ragged banner bearing the slogan 'Women for Life on Earth Peace March Cardiff to Greenham Common' waving above a white police car, which was being pushed along by a bunch of variously-aged women all showing a lot of flesh and laughing their heads off. The police inside the car were laughing as well.

At every county boundary we would be met by a new lot of police officers and a sort of 'hand-over' ceremony would take place. We would have to begin the training process all over again. They would want us to go here; we would want us to go there. They would want us to walk on the pavement, we would want to stay in the middle of the road – we were not just a big group of shoppers. The argy-bargy would begin, conducted by Karmen, fuelled by her particular penchant for men in uniforms. They would look at us in bewilderment and say, 'Who is your leader?' or some such form of words, and Karmen would say, 'Well we don't have one, not as such, but you can talk to me. The last lot were very good,' she would say, loudly. 'Very well-behaved indeed, couldn't fault 'em. You've got a lot to live up to.'

On one occasion, one rather pompous, tall officer from the Royal Berkshire Constabulary – a cut above the easy-going Wiltshire lot – said 'Right – here is the route we've decided for you.'

'Oh no, officer,' said Karmen, her eyes like black wells sparkling with stars of merriment. 'You've got it all wrong. On this march, we decide on the route.' For a moment he looked down, wooden-faced, humourless, at the small person in front of him. I was a helpless bystander. 'No,' I felt like shouting, 'don't look! Fall into those eyes, mate, it'll be ten years before you clamber out! You'll wake up gibbering in your sleep! You'll forget to wash the car on a Sunday!' He tumbled in, broke into a broad grin and said, 'All right, where do you want to go?'

We sat round that night in our big circle. Liney and Lynne explained their proposal. It was not very well received. Some women were enthusiastic but most, I think, were not.

Only a few were saying anything, so I was guessing at their reactions. Some thought we would simply make fools of ourselves. Thalia, her eyes shining, said she was all for it. It was a good idea but would invite police brutality upon us. 'Make no mistake,' she said, 'policemen's helmets will roll. If we start to get effective, they'll react. It's all very cosy now, this lovely relationship we've got with our police escorts, but they'll show their true colours all right.'

I suspected she was wrong, and that we would remain as we were now, beneath notice, for some time. Stirred up by this alarmist statement, all the talkers began to talk at once, and the quiet women stayed silent; it was clear there was no agreement in the air. The meeting was getting impossible to chair. There were two women who were from a women's group in Cambridge, who so far had been rather quiet, saying very little. One of them spoke.

'When something happens like this and we can't agree,' she said, 'what we do is this: we all go round the circle, and everybody says briefly what they are thinking, but nobody comments or tries to reply or react to them. Nobody is silent either. Everyone speaks in turn. That's all. Then we leave it until the next time we meet.'

So that is what we did. That first time we all sat round and each spoke in turn, many, perhaps most of the women there voiced misgivings of one kind or another about the proposed action.

'I only know,' said Margery Lewis, 'that this is not what I came to do. Coming on this march was a big step, but I felt sure it was right and now I know it was. This other thing, I'm not sure about. I wish my husband was alive, because we always used to discuss everything together, and he was a wise and thoughtful man. Now I don't know what would be the right thing to do.' Margery's husband had died not long before; she was sixty-five and they had been married many years. She spoke for many there.

Janet Tyrrell was one of the women who had brought their children along (because she had to – she was a single mother). She too was ambivalent in her reaction. 'I'm not sure if it really is the right thing to do. We could lose all the strength we've built up between us. Perhaps we should be satisfied with what we've achieved so far. We don't know what our influence has been. It might be more than we think.'

Several said they felt we risked losing something precious and important we had created between us, as a group: something only partially and inadequately described by words like trust and solidarity, something we had come to talk about jokingly as 'our spirit'. Perhaps we were achieving something, quietly and on a local level, that should not be overlooked, and to undertake a more high-profile action might jeopardize the goodwill and respect we had so far encountered along our route. We should be patient, maybe. Our message would take time. We had already achieved things; people in our families and the places from where we had come knew what we were doing and why. Everyone wanted to avoid breaking into two separate groups, but this began to seem inevitable.

Liney, Lynne and Karmen were disappointed. Now they had to decide whether they would go it alone, with those few who were in support, or not. I would have to decide what to do, which group to stay with. I felt disappointed, and dispirited too. We were walking – or rather romping along, by now, a good twelve miles a day, but still the adrenalin flowed. I had to borrow sleeping tablets from Margery, or I would have stayed awake all night.

Walking to Marlborough –
How Eunice spoke for us

The next day we walked through the Savernake Forest and stopped for lunch under the huge grey beech trees. Everyone was talking, in pairs and groups, about what to do. There seemed more difference of opinion than ever. We agreed that when we got to Marlborough we would have another meeting and air our differences in the same way. It seemed a good, calm sort of approach and got round the problem of the shy people not feeling able to say anything. But when we were all sat down in a big circle and the meeting began, I was shaking without understanding why this was, why I should be feeling so much tension.

Two young women who had joined us were animal rights activists. They said emphatically that they couldn't afford to get involved in anything illegal, such as being chained up, as that would jeopardise their other illegal things with the animal people.

Thalia referred again to a rough-and-tumble vision of rolling helmets and repression as the underlying fascist state revealed its true nature. General doubts were expressed one after the other: What was the legal status of such an action? Was it obstruction? Criminal damage? Trespass? Conspiracy? Breach of the peace? Treason? We had made a discreet phone call to a friendly solicitor during the day and were able to answer these questions. We might be charged with any or none of the above. Wouldn't the reaction of the authorities surely be swift and decisive – they could hardly allow women to stay chained up to such an important place for longer than five minutes? Those with jobs were concerned about a possible conviction. Even if only a few actually attempted to chain themselves up, we might all be charged with conspiracy to whatever crime it was decided to call it. Even if the law wasn't involved at all, whatever action a few took would reflect on us all and would affect how we all felt about the whole action so far and how other people reacted to it. Might we not just look very silly if we tried something like this and it didn't work?

About half the group had expressed their views, mostly doubtful, when Eunice Stallard, the white-haired grandmother from Ystradgynlais, sitting opposite me in the big circle, took her turn to speak – we were following, in strict discipline, the 'no comment' format.

'Well,' she said, and the rich tones of the valleys of south Wales rolled round the brown wood-panelled room. 'What's the matter with you all? What are we all so afraid of? We've got to do something more, they're just ignoring us. So what if policemen's helmets roll? What are we here for? What's worse than a nuclear war? I'll do it!'

A century and a half of rolling helmets, of people blocking traffic and roads and shouting and making a fuss about basic human rights, about decent living and working conditions, about the right to combine, about the right to organise, about the rights of the poor, about the rights of women, a century not yet over, for the days of the miners' strikes were still to come, spoke through her. So what, indeed. With those few simple words, Eunice cut through objections and misgivings like a scythe through a bunch of lettuces.

'I agree with Eunice…' 'She's right…' 'Eunice spoke for me…' and suchlike statements followed. Not one now spoke against the proposal. Those who had voiced doubts earlier said they agreed to back up whoever wanted actually to undertake the action. We decided that we would be represented by four women, Liney and Lynne (as it was their idea) and Eunice and Helen, as between them they ranged in age from twenty something to sixty something, and that just these four would chain themselves up. Apart from any other logistical consideration, we had very little money in the kitty and couldn't afford to buy chains for everybody!

We agreed to form a 'chain gang' group, which would meet to discuss the nitty-gritty of how to do it and what to do about weeing and worse. Above all, we now felt unanimous again, with the continuing exception of the two animal-rightists, who were sniffy and said we were mere amateurs dabbling in matters about which they declared themselves to be the professional judges. Theirs was the only view we ignored. For the rest, we had stayed together. Our loyalty and commitment to each other would continue.

As the meeting ended, I looked round at this group of young, middle-aged and elderly women, struck dumb by tears at their courage, their honesty, their consideration for each other's point of view, their concern for each other and the way they had reached this decision. There had been no posturing or speech-making, no considering of self above others, nor any self-conscious borrowing of religious rituals from ancient cultures, no chanting, no hand-holdings or 'unifying exercises', none of the paraphernalia which would follow soon enough; just speaking, listening, hearing, thinking, and deciding.

How quaint, how timid, our fears and misgivings seem now. 'Are these really Greenham Women?' I hear you cry out in dismay. But our very fears were also our strength – for we were not a bunch of battle-hardened political activists sharing none of the concerns and constraints of the rest of the population, eager to embark on the next protest, people with nothing to lose. No. We had friends, jobs, children, husbands, parents, interests and obsessions, homes and possessions – in short, lives like anybody's, vulnerable to disruption. As a group, we were, like most people, cautious. Going on the march had already been a big step, a major commitment. Now what had begun as one thing was about to turn into another.

Why a good society needs ironmongers

Liney and I were sent off by the top-secret committee, which then met to discuss How to Do It, to buy suitable chains. We found a nice, old-fashioned ironmongers in Marlborough.

Those were the days before B&Q and Do-It-All and Great Mills, the days when you could still buy small items like, um, nails and cup-hooks and suchlike, by quantity: such as 'I'd like

67

ten inch-and-a-half nails please,' or, 'Three cup-hooks please,' and the person serving you would say, 'Do make sure you use a bradawl to make the hole first.' The items would be served to you in paper bags, easily opened and harmlessly disposed of afterwards. Since these shops were always run by men in overalls, they were generously stocked not only with rivets, nuts and tap washers, masonry nails rawl-plugs and size 8 screws, but also with an attitude: the ever-optimistic cheeriness, the head-in-the-sand denial of life's ultimately tragic reality, of the small-time builder, bodger, and gardener.

They twinkled with blue-and-white lobelia and alyssum and seed packets, they flashed with galvanised iron and smelled of metal, linseed oil and paraffin. Their dark, cavernous interiors were always run by people who knew everything about fixing things up and who would be likely to interrogate you, with the best possible intentions, about the purpose of your purchases and whether you had made a wise choice and whether all the other tools appropriate to the task you had in mind were to hand.

So we had to have a story, while assessing the various lengths and weights of chains on offer without appearing to really take much interest in them at all, as we were under strict instructions (emanating from the ultra-paranoid Politburo-style 'chain gang') not to attract attention to ourselves or look suspicious in any way. We thought maybe we should pretend we had three very fierce dogs that needed chaining up, but we didn't think this seemed very plausible and anyway we couldn't stop ourselves from giggling as we surreptitiously measured how much was needed to go round our slim little waists. We had no idea what sort of length to get or anything. How were we going to fix the things? Ah! Padlocks – expensive. We probably had about nine pounds eighty-seven pence so all we could get was about three metres of chain and four of the smallest padlocks.

All the participants in the 'chain gang' were sworn to secrecy concerning the final arrangements, as some people were convinced that so sensitive were the security procedures surrounding military bases, such as that towards which we were wending our way down the A4, we must by now be under surveillance of a nature so subtle and advanced as to be undetectable. The proprietors of this and other hardware shops within striking distance of our route would have been alerted to our designs. Surely our purchase of several yards of chain from a traditional high street ironmongers would result in several van-loads of riot police, complete with dogs and riot-shields, awaiting us when we arrived at Greenham. It was a politically sensitive place. They would be keen to nip any potentially awkward developments in the bud, wouldn't they?

Nettles

Despite the risk of calling attention to our newly subversive selves, we decided to make a social call on another base kindly given to our closest allies, the Americans, at Welford. There is a slip road off the M4, which goes directly up to this place, between Hungerford and Newbury. It has a sign saying 'Works Access' but it is no such thing. It is there so that military vehicles can get onto the motorway quickly from this base. It wasn't built for the likes of you or me. It is a supply base, and during the by-now-notorious Iraq war of 2003, was used to store the bombs that were dropped on Baghdad by the B52 bombers that took off from nearby Fairford airfield.

We rang up the people in charge at Welford to tell them we were coming, and the purpose of our journey. The day was even hotter than the eight previous days. Outside the perimeter fence (eight feet of stout wire mesh on concrete posts, topped by three rows of barbed wire, a configuration that would become familiar over the as yet unborn years to thousands of women) was a neat mowed lawn, and little bushes and hedges.

A man and woman in US Army uniforms came out to meet us and listened while one of our number delivered a speech (now that we were all about ten feet tall, we could all say succinctly and clearly, without mumbling or referring to notes, why we were asking that 'Cruise' missiles not be stationed in our country) and gave us tea in plastic cups and 'cookies', of the type that would soon be all over our supermarkets and garages helping to make us more like the Americans, i.e. fat. We had picked a huge bunch of flowers from the hedgerows along the route, including stinging nettles for symbolic value. We gave them the flowers and they sniffed them, recoiled, and said, 'Thank you ma'am.'

Recently I was talking about all this to one of the other women, and she said that incident stuck in her mind as a point at which she felt something that came to be familiar, feeling faintly ridiculous and yet, oddly, paradoxically, powerful.

The flowers themselves were mostly golden yellow, powder blue and mauve. There were yellow dog-toothed hawkbits and cat's-ear, sheeps' bit scabious as blue as glaciers, and the papery flowers of field chicory like pieces of the blue heavens; deep mauve, feathery knapweed, a bit of creamy white, lacy wild carrot, some lemon yellow vetch. I guess the point is, if that American woman had ever walked these native lanes, if she had ever looked at the wild flowers, which still in those days adorned them, if she had ever paid them any attention, she would easily have spotted the nettles which were quite obvious, and would not have stuck her nose into them.

Arrival (i)
Greenham Common, September 5th, 1981

That night in Newbury the 'chain gang' met to finalise the details. A very cautious trip was taken by car to have a look at the scene. No one dared actually stop or get out, but the main gate was plainly viewed. The problem, it was assumed, would be actually getting across the fifty yards or so of grass out front before the police, who could be presumed to be waiting, possibly inside the base itself, could arrest those involved. The four women would have to run as fast as they could. The chains would have to be already wound round their waists, so that they could just hook on within a few seconds. They did lots of practice with their padlocks. As far as the running went, they were already fit from their ten days of walking. Other problems were anticipated, to do with the alimentary canal. Skirts would have to be worn for discreet peeing purposes, and no food and very little fluid would be consumed in the preceding twelve hours. I felt secretly glad that I wasn't subject to any such prohibitions. I was composing the declaration about our purposes, to be read out once the women had successfully chained themselves up, whilst gratefully sinking what I felt to be a well-deserved pint of beer in a pub in Newbury.

It worried me that we had no specific aim beyond the full cancellation of the 'Cruise' project and that our government put in hand multilateral nuclear disarmament. This of course was what we were going to achieve, but I thought, as this was a process rather than a single event, we needed some sort of interim, realistic-sounding 'demand'. So we settled on asking for a public debate, televised, between our representatives and the Secretary of State for Defence. This declaration was given to Karmen who would accompany the four women and would read it out, to whoever emerged from the base to hear it, at the first opportunity.

The operation would be monitored by our fully qualified doctor, who would try to make sure the women didn't get too dehydrated on their nothing-in-nothing-out regime. The women would throw her the keys of the padlocks. She would arrive in one car at 7.30am, and drive on past the base so as not to attract suspicion. The car would stop only briefly to let out her and Karmen who would walk the few yards back up to the gate, arriving to synchronise with the second car, the trusty VW Polo belonging to Marjorie Lewis, which would convey the four women with their ready-in-place chains. This would arrive at exactly 7.32 a.m. outside the main gate. We didn't bother to envisage what might happen over any length of time because obviously the Ministry of Defence and the Americans wouldn't let women remain chained to the gates of USAF Greenham Common for longer than a few hours at the very most.

There was one remaining problem, which had got a bit overlooked in all these preparations – what would the rest of us do? We expected to be joined by supporters from Reading, Newbury and London. Nobody knew whether the police would stop the march going to the main gate. A local bye-law prevented any gathering likely to involve more than a hundred people outside the main gate of this military airbase. Accordingly, the police told us on the morning of September 5th that we would have to go to the small gate at the back of the base, on an insignificant by-road.

'We're not doing that,' we thought. As we loaded our luggage into the van for the last time, a message came back to say the chaining had been successful. Greenham Common airfield is about a mile and a half from the town centre of Newbury. To get to it, you walk down a bypass road, a modern fast sort of road, which has since had to be bypassed by another bypass, through a couple of roundabouts and then you are on an old-fashioned country 'A' road, a busy road to Basingstoke (another town surrounded by a cat's-cradle of bypass roads). The first roundabout is where the small suburban road to the back perimeter fence turns off. As we approached it, I ran to the police superintendent at the front of the march. Well, he wasn't right at the front. In recognition of the fact that this was a women's march, the police had voluntarily placed a WPC at the very front, up there with our pink front banner and an image of the tree of life in a circle cut out of cardboard and painted, which a woman called Margaret carried very slowly, with a ram-rod straight back, right at the very front of quite a long, straggling crowd of women. I have to say, she looked terrific.

'Look here,' I said. 'We've been told we're meant to be going to the back gate but we want to go round to the main gate – I mean, we've walked all the way from Cardiff to get here and there'll be people coming to the front gate to meet us, so don't you think that's where we should be?'

'I don't see why not,' he replied. 'Mind you, there's some loonies of some sort trying to steal your thunder. We got a report earlier of some women chaining themselves up there this morning. Just thought I should let you know – they could still be there, we're just ignoring them. Just tell the WPC we'll be going straight on at the roundabout, then.'

The same neat little box hedges and shaven lawns as we had seen at Welford came into view, making a small patch of civilised parkland round the short entrance road to the base itself. On either side stretched woods of birch, oak, and pine. This was, after all, an ancient common. Through the trees, we saw for the first time, the fence.

At seven thirty that morning, the sort of morning when it seems the world quietly hums not with traffic but with bees and insects, a car had pulled up into the driveway sweeping round to the front entrance of the military air base known as USAF Greenham Common. It stopped briefly to let out its occupants, who immediately ran to the metal mesh fence at the side of the main, steel, double gates. The single policeman standing in front of the gates regarded this event quizzically, but then found his attention distracted by a small woman with large dark eyes who stood, neatly clad in T-shirt and light trousers, in front of him. She seemed to be wearing an odd kind of scarf, and was about to try to read to him from a piece of type-written paper she had taken from her pocket. Clearing her throat, she began:

'This is an open letter from the Women's Peace March to the Base Commandant, US Air Force, Greenham Common, Berkshire. We are a group of women from all over Britain who have walked one hundred and twenty miles from Cardiff to deliver this letter to you. Some of us have brought our babies with us this entire distance. We fear for—'

Aware that he was not taking in this bizarre declaration and feeling even more puzzled, he interrupted her with the words,

'Aren't you a bit early?'

This caused the young woman to look around in alarm, as if she were expecting something – several armoured cars full of military police, for instance. But seeing nothing to disturb the peacefulness of the scene, hearing nothing but the thrushes and blackbirds singing from the poplar trees and silver birches that bordered the neatly trimmed lawns on either side of the driveway from the main A33, she asked him what he meant by this remark.

'Well,' he said, 'the cleaners don't usually arrive until eight o'clock. You are the cleaners, I take it?'

'Oh my God,' said Karmen. She went over to the four other women, who now stood, looking tense and expectant, in their voluminous skirts and large shirts, beside the fence. 'He thinks we're the cleaners,' she said. Three of the women bent forwards at the waist shaking and giving out small squeaking noises. Eunice Stallard, white-haired, aged 60, from the upper Swansea valley, leaned away from the fence and shouted to the policeman, himself a member of a fast-disappearing linguistic group, speakers of the local Berkshire accent, 'Cleaners! We're not your cleaners! We've chained ourselves to your gates! We've marched 'ere to protest against nuclear war!'

The policeman strolled over to where they stood, now revealing iron chains (medium weight) beneath their clothes. 'So you have,' he said. 'What have you done that for?'

Good question...

Arrival (ii) September 5th, 1981, 7.45 a.m.

This is what Karmen told me happened next: 'You weren't expecting us, then?' said another of the four chained women. 'Well, not if you're not the cleaners,' said the policeman. 'My job is to let the cleaners in at eight, you see. I'd better report this.' He spoke into his radio and after a short while, the gates opened to let out a uniformed man who had been driven there from inside the Tarmac and concrete expanse of the base. The two men spoke together and then Karmen approached with the piece of paper, introduced herself and began again to read from it. The uniformed man stood in front of the gate and listened politely. This time Karmen got as far as:

> 'We fear for the future of all our children, and for the future of the living world which is the basis of all life. We have undertaken this action because we believe that the nuclear arms race constitutes the greatest threat ever faced by the human race and our living planet. We have chosen Greenham Common as our destination because it is this base which our government has chosen for 96 'Cruise' missiles to arrive at in 1983. This decision has been made without our consent. The British people have never been consulted about our government's nuclear defence policy. We know that the arrival of these hideous weapons will place our entire country in the position of a frontline—'

She had become aware of a line of about a dozen women, all dressed in black, who had taken up position a few yards away, on the other side of the gates from the chained four. They seemed to have materialised from nowhere, and were making a sort of moaning, wailing sound which was increasing in intensity towards a concerted scream. Things never go according to plan.

These were Reading Women for Peace, who upon hearing news of the expected arrival later that morning of the women's peace march from Cardiff, had decided that the most appropriate way they could contribute to the occasion, and show their support, would be to demonstrate the ancient and feminine art of keening, the making of a loud sound of grief. They had been practising their keening for weeks, and had decided to come early to get in some on-site keening inspired by the vision of the place to which the 'Cruise' missiles would actually be delivered. This, then, was the Reading Keeners, not to be confused with the mistakenly-identified 'cleaners' nor with the real cleaners employed by the base, who had also, by this time, begun to arrive.

Karmen was beginning to be exasperated. 'What on earth is that horrible noise?' she demanded. 'I'm trying to read something out here. Would you lot just mind shutting up for five minutes?'

A shocked silence ensued and Karmen finished reading our Declaration, the one which I had composed upon the pub table in Newbury the previous evening. Re-reading it twenty-five years later, I think it's fairly concise:

> 'We in Europe will not accept the sacrificial role offered us by our Nato allies. We will not be the victims in a war which is not of our making. We wish neither to be the initiators nor the targets of a nuclear holocaust. We have had enough of our military and political leaders, who squander vast sums of money and human resources on weapons of mass destruction while we can hear in our hearts the millions of human beings throughout the world whose needs cry out to be met. We are implacably opposed to the siting of 'Cruise' missiles in this country. We represent thousands of ordinary people who are opposed to these weapons and we will use all our resources to prevent the siting of these missiles here. We want the arms race to be brought to a halt now – before it is too late to create a peaceful, stable world for our future generations.'

The cleaners went through the gates. The officer likewise returned, bemused, to the inside. The policeman went home with a story to tell his wife. Groups of female cleaners are notorious for their weird pranks, and he was no doubt still unconvinced that this was not an elaborate joke. The keeners resumed their interrupted keening. Karmen sat down in the sun with the others to wait for the rest of the march to arrive from Newbury town centre.

September 5th, 1981, 6 p.m.
A hearth in the Forest of Arden

It was another lovely golden evening, but the September air already had that hint of autumn. We would need a fire to keep warm if we were going to spend the night out. I like lighting fires, so I set off collecting dry, dead wood, of which there was plenty in the woods, within a few yards of where the groups of women and the remaining local supporters sat around. We chose a bare-ish patch of lawn, and made a hearth with big stones. Soon we had a convivial fire, close enough to the fence to include the four chained women in the conversation. They regaled us with the account of their arrival, when the policeman on the gate had mistaken them for the cleaners. The four of them were still there in their chains, and by the end of the day we had begun to take it in turns to be chained up, to give everybody food and wee-breaks. (Where? In the woods, of course, which extended gloriously, for nine miles, either side of the neat lawns.) They weren't now chained to the gates themselves but to the fence on the left-hand side. The business of the base could carry on unimpeded by ourselves, as we weren't in fact obstructing anything. Throughout the day people had sat in the sun and chatted, speeches had been given by women who had never thought themselves capable of such a thing, supporters had turned up from Newbury, Reading, Oxford, and London. There had been a few intrigued reporters, one of whom had managed to contact some Ministry spokesperson who had said, 'They can stay there as long as they like – we're not going to do anything about them, no. Anyway, it's common land. We don't own it. Not our problem.'

That night I lay in my sleeping bag under the stars, propped against the fence, and couldn't sleep. My mind seemed to insist upon great travels, following first this then that path into the weeks and months and years to come, exploring every possible scenario. It always returned to the same place: sooner or later, whatever happened, they – the people in power – would have to listen to us. No longer could we be ignored. Now we would have to stay, and we would inevitably, in time, gather support. We had done it, whatever it was. Of course! What use is protest until it has focus? And what a place to have for a focus – not some concrete city of shops and offices, but a sylvan corner of the Old English Wildwood, a patch of primary woodland with great trees and brambles and fungi, an ancient common that had been seized from the public and now dedicated to the purpose of military-sanctioned mass murder. What a great campsite! We had stumbled upon none other than Shakespeare's Forest of Arden! I was amazed, my mind like a runaway horse galloping through the hours until the first bird began to sing in the tall poplars and the sky behind the gently rustling leaves turned back again through indigo to violet to pink to green to yellow to blue. It was going to be another perfect hot day.

Part ii
The Witness

Woman warming her hands at the fire, Greenham Common

Chapter 8

Solange's story

It is twenty-five years since the events I have described here. We still have nuclear weapons. Their possession and deployment makes no more sense now than it did then. Nuclear proliferation looks likely to run beyond anyone's control. The thinking, concerned people of the rich, nuclear-armed nations, have failed to prevent the spread of these weapons of mass destruction, have failed to convince politicians of their clear, utter, absurdity.

Perhaps we got side-tracked. One result of lying beside that fence in my sleeping-bag would be to plunge me into a world of assumptions. The biggest of these assumptions, one which persists to this day, was this: that because I and so many others were opposed to nuclear weapons, we were also opposed to all forms of military force, all war, in all circumstances. I would become part of a movement to disallow nuclear weapons which allowed itself, willy-nilly, to be called 'The Peace Movement', with the assumed aim of the renunciation of all our armed forces. I never felt comfortable with this label, or represented by it. This is despite the knowledge that armed conflict is the cause of most of the misery and poverty in the world, and that these wars which make arms dealers rich and whose victims are overwhelmingly women and children are mostly fuelled by greed and testosterone, and that the US-led wars of revenge for the attack known as nine-eleven are a disaster.

The journey which had brought me to lie awake beside that fence that night had begun before I was born. The cliché phrase 'where I am coming from' is useful here. The biggest influences on me were, quite simply, my mother and my father. This is where I am coming from. I am not coming from 'The Peace Movement'. I, and the rest of us, are coming, whether we like it or not, from The War.

Before going on, I want to go back. I want to climb back into their world, to think myself back into that time without knowing what is coming next, to feel a faint echo of what that felt like. I can't even really say why it's so important to do this, except by doing it. Come, let's go. This is an interlude, an interruption of her own story by one who is often accused of interrupting others, an investigation if you like. History isn't pre-ordained – it's spring, 1940 and the future hasn't happened yet. There are questions to be asked, questions we in the full-fed world, who know so little of ourselves, don't get asked, dilemmas we don't have to face – or not yet, anyway.

This is how the war began for my mother, a teenager in Northern France in May, 1940.

Solange, May 20th, 1940

A single black plane, like a hornet, appeared suddenly almost between the trees lining the road, which was blocked as far as the eye could see by slow-moving traffic. The traffic was a motley, strange-looking column, all going one way, at right angles to the morning sun which painted the trees' shadows in bluish stripes across the scene. There were carts, many pulled by horses, some by small tractors and others pushed by people, lorries crammed with people, bicycles and cars with running-boards and curvy, ample bodywork, aluminium hardware strapped onto their bonnets and spare wheels. Everything was piled high with every sort of household item; cars with mattresses and suitcases on their roofs and carts and trailers with small dogs and children on top of teetering piles of furniture, sacks and baskets.

Marie, Solange's mother, saw it first, from where she sat squashed into the back of a tiny grey Citroën car.

'Heuh!' She exclaimed. 'Il y a un avion qui vol rudement bas.' There's a plane flying terribly low.

Rat a tat tat! RATTA RATTA RATTA ! TATTA TATTA TATTA TATTA! Screams erupted from the line of refugees, immoblised in the heat of a clear day in May.

'Mon Dieu! Il nous a mitraillé.' My God! We've been machine-gunned.

'Il a mitraillé le convoi.' It's machine-gunned the convoy.

'Il y a des blessés là bas.' There's people wounded up there.

'Il chasse les Anglais.' He's after the English.

'C'etait un avion Allemand. Il y avait un swastika.' It was a German plane. There was a swastika.

People were getting out of cars, looking up at the sky, looking at their cars. A couple pushing a hand-cart began to shriek. Their child had been hit in the back. Others gathered round them. The women – most of these people were women, children, and elderly men – wore summer dresses printed with jazzy dots, stripes and little modernist motifs. There was confusion. No one knew what to do. A cart had overturned, and mattresses, a kettle, and a red armchair, lay skewiff across the road. There were even prams and wheel-barrows with suitcases, and baskets full of ducks and chickens piled on top in this strangely medieval-looking scene, a tableau made for Breughel.

'Un médicin! Est-ce qu'il y a un médicin, une infirmière ici?' Is there a doctor, a nurse here? a woman shouted, but there was shouting everywhere now.

'Il revient!' It's coming back!

As the Stuka appeared, anyone standing on their feet ran and threw themselves into the deep ditches on each side of the road, some rolling over and over in the long grass, nettles, and ox-eye daisies.

Again they listened in disbelief to the staccato pounding as the pilot flew as low as he dared, dead straight up the road, wing-tips at tree-top hight, firing. The plane screamed off into the silence of the wheatfields, the rich plains of Picardie.

The silence went on a long time. Even the newly-wounded and the children seemed to hold their breath. The horses began to graze the sides of the road. The bees continued to gather nectar. It seemed only they and the butterflies, of which there were many, moved.

Eventually the mother whispered to her daughter. '*Solange, tu es la?*' Solange, are you there?

'*Ouai*' Ye-es

'*Tu es blessée?*' Are you hurt?

'*Non*' No.

'*Et toi?*' And you?

'*Non*' No.

'*Qu'est-ce qu'on va faire maintenant?*' What are we going to do now?

'*Eh beh, on peut pas rester ici. Faut continuer.*' Well, we can't stay here. We'll have to carry on.

They clawed their way up the steep bank, peering cautiously over the top. Uncle Albert, the driver of the car, was fingering a small round hole at the back of the car. The bullet had only just missed the petrol tank. Others had not been so lucky and the smell of leaking petrol began to fill the air. People were re-emerging and hurrying now, rearranging loads, shouting at children who had begun to whimper. People now sat, bewildered, next to those who had been wounded, or tried to drag them in under the trees lining the road. Some began to turn their cars and carts around, saying that if this was going to happen, they'd all be killed out on the roads, and they might as well be killed in their homes. Shouting, screaming and crying broke out again.

'*Ce sont les Anglais qui bloquent les routes.*' It's the English blocking the roads

'*Mais non, ce sont les Francais qui ont retiré d'Amiens.*' No, it's the French army retreating from Amiens..

'*En Belgique ils ont bombardé tous les convois. Voilà ce qui'ils commencent ici.*' In Belgium they bombed all the convoys. Now they're starting here.

'*Où est l'armée Francais?*' Where's the French army?

'*Beh, ils ont quitte Amiens hier. Les Allemands ont bombarde la gare – n'ya plus rien qui reste. On dit qu'ils vont tous sur Dunkerque. C'est fini, tu sais.*' They left Amiens yesterday. The Germans bombed the station. There's nothing left. They say they're all going to Dunkirk. It's finished. I'm telling you.

'*Où sont les Anglais, quand on en a besoin?*' Where are the English when we need them?

'*On dit qu'ils sont à Albert, le front est la. Un Monsieur qui a quitte Cambrai hier a dit qu'il a vu les chars Allemands en traversant les champs , et rien qui ne les a empeches.*' They say they're at Albert, that's where the front is. A man who left Cambrai yesterday said he saw the German tanks crossing the fields, with nothing stopping them.

'*Où ch'est qu'ils vont?*' (Most of these people spoke in Northen accents, which turned an 's' sound into a 'sh' sound). Where are they going?

'*Eh beh, ils vont á là Manche, comme nous.*' Well, they're going to the coast, like us.

'The English', 'the French', ' the Germans' do not here refer to holiday-makers or particular ethnic groups. These words refer to armies. The pilot of the plane who shot at the line of fleeing refugees would have enjoyed a scene, I imagine, similar to the anthills I used to delight in, I'm sorry to say, poking with sticks when I was a child. This anthill would have looked as if the top of it had been suddenly lifted off. All the roads leading west out of every town and village were full of people carrying belongings in much the same way the ants would scurry about, apparently randomly, cumbersomely lugging their big white eggs with them. The armies of Britain and France were in groups, moving hither and thither, some in the backs of lorries, some in small groups of tanks, some dragging wheeled guns, some in columns of armoured cars. Some that day were moving towards the town of Arras, some were stationary, preparing to defend a canal bridge here, or a road there, against the steadily advancing German tanks, which used the novel approach of bypassing the blocked roads and advancing, in places, straight across the undulating fields of ripening wheat.

A week earlier the first people had crossed the red and white stripey road barrier on the frontier between France and Belgium. My future-mother, Solange Dhulst, and her mother, Marie Dhulst, had stood outside in the street to watch them, people with grim exhausted faces pushing their furniture and mattresses on handcarts, cars piled high with stuff, even tin baths and chairs strapped to the bonnet. They made for the Mairie, for churches, they slept in the streets and under the market tarpaulins in the main square. And during the week there had been jolly, joking lorry-loads of British soldiers, going the other way into Belgium. The roads were all cobbled with shiny, black, square paving-stones, and anything wheeled made a tremendous shake, rattle and roll.

Then the station at Arras was bombed, killing some children whose parents had been sending them off to stay with relatives in the country. People were starting to do this, put their children on to trains, on their own. Uncle Albert called at my grandmother's house on Saturday and told them he could take the two of them in a car. They had to be ready to leave the next morning, Sunday the 19th of May.

Solange wrote a 'things-to-take' list, in a little book with a brown paper cover. I know this because she kept the book and I still have it. She wrote in ink on squared paper, as in all French note-books. These are the things a nineteen-year-old took with her when she left home because a foreign army was invading her country:

> paper, envelopes, stamps, ink
> 1 tube toothpaste, mug, toothbrush
> scarf, beret, mittens
> 1 warm coat, 3 bras
> 4 pairs woollen stockings, 1 tube Vaseline
> 2 nightshirts, 1 support stocking
> 1 pair shoelaces, 4 hand-towels
> 1 woolly shirt, 1 tube 'Brontyrol'

1 dressing-gown, 1 wash-glove
1 dozen sanitary towels, 16 pocket hankies
3 [2 is crossed out] pullovers, 1 skirt
3 silk shirts
3 vests
1 jacket
1 pair slippers
2 pairs shoes
1 wool vest
4 pairs of knickers [at last! – I thought she'd forgotten them!]
1 pair scissors
1 pair silk stockings
1 (pretty) pinafore
2 pairs knitting needles and knitting

She wrote the date of their departure, May 19th, the place they spent the night, and a little paragraph about the machine-gunning, the bombarded convoys, the blocked and impassable roads of the 20th as they tried to escape west. She wrote nothing else about that journey. The rest, and all the other stories about the war, she told me when I was grown up, before she died.

Motivated now by fear and panic to use the full width of the road and its verges, the refugees began to move. No more planes arrived, but as the day wore on the noise of explosions could be heard getting louder, closer and more frequent to the south, as they neared the town of Amiens. Albert decided to get off the main road, the *Nationale*, and plunged into a maze of tiny lanes, making for the town of Abbeville where the river Somme widens as it nears the English Channel.

Every village presented people on the road staring in disbelief and others turning out the contents of their houses into carts and, rarely, vehicles, some even throwing things out of upstairs windows. By three o'clock, avoiding the town centre of Abbeville, they crossed the Somme at the village of Pont-Remy. They continued towards Dieppe, the booms and bangs from over the horizon slowly diminishing.

An hour or two later, what looked like little puffs of smoke on the southern horizon, already turning golden in the afternoon sun, resolved themselves into the columns of dust, as far as the eye could see, raised by the tanks of General Guderain's divisions, which together with those of Rommel would cut off the British and French armies and force the evacuation of Dunkirk. They too, were going to the seaside. Guderain drove into Abbeville in advance of his tank division, 2nd Panzer, at five o'clock that afternoon, May 20th, 1940. Given a free hand, he would have been there a whole day earlier. Days in May 1940 in Northern France were like the days of our childhoods, when whole lifetimes of experiences happen in a few hours. A whole twenty-four hours, then, really was a long time in the Battle for France, upon the outcome of which would depend, not only the fate of my own family, but that of whole populations – of Britain, of Russia, of Europe's Jews.

My great-uncle Albert drove down lanes that would become deeper, greener, and more drenched in the fragrance of honeysuckle and May blossom as they drove into hilly, wooded Normandy, and a landscape wrapped in as profound a peace as you could imagine. Here the cows still lay, drunk with contentment, in fields frothy with flowers, and processed in the evening with swishing tails into timber-framed barns to give milk for cream and Camembert. The desperate mooing of unmilked and abandoned animals with bursting udders, which had accompanied their two-day journey across what hindsight and a Michelin map would reveal to have been a battlefield upon which the fate of Europe had been decided, receeded and joined other sights, sounds and smells in the realm of nightmare and foreboding.

General Weygand, recalled from Syria to take charge of the French forces, tired after his journey, spent Monday May 20th 1940 asleep in bed.

That night, a farmer, astonished to find that war had found his corner of the countryside, would allocate Uncle Albert, Marie and Solange a haybarn in which to sleep. Here on top of a great pile of the previous year's hay they slept like babies, a slumber of such relief that even when the rats running over their bodies woke them up from time to time, they merely sighed contentedly and drifted off again until a milky, misty sun came up. It was the first night Solange had ever slept without the constant whirring of the machines from the factory across the road, the first unforgettable sound of a night whose silence is punctuated by no more than owls – hunting, courting, owls near, owls afar.

No one can ever believe that a plane will come out of a clear blue sky and try to kill them, until it does.

Chapter 9

Zone Interdite, 1942-1943

Marie and Solange spent six weeks by the seaside after they evacuated in May, 1940, staying with a distant aunt in Normandy. It was the first holiday they had ever had. My young future-mother grew strong and tanned and acquired a love of paddling by the water's edge. One day there was a body washed up on the beach, and the next day the German commander summoned all the refugees to the town square and told them to return to their home towns, where they would be issued with ration cards on production of identity papers. He spoke arrogantly, in bad French, and told them that the glorious Third Reich would create a world of order and progress, a civilisation which would last a thousand years.

Uncle Albert drove them back to Tourcoing, a French industrial town on the Belgian border. The official title of this region would become the *Zone Interdite* – the Prohibited Zone. Although part of France, it was administered by the German occupiers as part of Belgium.

Geopolitically, this is Flanders, a land whose flatness has kindly lent itself to successive invading armies throughout its inhabited history. There are deKeyzers in Belgium, and deKeyzers in France. There are deRhykers and Huyts and Loos. There are as many H's and K's in combination in the cemeteries as you could imagine. Why does a certain landscape favour certain letters of the alphabet? Why do the people of the North favour the onion over garlic, why do they love chips, why do they eat horsemeat to the extent that a horse's head protrudes, elegantly sculpted, from the pediment of half the butchers' shops that sprinkle the dark, liver-red brick streets of terraces?

By the cold midwinter of 1942-1943, down one of those streets, glowing in the pink light of a disappearing midwinter sun people hurry against the plummeting cold. Before this time, and after it, they would need to pick their way around tiny piles of dog-shit (evidence of the typical size of the dog as much as of the diet) but the dogs, and the cats, have disappeared. There are holes in the square cobbles which someone has attempted to fill with asphalt, and in their nostrils the sweetish smell of drains, burning coal and various other *je-ne-sais-quoi*'s. The traffic is sparse, the occasional car making a roar as it passes over the cobbles. Instead lorries carrying helmeted, uniformed soldiers or armoured cars carrying officers, rattle along at top speed. The most numerous mode of transport is the bicycle, the most popular head-gear the black or navy beret, the age-group most conspicuous by its absence, men in their prime. The gutters are deep and uneven, and filled with rolls of fluff from the factories, whose vast blank brick walls line many of the streets, including this street,which is almost like a narrow canyon between houses on one side and a continuous factory wall, turning the corner, on the other. It is the factories that provide the soundtrack as well, day and night. A sort of constant shushing and murmuring, punctuated by clacks and thwacks, and sirens which sound off at varying times.

It is the factories which, for all that the worst kind of exploitation of people's minds and bodies takes place within them, have for fifty years provided the work which is the basis of the self-respect, pride and self-confidence these hurrying people undoubtedly possess, not only men but women too. Everybody works in the factories, making carpets, churning out pink bras and silk stockings by the million, sending floral tablecloths, overalls petticoats and pinnies with all the latest designs – little modernist dots and dashes, bold jazzy stripes, fabrics covered in faces or zigzags interspersed with triangles and lozenges, whizzing round the world from Guinée to Tahiti to Martinique. Mucky old fleeces from sheep that have cropped the grass on cold, wet hillsides, fleeces shorn on a Pennine farm, once found their way here, by boat and train, and got processed into malleable, brilliantly dyed balls of wool that are sold to the half of the population, which constantly knits. Oh yes, people had been poor but they were not destitute: they earned, and they could choose to look smart and fashionable. They earned, and when the rent was paid – which it generally was – they could choose to eat well, for most of their money was spent on food and, of course, on drink, much of it originating in the Bordeaux region.

A house in the Rue de Renaix

At the moment I have chosen to revisit Tourcoing, things appear similar – but they are quite different. Since the factories have reopened (after the Armistice, after the people came back to find their houses much as they had fled them in May 1940) it is mostly heavy woollen great-coats, the double-breasted sort with the big flappy collars you see in the photographs, that the people make, and army uniforms, and sheets and blankets, tents, webbing belts, anything useful for the war effort. It all goes to Germany, helping the Germans consolidate their efficiently-administered control of the whole of Europe, Norway, North Africa, and European Russia. They control all this in the name of a clean, wholesome, healthy vision of mankind at its pinnacle of excellence, blond, fair-skinned, racially and ethnically 'pure'.

The narrow terrace brick-built house, darkened by the high wall of the factory opposite, on Rue de Renaix, has a front door, which opens straight onto the street, and a window, which despite being grilled is nonetheless secured with a pair of stout wooden shutters, themselves kept in place by a bar operated from the inside. It is just as well there are shutters to make opening the door a matter of time, for this is a country under occupation, and the young woman standing in the room has already put herself at more risk than she probably realised. Or did she realise it? Risk, past and future, is just one of the thoughts going through her mind at this moment, this midwinter evening.

The floor of the passage leading straight through the house from the front door is tiled in black and white, a geometric pattern reminiscent of the interiors of Dutch masters. To the right is a room that fronts onto the street and is never used. It has a large heavy brown sideboard, in which a collection of heavy linen tablecloths are kept, and a tin tray with wine glasses, real crystal with gold rims. There is a sagging brown velvet-covered settee above which are hung two photographs, black-and-white of course. One shows a couple, grim and unsmiling, staring straight to camera, both with hair parted down the middle. It is a wedding photo! The other, equally grim, shows two women in the stiff high-necked garb of the 1880s, hair piled on top. They look guarded and sinister. People always did when they had spent all morning getting dressed up for this trial, this defining test, this studio photograph in front of the faded-out background, an idyllic country scene such as none of these people, though of sturdy peasant stock themselves, had ever seen.

The passage leads into an altogether jollier, if cluttered, room. Here cut-out advertisements have been used as pictures, such as the red laughing cow, *La Vache Qui Rit,* which advertises the famous soft cheese, and a calender advertising the Post Office, red and blue, hangs on the wall. A pair of wooden Swiss chalets, luridly painted, display *'petits mots'*: *'La bonne humour ne coute rien',* *'Une sourire peut tuer une soupire'.* The room is heated (not now, of course, but normally) by a tall maroon enamel stove with a curvy, sexy top, beneath which is a polished hot-plate for boiling a kettle. On the wallpapered walls, which show mildew in the corners, hangs a wooden clock-case and a pendulum clock that ticks loudly, ponderously. There is a big saggy armchair, with wooden arms and a knitted cushion, in the corner, but the centre of the room is the table, which is always covered with an oilcloth of a garish design. When not in use the chairs, which are cane-backed and seated, are kept against the walls, as if in waiting. Perhaps they are waiting their turn to be burnt, for that will come. The radio, a brown bakelite construction with a webbing front, is on a side table, sitting on a fringed cloth, under the 'P.T.T.' calendar. The kitchen beyond is almost half-outdoors, a much smaller room, with a lean-to roof, a small table, a wooden double-doored cupboard, an enamel pail, a wide shallow sink with a pump handle above, a drawer, a blue enamel gas cooker with two scoured shiny aluminium pans sitting on it. Beyond this the house sort of collapses into a series of lean-tos and outhouses, running along the side of an ashphalted, gritty yard with a brick path. One houses the toilet, which they call the 'water', pronounced to rhyme with 'hat air'. It has a wooden seat, which has a round hole in its centre and a cover you lift by putting your finger into a hole in that. Below this is a glistening black hole, from which a strong smell arises, obviously, and the sound of running water from the sewer some ten feet below. Beside the seat is a rusty tin kept full of rain-water, and a pile of torn-up pieces of the local newspaper, La Voix du Nord. The hole, equally obviously, is encrusted with old shit, but a strong smell of french black tobacco moderates and even mingles with the sewage smell to create a rather savoury, certainly unforgettable, aroma. Next-door is a further sort of cubby-hole for vegetables, and here are the pails for washing, and a ridged wash-board, and a bucket of what my grandmother used to call 'savon noir', 'black soap', which is some sort of by-product of the coal industry, smelling like Wright's coal tar soap. Memère attributed almost miraculous curative and cleansing properties to this stinking sticky dark-brown stuff, particularly when it came to hair washing. Finally there is a tiny piece of frozen dust where, since the previous summer, the two women have tried to grow beans.

In this house, Solange and Marie Cuvulier-Dhulst, my mother and grandmother, hid a British soldier for six months from August 1940 to February 1941. He had got left behind in the chaos of the retreat to Dunkirk. It was probably my grandfather, Jean Dhulst, who had picked him up and brought him to be sheltered by his ex-wife. Having deserted from the French army he had joined the resistance against the German invaders. By this time he and Marie had been divorced for some time – when drunk, which was often, he had beaten her and their daughter and after twelve years of suffering Marie had walked out. The Catholic Church excommunicated her for her pains, allowing her back only for her funeral.

According to local records, there were quite a few of these British soldiers, whose presence had to be kept an absolute secret even from the closest and most trusted of neighbours and family. Although at that time there was, historians tell us, no organised resistance to the German occupation, someone managed to find the contacts to get the soldier out and safely back to Britain. The route from Holland, Belgium, and the North of France, using safe houses and with groups travelling by night, went down through France to the Pyrenees, across to Spain, then to North Africa and then onto a British warship.

The Belgian group which organised this escape route, known as the 'Comet Line' would last two years before it was betrayed by an informer. But in that time it saved the lives of hundreds of British soldiers and Nazi resisters.

La cuisine Française

Solange worked in the factory opposite the house in the *Rue de Renaix*, until she went down with pneumonia in November of 1942. She had thought then that she would die. Yet she had fought to live, and had filled her mind with food when all Marie could make was soup made from potato peelings and other vegetable scraps. The rations entitled the population to, at most, 1,100 calories – about half the daily normal human requirement. They had coupons, but the bread often ran out before they could get any. There was no more butter, no fat, no milk, eggs, and no meat. Sometimes they ate rats, if they could catch them.

Every September weekend mother and daughter had got up at

dawn to be in the queue for the first '*Mongy*', the tram which left from *La Place St Christophe*, and rattled and swung its way down twelve kilometres of boulevard all the way to Lille. But they got off after fifteen minutes, at the stop called *Les Trois Suisses*, where there was still a burnt-out British tank leftover from May 1940. Here on the boulevard was where the factory owners had their houses, each one like a perfect château in miniature – you could almost see Rapunzel letting down her hair and princes hiding in those thick high hedges. But they plunged down a side-road where terraced houses gave way to individual one-storey cottages, some very decrepit, finally revealing that vast flat expanse of Flanders, of fields delineated by reed-filled ditches, of distant lines of trees; a vista criss-crossed by slowly flapping herons.

This was *la chasse aux pommes de terre*, the potato chase. Carrying shopping bags and hessian sacks, they joined many thousands of others tramping from farm to farm begging a few potatoes. It was the only way. The crops were being grown, all right, but the size of each farm had been noted, the yield had been noted, and the expected amount to be delivered to the occupiers had been given. A farmer couldn't stand there when the squads drove in and say, 'I haven't got any', when clearly he had. Sometimes the women were told they could go and dig some of the precious tubers up themselves, which they did with alacrity. Sometimes they would go out with cousins or more distant relatives, to where someone had found a new contact, so-and-so's maiden aunty's god-mother's uncle who worked on the land and had saved something back. The war turned them all into a nation of back-yard scavengers, skilled in detecting edible wild foods. In spring they ate hog-weed shoots, sorrel from the fields and roadsides, cow parsley. Dandelion replaced lettuce, and when coffee became scarce, even dandelions became scarce because people dug up their roots and roasted and ground them up as a substitute.

There was no treatment for pneumonia, which kills people if they are weak. Solange lay in bed under as many blankets as they owned. She was burning with fever and feeling icy cold. She wrote a list of every French dish she could think of. In her neat school-girl hand-writing, she copied down the classic texts:

Soupe aux marrons
Potage aux concombres
Morue Provençale
Oeufs niçois
Coquilles de Cabillaud
Conseils sur les divers cuissons des poissons
Sachez connaitre le gibier
Grives au vin blanc
Faison cocotte
Terrine de lapin de garenne
Paté speçiale
Patéen croute

And so on, altogether eighty detailed, complex recipes. She lived and dreamed food, she thought about it all the time. No one was eating like this, except possibly the German élite in Paris. Perhaps no one ever would eat such dishes as *Cotelette de veau a la Milanaise,* or *Civet de Lièvre*, again, but she wrote in the knowledge that her writing constituted evidence that here, in France, once upon a time, they had eaten like this. She embroidered also, using up the gloriously coloured silk threads she still had. She embroidered tablecloths. It worked. Beauty and the art of cooking fought a battle with death for her spirit, and won. She lived, but she could only now take shallow breaths.

Doctor Pommier had warned her, had said if she went back to work in the factory, she would die, because of the dust. 'You must consider yourself a permanent invalid,' he had said. He had told her a year earlier that she must ask for a transfer from her position. Her job meant carrying the heavy coats right through the dust-laden factory to the other end, where they were finished. She had asked the foreman, but he had refused, pointing out that there were plenty of others would be glad to have her job if she didn't like it. So she had to carry on. Her lungs would never recover.

"Ici Londres" – the death of hope

The occupying forces had begun making spot raids on houses, sealing off streets. These raids were carried out by various sections of the German military. There were many sub-sections with different uniforms, and things sewn (by factory machinists like my mother) on those heavy-duty wool jackets – black crosses, death's heads, and of course swastikas – but the French generally used the word '*Gestapo*' for them all. They were looking for people who might be in hiding: deserters from the French army with no papers (such as Solange's father). They were looking for Jews who might not be identifying themselves with one of these things sewn firmly across the upper left chest, over the heart, and for households who might have suddenly acquired an extra child. It is a full year and a half since the first decree, from the *Mairie*, ordering all Jews to buy a large yellow cloth star with the word '*juif*' in black across it, went up in the streets. They were helped greatly in this business of rooting out fugitives and anti-Nazi elements by the reports, suggestions and denunciations that came in, some anonymous but many not, from the local population.

Rumour told that they acted with their customary speed and the first thing they did is switch on the radio. If you were found tuned to the BBC you were taken away.

'*Ici Londres*' broadcasts began on the BBC, to which Solange and Memère were avid listeners. Two years earlier, the voices of Churchill, and the young General de Gaulle, who had managed to escape to Britain, had inspired hope and urged resistance. America surely, would enter the war.

But now, there was no hope, none at all. The Americans had come in, but too late in the day to make a diffference. The battle of the Atlantic had been decisively won by the German U-boats. With the sinking of over 600 Allied ships, Britain was perilously close to being completely cut off from its life-line to American supplies. The British were reported to be close to admitting defeat. Rommel had pushed them back in Africa (they know all about Rommel in this part of the world) and the glorious Reich would shortly achieve a decisive breakthrough at Stalingrad, where illiterate, third-rate badly-led undernourished Russians were no match...yet had been fighting...but a few pockets of Russian resistance remained...

In the depths of winter, and not just any winter, but the exceptionally bleak, cold winter of 1942-1943, the world around the house in the *Rue de Renaix* spun. Outside, Orion the hunter blazed in the sky, the bull above him, the dogs at his foot and shoulder; the soft necklace of the Pleiades clearly countable. The stars were so brilliant because it was so cold and because of the blackout.

Orion was in heaven. Below him, Europe was in a hell that was slowly unfolding and revealing itself, piece by piece. It looked almost normal. But some were starting to guess. There were the trains, for instance...

Chapter 10

The train

It was the golden age of rail travel. Everything and everybody travelled by train. About four months before this midwinter, sometime in the hot sunny summer of 1942, people had started talking about the strange trains. Because this was a border town, and because there was a lot of rail freight of both a military and an industrial kind, trains would often be halted in the open sidings outside the station. One hot day a rumour spread in the factory about a goods train, stationary in the sun, which was carrying a cargo of people. Solange had gone down there on her bike (frock, socks, sandals, basket on the front) in her lunch break. The track ran along the street, like a tram line, and there, high up on its wheels, the train stood. There was a line of wooden goods wagons with narrow slits high on their sides and central double doors – they were normally used for transporting animals. Barbed wire had been laced roughly across these openings, but despite this many hands were pushed through the slits and from inside people were shouting for water, for help. Children were being held up to the narrow openings. The people inside appeared desperate. Scribbled notes, with addresses, were thrown. Many townspeople, of course, walked by on the far side of the street and took no notice. Some, including my future-mother, stopped, which encouraged others to pause, notice, and gather, forming a small crowd.

This is some kind of bottom line, isn't it? Will you be a witness, will you choose to know about suffering, and carry its truth in your human heart and in your human memory – or will you shrug and see nothing because there's nothing you can do?

Merely stopping to look was risky, for the German guards were armed (with machine-guns) and patrolled up and down the train. However it was hot, they were bothered, and they could not be on both sides of the train at once. Some of the young women would try to distract the guards, so that others on the other side could try and throw something up to be caught by an outstretched hand, or even risk the run up to shove a bottle or a piece of bread into one of those hands. Eventually (whistle, squeal, clang, lurch, rumble, the contents by now giving off various unpleasant whiffs and causing the guards, sweating in their heavy uniforms, to put their sleeves over their noses), the line would clear, the coal would be loaded for the engine, the French or Belgian driver would climb into the black, oily cab, and the train full of Jews carried on, travelling east, to where there were work-camps for them. There were rumours about the nature of these camps, but who knew what to believe? There were rumours that when the trains arrived wherever they went in the East, the old people and the children were taken off and never heard of again, leaving the able-bodied to work in bad conditions. Other people said they were all going to be settled somewhere in Poland, or that a homeland somewhere in Russia was being prepared for them, and they were mostly illegal immigrants to France anyway, 'So why should we have to have them here?'

How life nearly ended for Solange

Solange is standing in the tiny kitchen at the back of the house in the *Rue de Renaix*. It is the end of December 1942. The temperature is glacial. She is wearing a coat, several woolly jumpers, a thing called a bodice, a silk petticoat, a thick skirt, stockings held up by pink suspenders, flannel knickers with no elastic round the legs, the wooden clogs she wears for work. She has a glass of water in one hand and two small tablets in the other, which she has taken out of a cupboard on the wall. Don't worry, she can't see us: we are ghosts, spies from a future which may not yet happen. She is staring at the tablets and thinking, thinking – the truth is, I don't know what she is thinking. Sitting here over half a century later, after a lifetime of peace and plenty, with soup bubbling in my pan and only a pleasant feeling of anticipatory appetite to fit the word 'hungry', I have to imagine what it is to look out upon a world which has a swastika as an image of excellence, modernism, and efficiency, supported by many upright, respectable people, people practiced at not seeing the parts which don't fit this picture, citizens who can easily overlook the truth lying in the corner like a little bog-burial.

She is certainly thinking about her father, Jean Dhulst. He leaves his ex-wife and daughter alone, now, but keeps some of his things here as he has no place of his own to live, no official existence, has false papers he would rather not have to show at the frequent road-blocks and inspections. She is wondering whether it is not anyway a matter of time before someone, somewhere, gives 'them' a tip-off, and the Germans come looking for him and take her and her mother away when they can't find him, for these are his tablets she is holding, not hers.

These are the so-called 'suicide pills' issued to members of the various resistance cells, so as to protect the other members from betrayal by a captured member under torture. Whatever the nature of Jean Dhulst's activities during the war, the truth has died with him and with those other members of his generation who are now also dead. And what does that word 'issued' mean? Who got hold of them (probably cyanide) and who gave them to whom? If Jean had been given the pills, he must have had information worth protecting.

The popular view of the French 'resistance' is that large sections of the French population were involved in various forms of non-collaboration with the occupiers, loyally protecting the activists who carried out sabotage. Unfortunately this is not what took place. Only towards the end of the war, once victory for the

Allied forces appeared to be just a matter of time, did resistance, whether passive or active, become widespread. Those who took action in the time of no reasonable hope – they must have been interesting people. They operated in tiny 'cells' of two or three people, who trusted one another, knowing little of what other groups were up to. It wasn't just themselves they put in danger, it was their entire family and countless, nameless others who would be taken hostage the moment they did anything that effectively damaged the German occupation. Sometimes Solange would be asked to deliver a coded message to a stranger in one of the many dark, dingy cafés that were still a feature of every French street corner in the 1960s. But as such men began to organise and undertake bolder acts of sabotage, particularly of the transport system – by blowing up the railway lines, the Germans began to take ever more savage reprisals.

For every German soldier killed, if the perpetrators did not give themselves up, ten hostages were taken at random from the streets, to be shot if they were lucky, or publicly hanged if they were not. Often people were taken from cinema queues. Solange did go to the cinema and she went dancing, with her girlfriend Raymonde. This was life now, and they were young, and life had to go on. Or did it? Posters on the walls proclaimed that the entire family, including in-laws and second cousins, of every person suspected of anti-Nazi sympathies, would be rounded up; the male members executed, the women sent to corrective labour, the children to 're-education'. What future did Solange have? She was already as thin as a stick, and weakened by pneumonia. Would the young, blonde and blue-eyed women like her be selected to be sent to Germany for breeding – as was rumoured? It was very possible. There were recruitment posters up everywhere for those fit to work and willing to go to Germany, to fill the spaces left by the recruits to the army. Soon, it was also rumoured, this would be compulsory. Germany could now put vast resources into battle, for not only did it have the manufacturing economy of all Europe, but also all its citizens, willing or unwilling, whether as fodder for factories, for front lines in battle, and even for breeding more

Aryan humans. French citizens in a French village, for instance, were employed in a chemical factory making a poison gas to a new formula called Zyklon 'B'. The Reich could afford to lose the odd battle here or there – they had the time. This was after all the dawning of a new era, and there were many, many, many, and not only in Germany either, who believed this to be so. Whatever this was, war or dictatorship, it was going to go on a long time, maybe the rest of her life, maybe several lifetimes. There was no escape to another parallel world somewhere else, where people did not live in terror of informers, or where there was enough to eat. When would it be her turn for the train, for work in the factories of Germany until, weakened as her lungs were, whatever happened to the unfit would happen to her?

Solange is hesitating – this could be her only chance of a quick death now, before her father comes to collect the pills she is holding in the open palm of her hand. And I am wondering – what did she know?

The turning point

This is what happened in the deep midwinter of the war, when my future-mother decided not to take her father's suicide pills. This decision coincided, I now realise, with the very turning point of the war itself, which is geographically situated somewhere in the middle of the frozen rubble of the battle of Stalingrad, and spiritually within uncounted numbers of human beings of whom my mother was one. Had things gone another way, not only would the whole world be different, but my own story would also have come to a premature halt.

I know about this long moment of hesitation, when Solange took a pair of pills from the cupboard and stared at them. I know she was on her own and her mother was already upstairs in the bed they shared for warmth, the bed in which two months earlier she had nearly died. I know, because when I was old and sensible enough (which took a fair while) to listen and to want to know, she told me about it.

Did she know that Von Paulus's army, the German 6th army, the same one that had entered Paris in such triumph two and a half years earlier, was surrounded, freezing cold and already reduced to eating frozen, raw horsemeat, beseiged by Russian troops in Stalingrad? No, in late December, or even as late as New Year's Eve, she could not have known. The Germans were broadcasting on their ubiquitous loud-speakers cheery Christmas greetings (*Achtung! Stalingrad!*) from the Stalingrad front on Christmas day. Only later were these found to be completely fraudulent – Von Paulus, seeing no way to escape mass slaughter of his troops or death by cold and starvation, had already asked, and been refused, permission to surrender from Hitler.

In the depth of the year, in the world's northern latitudes, at the point of lowest ebb for the spirits of the occupied people of Europe, at the very point when my mother Solange seriously considered suicide, *the Russians were starting to win...*

Did victory at El Alamein a month before signal that the fortunes of the Reich were on the turn? Probably not, as battles had been won and lost and won and lost for many months in the North African desert and anyway, out there was Rommel and Rommel was a winner. How was she to know that he, too, had told Hitler that the war in North Africa was unwinnable, and how could she have read Rommel's letter to his wife, which we can now read, in which he complained of the lack of everything, including petrol 'without which there's nothing to be done'?

During November and December of 1942 the events that we now call atrocities were becoming so frequent as to be everyday occurrences. In Poland, the compassionate were being killed by the village-full for harbouring a household sheltering Jews. A favoured method was to shut everyone into a building of sufficient size and burn them alive. In Russia, too, men, women and children were being subjected to medieval tortures and death by burning or public hangings for being suspected of helping partisans.

The biggest atrocity, the one which will be remembered for all human recorded time, was now half complete. Within this past year of 1942, nearly three million Polish Jews had been murdered in the camps of Sobibor, Treblinka, Chelmno, and Belzec. Now the work of removing the Jews from other German occupied countries was getting underway. It had begun that summer in France, and in December three trains carrying 2,500 Jews left the Westerbork camp, in Holland, for a camp in eastern Poland known as Auschwitz. They were among the first to receive what was called 'Special Treatment'.

On December 17th, the three Allies: Britain, the Soviet Union, and the United States, issued a declaration which summarised what was then known about the fate of Europe's Jews: 'The able-bodied are slowly worked to death in labour camps. The infirm are left to die of exposure and starvation or are deliberately massacred in mass executions.' The BBC had broadcast news of what was happening to the deported Jews of Poland six months earlier, the day after 22,000 Jews from around Paris had been rounded up and deported. The word 'extermination' was being used for the first time.

Solange listened to the BBC nightly broadcasts in the French language. She knew, then, what was happening, and it must have made her feel sick with fear. Yet still she took the risk of choosing to know, of being a witness, of caring about the truth.

She thought of Marie, that solid, practical, kind woman, coming down at dawn to light the paraffin lamp and finding her on the floor. What would she look like? Would her body be contorted, what would her face be like? Would her tongue stick out?

The war had isolated the two women. The various secrets they shared – the British soldier, the listening to the BBC, the knowledge that Jean Dhulst was involved in things they were not meant to know about, any of these, should they leak out, would be enough to have them both arrested, and beyond arrest lay the land of nothing but rumour, rumours of people's faces being unrecognisable as they were led out to their execution, of prisoners' skin being taken, before death, for skin grafts for wounded German soldiers (there was even a rumour that this had been done to someone's child) and so on, and so on.

Solange knew Marie, ever the cheerful and practical optimist, would never do what she was contemplating. She would be left alone and completely defenceless. She thought of her mother carrying on living on her own in the dark, cold house, sitting down to eat the bread and soup at the table on her own. She was crying because she could see her own mother crying, and in the crying her resolve began to change. Astonished at her own courage, Solange knew she had amassed and gathered together, from wherever she could find it within her being, the nerve to kill herself rather than continue to submit to humiliation, to degradation and slow starvation. She both knew she could do it, and that she would not do it because in doing so she would have to abandon Marie, who had never abandoned her. Together they might find some way of continuing to exist. If she was going to die soon by one means or another, she may as well make a gesture while she was alive.

Reluctantly, Solange realised that she was still, in what had become a habit, returning the polite communications of the various German uniformed soldiers and officers she passed in the street or on the the tram. It was almost as though people had in two years begun to accept them as normal, and little by little had come to accept as just a part of life, now, all the other things the Germans had introduced into daily life – the night-time disappearances of people with left-wing sympathies, the yellow stars marking out Jewish people; then, town by town, first Lille then Roubaix and now here in Tourcoing, the 'resettlement' of these people, to a place from whence no postcards or letters were ever sent. They accepted increasing pressure on the able-bodied to 'volunteer' for work in Germany, they turned a blind eye to the ubiquitous red, black and white Swastika flags, to the renaming of streets and towns and villages and all the street directions written in that heavy, medieval-looking German script, and they grumbled in whispers only about the steady reduction in food rations and simply unavailable food and fuel. She realised that if all these things had happened in the first month of the occupation, people might have protested, risky though that would have been.

But they had accepted it all – death and degradation by stealth, delivered by proclamations written in that same Gothic script, by endless radio announcements, by loudspeakers in the squares and streets, and always to the accompaniment of cheerful, big band marching music, as if they were the children being led by the pied piper. No, she would at least do what she could in her own tiny way to refuse cooperation, even if that only meant refusing to speak to them until she died, even if she could only make a pointless gesture.

She put the two pills back in the cupboard, and went to the back door to the yard to listen if all was quiet. Maybe there would be a plane, and the sound she longed to hear – the sound of falling bombs. But there was only a sky blazing with stars.

Chapter 11

The news is new – January 1943

Turning points, which happen all the time, without our even noticing, are interesting things. If facing death requires the greatest courage of all, then consider the position of the suicide. Is suicide an act of great courage, or great cruelty of the grossly negligent variety? In considering the feelings of her own mother, my future-mother Solange had decided in favour of the latter view. But her mind had gone through certain motions. In her mind, she had taken the decision, and then had changed her mind. It would remain in its altered state, a state that can affect anyone who has knowingly had a close encounter with death. It takes the form of an enhanced appetite for life. Colours seem sharper, the stars brighter, food tastier.

Emboldened by the knowledge that she was capable of taking her own life, Solange began to take more risks. Her friend Raymonde came round in those January evenings and they would tune in to the broadcasts by de Gaulle broadcasting from London, the news of the war on the BBC. Suddenly, the news was worth listening to...

The rumour that was true: Germans stationed in France were sent to the Eastern front in an effort to lift the seige of Stalingrad. January 8th: 490 German planes were shot down over Russia. Stalingrad remained beseiged. Von Paulus rejected a Russian surrender ulitmatum. What nobody knew until years later was that the German 'Enigma' code had been broken by the wizards at Bletchley Park. The allies now knew about the German aircraft both in Russia and in North Africa. January 14th and for the next few days: Churchill and Roosevelt met at Casablanca. They reaffirmed that unconditional surrender of Germany, Japan and Italy was still their aim. They would continue to support Stalin to the full.

To these women, brushing each other's wavy brown hair as they stayed close to the radio (you kept it turned down really low, even though it made no difference to risk of detection, since most 'detections' were delivered by people who knew you and disliked you), to these listeners, what they understood from this bit of news was that Churchill and Roosevelt thought they could win the war, something that was not in the least bit obvious to anyone attempting some sort of objective view.

January 30th, what everybody had to listen to: Goebbels made a broadcast that was relayed in the streets and repeated endlessly on the radio. It was the tenth anniversary of Nazi rule, a big day. Flags in the streets, processions of troops. Music, celebrations. 'A thousand years hence,' he screamed, 'every German will speak with awe of Stalingrad and remember that it was there that Germany put the seal on her victory.' Many people in Tourcoing stayed indoors, didn't look at each other, and didn't refer to the deafening loudsdpeakers playing up-beat martial and stirring classical music. January 31st, Von Paulus surrendered at Stalingrad. The German 6th army, which had been dying of cold and starvation and splintered flesh and bones inside the city of Stalingrad, was the very same which had so confidently carried out the 'blitzkrieg' invasion of Holland, Belgium and France in May 1940. The BBC lost no time in reporting the surrender. 160,000 German soldiers were already dead in the ruins of the city. Only 90,000 remained to be marched east, as prisoners of the Russians. Few survived. It was a massive defeat.

Raymonde, who always wore the darkest most brilliant red lipstick on those thin, sarcastic lips, how high she must have raised her glass (whatever was in it, knowing those two, they must have found something) that night.

Did they dance, Solange, (aged twenty-one and gorgeous, with perfect cupids-bow lips, with honey-coloured wavy hair, with intelligent blue eyes), and her life-long friend Raymonde, (with scimitar lips and dark, flashing eyes and hair to match) when they heard on the evening of 31st January, 1943, the news of Von Paulus' surrender to the commander of the Russian Don front, general Rokossovsky (I mention his name because I feel it is merited)? Did they tune in to the usual radio station, which could be guaranteed to be playing the big band dance music of the time? Surely they danced, ballroom style, round the tiny dark living room, in each other's arms, with Marie looking on, smiling.

By early February 1943 something (I had previously written everything, but that was not true – in some ways, nothing would equally well have applied) had changed. In the 'Zone Interdite', the STO – 'Service de Travail Obligatoire' – made work in Germany compulsory for all men aged eighteen to twenty-three. In Vichy France (the southern half of France that was run by a puppet regime loyal to Germany), a brute called Joseph Darnand had been put in charge of a French police unit called the Milice. They set about finding, killing and torturing resisters to German occupation, rounding up the remaining Jews, making public examples of those with the courage and compassion to hide Jews in their houses. We would not, we say to ourselves, count ourselves among that number. We are not made of that stuff. Yet that stuff, whatever it was, was becoming not less, but more widespread it would seem, for on February 16th a US airman, shot down somewhere over France, was greeted as his parachute came to the ground by French women already carrying the clothes for his disguise and successful escape.

Solange and Raymonde, arm in arm out on the Grande Place de Tourcoing, shouted 'Stalingrad!' at a group of German soldiers in the street. The soldiers gave chase. The young women ran away, skidding on the ice, escaping down the streets they knew so well, laughing even as they knew they risked death by shooting. In a mere six weeks, Solange related to me many years later, everything about their mood had changed, in a way she could not possibly have predicted. Suddenly, there was hope.

A kindly couple who ran a small chemist shop offered my future-mother a quiet, clean, job working behind the counter. She was still there at 6pm on 4th September 1944, when British soldiers entered the town.

Chapter 12

Colin

*Barrow-in-Furness Communist Party
Branch Committee, March 1940
Meeting to discuss arrangements for the Peoples'
Convention for Peace.[1]*

Several men and two women are crammed into a small front
parlour of a terrace house. The house is in a ship building town
called Barrow-in-Furness. It is a grimy, grey, slatey place beside
a glinty seashore, with a view of not-so-distant blue mountains
known as the Cumbrian fells, later to become the Lake District
National Park. It is cold outside and sleeting a little. Their heavy
brown and navy coats hang with the men's caps and the women's
hats (for nobody walks around bare-headed at this time of the
year, and everybody travels by bus and on foot) in the hall. The
room is heated by a small coal fire in the grate, and there is a
smell of paraffin from a columnar paraffin stove that was used to
warm it up before the fire was lit. There are two settees, covered
in a faded floral print, a rocking-horse, two stools and a brown
armchair in which sits Frank, the owner of the house. He seems
older than the rest of the gathering. A small table has been set up

1. I am greatly indebted to my father's friend, John Marshall, for his detailed
memories and comprehensive descriptions of this and other such meetings of
the time.

across one corner and two people, a blue-eyed intense-looking young man and a middle-aged woman with frizzy hair, sit behind it, facing the others. They are the chair and secretary of this group. Across one corner of the room a bright red flag is draped, with a small hammer and sickle emblem in one corner. Both the alcoves are full of bookshelves, and one of those alcoves displays the red and orange spines of the cloth-bound books issued by the Left Book Club. One entire shelf is occupied by the *Complete Works of V.I. Lenin*, and the *History of the Communist Party of the Union of Soviet Socialist Republics*, by V.J. Stalin. Beside the fire is a stack of magazines entitled *Russia Today*. The top copy shows a photograph, soft-focus black-and-white touched up with vermilion red and turquoise blue, of several hundred men and women in bathing costumes performing gymnastics on a beach beside a brilliant blue sea. A general discussion is taking place before they get down to the business of the meeting, which is to finalise the arrangements for the 'People's Convention for Peace' to take place in the the the nearby town of Ulverston.

'War is always a reactionary business,' the woman behind the table, Lizzie McGuire, said to the other woman, also middle-aged. Both women wore slacks. 'And in the end, it's always the working class that suffer. Look at the last time. We were too late waking up to that. We didn't protest then, and look what happened.'

The small smoky room filled up suddenly with the glistening ghosts of young men, some as young as seventeen, known personally, and related, to each one of the living people present. The young man beside Lizzie did not need reminding of his five single, maiden aunties, every one of whom had lost a fiancée in the Great War. This young man works as an electrical engineer, but seems too well-spoken to be a factory worker, and also too slight and mild-mannered, beside some of the more forceful, heavy-weight men present, to be an obvious choice for chairman. It is his experiences that have earned him the respect of the others and placed him in this position. He has travelled extensively in Germany and Eastern Europe, and visited Russia – this alone makes him unusually energetic, enterprising and curious. During successive visits to Germany from 1933-1938, he has witnessed the rise of Hitler and knows, as few others do, the brutal nature of the Nazi outlook on life. So convinced is he of Hitler's aggressive intentions, he has already persuaded his employer to move the factory from its site near the Liverpool docks to one in Barrow, away from obvious targets for bombing (shortly after the factory was moved, the vacated site was indeed bombed).

He is utterly dedicated to peace and friendship between people of all nations. It is not simply a fine-sounding slogan for him, it is an extension of his own friendly, open nature, something he has made the very cornerstone of his own life. Now, like many other high-minded people, he is in a state of turmoil which began with the signing of the Hitler-Stalin non-aggression pact in September 1939. The Communist Party had saved his sanity three years earlier; now the Communist and the thinking human being were not co-existing so easily.

'Lizzie,' he suggested, 'why don't you speak for the branch? Put the mother's point of view. You might get enough interest to start a 'Mothers For A People's Peace' committee.'

'Oh I don't know, I haven't done a lot of speaking you know – I'm not sure what the line is on separate committees for women.'

'Look it's meant to be a broad coalition isn't it?' Another man, also a Lancashire dialect speaker, smartly dressed in suit and tie, spoke up. 'Don't we want to encourage non-Party people to get involved?' Someone passed round a packet of cigarettes. Most present took one and lit up.

'Well yes, exactly, comrade – that's why we've got the MP for our main speaker,' replied the young chairman 'because he's not Party – I know he's Labour, but he's not keen on the war. He knows that most people here don't want to fight another war, don't want to see that carnage repeated. He'll talk about how war just benefits the arms bosses—'

'Only problem with that, comrade, with all due respect, try telling that to the lads down at the yard – there's more work than they've seen in their lives, they're pigs in shit, war's good so far as they're concerned.'

'The war's got a lot of support with working class folk. Lizzie was spat on last Saturday in town, selling t'paper,' another man interjected.

'People are bloody ignorant, is what's what,' Frank spoke from the armchair in a loud, confident voice, with a ringing Lancashire accent. 'I see it down t'Works the whole time – half of them cow-towing to anyone in a bowler 'at and t'other half rushing off after the bloody Trots thinking they can have a rent strike with no organisation behind them.'

'Yer've not seen ignorance until yer've seen an ignorant Aussie.' proclaimed a huge, obviously Australian, man with a neck covered in folds of flesh – the most well-fed looking person in the room.

'Hm!' came a plosive noise from behind the desk. 'Comrades, can we keep the tone of discussion serious!'

At the same time, Lizzie spoke – 'I went after her. "You do realise," I said, "your son could be killed for no reason at all – we should be fighting for the united working class, not another bosses' war. I'm not saying I agree with Hitler," I said, "but it's up to the German working class to defeat him – this war won't change anything," she just looked at me then—'

'I should think so indeed!' said the young chairman from behind the desk. A young man who so far had said nothing spoke up tentatively from a chair at the back of the room.

'I do accept that the need for solidarity with the USSR is obviously, well, obviously important, but can we really trust—'

'What's your point, then, comrade?' Frank stared at the speaker. The Australian butted in, 'My family's Jewish yer'know, we've got relations in Germany we haven't heard from since two year—'

'Can we not have interruptions, comrades please!' said the chairman.

'Look, revolutionary pacifism in the present situation, as expounded by Comrade Stalin, is quite clear,' there was a rumble of assent. 'Further sacrifice of working class life is unnecessary and can only hinder the final establishment of a truly communist state in Russia. Once that is established, the masses themselves, throughout Europe and in this country, will realise where their true interests lie. This is not some little skirmish we're in here, this is mankind's—'

'Aye but they won't realise nowt if we're not united and they won't suddenly see t'light by themselves – it's leadership what counts, which is why we follow comrade Stalin.'

'Quite so – thank you comrade Robson,' said Frank, looking annoyed nonetheless at the interruption of his flow.

The speaker from the back of the room saw his opportunity and seized it, continuing in the face of stares from the rest of the company. 'It's just that – I know I may be saying this in ignorance of all the facts, of course, but so far, Hitler has shown himself to be ruthlessly following the aim of German expansionism, if I may so put it. So this is my question really, as a number of promises have already been broken and treaties ignored…what if he decides to attack the Soviet Union?'

Several people replied at once.

'This is totally and utterly diversionary, comrade…'

'Meaningless speculation…'

The woman behind the desk spoke. 'Only a fool would open a second front, and whatever else Hitler is, he's not a fool.'

'The point is, comrades, this is a typical diversionary tactic such as we see all too often deployed by our so-called friends, followers of so-called comrade Trotsky, whose programme has been utterly discredited and has himself been shown to be objectively serving the cause of the capitalist class in his efforts to sabotage the achievements of the Soviet Union!' The speaker, Frank, rose from his chair and pointed at the young doubter. The chairman looked anxiously at Frank, then at the doubter, George. The tidily dressed man spoke slowly and deliberately.

'The working class united can achieve anything it wants, anything; there's no force on earth can stop it; when we start dividing we get nowhere. We can be sure comrade Stalin hasn't taken these decisions lightly – he knows the facts, knows the dangers – if he gives us a lead, how can we sit 'ere an' say, oh hang on a minute, maybe we won't follow the line, maybe we'll support the war after all. I mean, this is it – look at us, 'ow many are we in a little town of 'ow many thousand, and 'ow many other tiny little groups are there like ours, struggling to get folk just to see sense – what good are we on our own? I mean, do we know better than comrade Stalin?'

Assent murmured its way round the room. The dissenter was silent.

Frank spoke again. 'This is a diversion from the main business of our meeting tonight, which is to discuss the planning for the People's Convention for Peace. However, the comrade has shown himself to have possibly fallen prey to those spreading confusion and we should take this opportunity, I stress briefly, to clear this matter.' The meeting had suddenly taken on a more formal tone. People sat upright and looked at the young dissident, who had assumed a slightly cheeky look of bravado and pretended to listen to Frank with his head held slightly askew in a skeptical manner.

Frank explained, again, why the current role of comrades loyal to the USSR in its struggle to consolidate the achievements of the first worker's state, was to seek by whatever means possible to influence the British working class towards an understanding that its true long-term interests could only be served by supporting the USSR, and that this was incompatible with the jingoistic fervour, nationalism and waste of resources, necessary to wage prolonged war against a powerful and well-armed enemy. The aim of the USSR, the very foundation of its existence, was to benefit workers everywhere, and anything which threatened the position of the USSR would ultimately threaten the workers of the world. Loyalty to the strategy laid down by the leadership of the USSR was the least that could be expected of those who wished to join the struggle for a world free of exploitation. 'We deal with reality as it is, we can't afford to waste time on fanciful speculation. Solidarity is our strength, speculation our weakness. Are you clear now, comrade?'

'Of course fascism has to be defeated. I mean, I've seen it, believe me I know what Germany is capable of, but this war isn't the only way to do it. Only the united working class acting in solidarity can defeat the forces of reaction. Comrade Stalin is right, comrades.'

The speaker was that blue-eyed young man who sat behind the desk, the one who had persuaded a factory owner to move to a place of safety, and who, as we will hear, had chatted-up the driver of a train bound for the Poland-Russia border, four years earlier. This was Colin, my future-father, spending his days inventing the three-pin electrical plug and his evenings chairing meetings.

Colin nodded his head earnestly and rapped lightly on the table. Lizzie McGuire put on her reading glasses and picked up a pen.

'I call this meeting to order – the agenda, comrade McGuire – would you read it out please?'

Chapter 13

May 1937 – Eastwards from Berlin!

'A new generation of workers is rising in the USSR,
healthy, buoyant in spirit, able to make our Soviet
country a tower of strength.'

J. V. Stalin

My father, Colin, was a keen photographer. In the first half of the
twentieth century, photographs were stuck into albums, usually
large books of thick, funerary black pages, and the photographer
would write brief captions or commentaries with a pen and white
ink beneath each image. After all, the pictures were telling a story.
These black-and-white photos were sometimes brown and white,
or greenish all over, for he developed his own pictures, eager for
them to tell their stories of a Europe of, among other things,
dazzling beauty, where the cart pulled by horse or ox was a far
more common means of transport than the car.

One album begins with a shot that must have been taken
from the driver's cab of a train. Colin had taught himself to speak
French fluently, then German, then Russian. He had talked his
way into the driver's cab of a train leaving Berlin on a grey day
(there are no sharp shadows) in 1937. The image is simply the
converging lines of the track forming an inverted V, for the line
extends forward across a vast plain. It is an image that conveys an
almost breathless excitement, a true sense of speeding towards
some great discovery. The caption reads, 'Eastwards from Berlin!'

For Here Be Dragons... Think of it – where was he going? To Russia, or rather The Union Of Soviet Socialist Republics. Did just anybody go to Russia in those days? No. So how did Colin get to be going to Russia? He was a member of the Communist Party, so he was on a special Party delegation or somesuch. He had a pen-friend he intended to look up in Moscow, a young man with whom the Party had put him in contact to help him with his Russian language skills.

When Colin reached Moscow (we have photographs of curved modernist park benches with men in uniform seated on them and huge banners behind them showing the smiling, benevolent faces of two men – Lenin and Stalin), he travelled on a bus to the part of the city where this young man lived. He showed the address from which he had but recently received a letter expressing enthusiasm for his forthcoming visit, to several people in the street in order to verify that he had found the correct block of flats. Arriving at the flat, he could hear a radio playing inside, which seemed to indicate occupation. Yet knock as he might, he could get no answer. He tried the neighbouring door, which was answered by an elderly woman. He enquired if this was the right address for so-and-so. Appearing terrified, she said nobody of that name had ever lived there. Insistent, he produced his most recent letter from his correspondent. 'No! He's gone! He was never here!' was the contradictory reply. 'Go away please!' she whispered to him, in a voice barely audible.

The worker's state – in which
we find out what left-wing politics for most of the
20th Century was at least meant to be all about

(Author's note: please resist the temptation to skip this section.)

'The factors which have promoted the USSR to a foremost place among the economic powers of the world, second only to the USA, are its vast natural resources, the rapid increase and cultural development of its population, and its social system, which precludes the possibility of economic crises and under which any increase in production benefits all citizens.'

E. Varga
The USSR as a world economic power
Moscow 1939

The incident of the missing pen-friend struck a puzzling and jarring note for Colin. For the strides made by the beleaguered state, the first in the world to be run by the working people, for the working people, were impressive. This was, it was claimed, a true 'workers' paradise', rightly feared by the Capitalist world, eager to suppress the truth.

Hours of work had been steadily reduced and wages increased. This, coupled with an efficient, planned food distribution system, meant that the population was well-nourished and healthy and enjoyed the benefits of entitlement to regular holidays in state-owned sanatoria, formerly only the preserve of the elite few. No longer was health-care a matter of wealth, available only to the ruling familes or the children of the bosses, as in the Capitalist countries. All workers by hand or brain were entitled to the best that was available. As a result, deaths from disease had steadily fallen and the growing roll-call of achievements of Soviet sportsmen and women had testified to the improvement in the health and well-being of the entire nation. In fact, according to the state statistical bureau, the average stature of young Soviet workers had increased by 1.07", while their chest measurement had increased by 8.6".

No longer were non-Russian peoples, such as the Tadziks, the Kazahks, or the Jews, oppressed and forbidden their unique cultures, as had previously been the case under Tsarist rule. The October Socialist Revolution, which transformed the Russian Empire into a free democratic state, into the fatherland of all labouring people, had put an end to all national oppression. All nations were represented in the Supreme Soviet, the collective governing body where previously illiterate peasant farmers from the Ukraine sat, on equal footing, beside blast furnacemen from Magnitigorsk or pile-drivers from Omsk. Women also partook fully in society, for the first time in the industrialised world. They enjoyed rights to maternity care and paid leave from work, and full civil rights of participation in society at every level. All forms of discrimination on sexual grounds were banned.

Education was now a universal right. Whereas before the Revolution three-quarters of the population had been illiterate, now the entire population was literate and able, if they had the ability, to attain the highest standards of excellence in the arts, science and engineering. Class and poverty were no longer a bar to progress in education. Indeed, reading seemed to be a mass activity and on trains and underground, many could be seen reading not only the daily newpapers but serious books by classical authors. Production of paper and books was prodigious and 'Dom Knigi' in central Moscow (literally 'Books House') was the world's largest bookshop.

Work was the centre of life in this purposeful, sensibly run economy where wasteful competiion had been eliminated and the people were able to receive the full benefits arising from their efforts, unlike in the past when long hours and ceaseless drudgery in primitive conditions merely served to increase the wealth of a self-interested élite. Now there were plans for the whole population to take part in the transformation of this backward country, incomparably rich in mineral and agricultural wealth, into a mighty industrial nation. Everywhere the targets set were oustripped by the enthusiastic workers. Those who achieved the greatest output, nicknamed 'Stakhanovites' (after a worker named Stakhanov who broke all production records in his machine tool factory), were regarded as heroes and their numbers were growing as workers grouped together to find the best possible means to raise productivity, thus creating a true socialist culture of the workplace.

As a result of the greater efficiency achieved through the

collectivisation of farming, the Soviet Union was now the world's largest producer of grain. The years between 1929 and 1937 saw a seven-fold increase in industrial output. Construction of railways and canals was outstripping even the pace set by the first two five-year plans, further enabling industries to expand in efficiency and output. The elecrification of even the most remote corners of the vast land mass of the country was now nearing completion. This formerly backward, underdeveloped country populated by undernourished, illiterate serfs and run by a small corrupt aristocracy, was now the foremost industrial power in Europe, the first in gross industrial output and the world's leader in the development of health, education and welfare services for the benefit of all its citizens.

The evidence of transformation was everywhere to be seen. Construction seemed to be taking place on all sides. Even in the capital, obsolete buildings were being torn down and new ones were rising on all sides. Bridges, roads, railways – an underground system whose sweeping escalators and vast palatial stations made the clanking London Underground seem pathetic, was almost complete. Everywhere gangs of workers could be seen, all wearing the same clothes to emphasise their equality, and so intent upon their various tasks that they even avoided all eye contact with passers-by.

Ignoring the prohibition upon the taking of photographs of construction sites or bridges – a temporary measure, the guide explained, part of the need for security on the part of a state whose further progress could only be hampered by the covert or overt action of its many enemies – Colin snapped from his hotel window the scaffolding surrounding a nearly-completed bridge over the river Moskva, a busy and impressive scene which would surely convey to the members of his small Party branch in Barrow-in-Furness the dynamism of this country intent on building the world's first truly communist, truly fair and just, state.

Of all those factors that had made such a remarkable transformation possible, in a mere twenty years, the most important was a social system that precluded the possibility of economic crises (such as bedevilled the economies of the Capitalist countries) under the wise leadership and guiding hand of Joseph Stalin.

Set beside such staggering achievements – resulting in a transformation for the better of the daily life of the entire population of almost 200 million people in a country that had the largest land mass of anywhere in the world – how insignificant seemed any doubts or unease arising from the failure to locate one mere individual. What an irrelevant pin-prick the incident came to appear, something hardly worth a mention. Some explanation, of which Colin was as yet unaware, surely existed.

Ulverston, 1943 – Colin goes to war

Colin had been living with his mother Mary all his adult life, apart from the times when he went off on travels round Europe. They lived in a house in a town called Ulverston, within sight and sound of the outlying fells of the Lake District. Great bare hills, green in summer with grey splotches where rocky crags protruded like ribs through a velvety skin; in winter, gold and orange from the dead bracken, flecked with scarlet blazes of rowan trees, black where the rocks and mine workings made gashes; in the distance, further, craggier, higher mountains. Water tumbling, and in spring the crazed baas of sheep and lambs calling everywhere. The nearest high mountain is called Coniston Old Man, and it's huge, gashed sides are full of mines. More sounds: the squeak and whistle and shunting and chuffing noises of trains, and the sound of boot-clad feet walking. The sulphur of coal fires, and that smell that comes off the tops of the fells.

The reason that Colin was still living with his mother was that his father had gone off with another woman when Colin was a tiny child. This son-of-the-gentry had made money in India, fathered two sons on a gentle wife, and then gambled away the money and begun an affair. He left his wife to fend for herself, but paid for his sons to be educated at a minor public school in

Yorkshire, so that they too could become gentlemen like him. In the case of son number two (the boys were called Pettitt One and Pettitt Two throughout their schooldays), this strategy for continuity badly backfired. Colin grew up resentful of the Greek and Latin classics, which formed the bulk of the education at this nasty-sounding establishment, and developed an eager curiosity about other countries and cultures that was the very antithesis of the imperial arrogance that was his natural inheritance. He was kind, compassionate and caring of his mother, and no doubt a disappointment to his father in that respect also. By the time he was eighteen, he had taught himself French, German and Russian, to a level of advanced fluency, as well as the new science of electronics, and gone to work in a factory in Liverpool. Here, seeing for the first time the depressing squalor of the lives of the urban poor, he had suffered a nervous breakdown. He was rescued by the friendly good cheer, genuine comradeship and compassionate, positive outlook of the young men and women who stood on street corners selling 'The Paper'. By the time he was in his early twenties, he was an active member of the Communist Party.

Colin's mother never shared his politics, but she loved her son dearly. When they held meetings in the house, she would always serve tea and biscuits to the 'comrades'. He didn't argue with her or try to convert her. As long as she was alive, he could not contemplate joining the war effort, any more than he could have gone off to Spain to fight in the Spanish civil war, like so many of the other young men of the time, like some of his new-found comrades.

As we know, that uppity young man at the back of the meeting in Barrow-in-Furness was right. On June 22nd, 1941, Hitler attacked Russia, and the comrades in the Communist Party could now follow their consciences rather than a 'Party line.' Now the Barrow group collected clothing and money to help the Red Army. By the end of 1941 the city of Leningrad was surrounded, and the seige begun. In an increasing agony of frustration, Colin rattled collecting tins on Liverpool street corners. He wasn't called up to join the forces, because his occupation – electrical engineer – was considered more important. His friends, one by one, left for a training barracks, for North Africa, for Arctic convoys across frozen Lake Ladoga. His elder brother Freddie joined the RAF.

His mother Mary died of a heart attack in the toilet. He found her, blamed the family doctor for not telling him she'd had a weak heart, and fell into a profound grief. But he was free, and at the earliest opportunity, in early 1943, he presented himself for armed service. He was a gentle man, but he knew bullying first-hand and hated it, he knew arrogance and hated it, he knew cruelty and hated that. He had seen the rise of fascism in Germany. Because of those travels of his, he was one of a tiny handful of British people who knew more of the reality of the Nazi regime than most of the politicians conducting the war. He had seen first the brown-shirts, and then the black-shirts, parading in the medieval streets of Nuremburg. He had seen the way the people he had come to know had changed, how they had become afraid of talking openly, how they had learnt to blame the Jews, how they had become evasive about certain things, how decent people had come to support Hitler. He hated what had happened to them and had concluded that the only way to combat fascism was by confronting it in war. He was the most peaceful person I can think of, but he volunteered to be a soldier, to learn how to stick a bayonet into someone and how to shoot a gun at another person. He did this because he wanted justice, more than anything else, to prevail. He wanted the victims of this racist, bullying "ism" to be defended.

He still knew nothing of the victims of the Marxism-Leninism which so inspired him.

Recently I spoke to a young relative of a Polish survivor of a Soviet prison-camp, collectively known as the 'Gulag'. We were talking about the subject, because we had just visited Auschwitz together. In many of the huts, the remains of the rusting iron stoves that were meant to provide warmth to the inmates on their straw mattresses beneath filthy blankets, have been cast into the corner, forgotten. The winter temperature in Silesia can drop to 25°C below. Talking of the Gulag, 'Think of Auschwitz,' the survivor had told his niece, 'and add to all that 50°C below in winter.' The same generation as that which in Britain sent letters of heart-felt encouragement to the 'Greenham Women', held a very different view if they happened to live in eastern Europe.

Chapter 14

Luck and individual determination continued to lock horns, like a pair of rutting stags, in the battle to provide the decisive factor that would make the Peace-camp a reality. At first the lackadaisical response of the authorities, from the Americans running the base to the local authority and the British Government, caused us an immediate practical problem because it meant we had to stick around at the end of the march for longer than we had anticipated. Most of us had jobs to go back to, lives to lead. We were not immediately facing a situation of arrests, followed by publicity and a trial, all of which would have given us a chance to make our case to the public. Instead we had a patch of grass (conveniently mown) some neat box hedges, an open fire, and a water tap under a man-hole cover the other side of the main road.

The British military person officiating at the base had shown us the tap, when after three or four days we were still there, and the numbers of young children had increased. He regarded our presence as a purely practical question, to be dealt with as a health-and-safety issue – much to Karmen's delight; she still commandeered uniformed men as her special zone of responsibility.

'He says they're Camp One and we're Camp Two,' she reported, having been invited inside to conduct negotiations regarding our presence. He suggested we dig latrines at a distance in the woods, and showed us how to get at the man-hole so that we could pour our sewage, collected in an Elsan bucket, in with theirs. We did this. He seemed quite enthusiastic about us, as though we were a troupe of Girl Guides arrived on his doorstep.

A few Newbury sympathisers turned up and lent us a couple of tents and some cooking pans, as we had none of these. Some of us went home to collect more tents and supplies, and returned, leaving puzzled and irritated partners at home. Others went home promising to return at the weekend. We put up some placards on the main road to say why we were there. Kiddies scooted around on plastic cars, kettles were endlessly boiled, a lot of lentil stewy type meals were cooked. Effie picked blackberries and cooked them with custard. The few reporters who came only wanted a picture of a chained woman for a local paper. I felt at my wits' end. Life at the other end of the M4 motorway was tugging me, urgently, and here I was hanging around, waiting for I didn't know what. What the hell were we going to do? There weren't enough of us to invade the base or anything and anyway if we did they'd probably just make us a cup of billy-bag tea or something, or start showing us how to construct bivouacs using bended saplings and bits of plastic. I knew I couldn't just live there, indefinitely. My life had been completely taken over by this campaign for the whole of the previous year, and already I felt too distanced from my two small sons. I couldn't commit myself to staying, but I couldn't just walk away and say 'Oh well, we tried' either.

Helen John, however, knew just what she was going to do. The contemptuous response from the Ministry of Defence: 'They can stay there as long as they like,' had stirred her characteristically dry humour. 'I wonder what those birch trees are going to look like in the snow?' she thought to herself. She considered that her four teenage children were quite big enough to look after themselves at home, that her husband was more than capable of caring for the youngest, and that this way she would be doing far more in a wider context to ensure them a future, than she would, as she would put it, stirring their porridge at home.

The dry warm weather continued for the first two weeks

after our arrival at Greenham Common. Women continued to take it in turns to be chained to the fence. New women arrived, drawn by word of mouth, and being chained up for an hour or two became quite popular. To me it seemed to have lost its point, so when, after we had been there a week, Newbury CND held a fundraising jumble sale, some of us went in and brought back a bundle of old clothes. We made these into four stuffed life-size dolls, and chained them up to the gates. Several papers had sent along journalists but all they wanted was a chained-woman image, no words. So the next reporter who strolled up was directed to the very life-like looking dummy women, who he began to photograph.

'OK – very funny,' he said. 'What's the idea?' We explained that all that seemed to be required were dummies in chains, so this was what we were supplying.

'Fair enough,' he said. 'So – why are you here?'

This was the first time since our arrival I recall any of them taking out their note-pad.

The first 'Cruise' missile to arrive

You have to picture a little raggedy encampment of a dozen or so tents of various sizes, with a lot of people, including the lads who had marched with us from Cardiff, hanging around. We had lots of curious visitors from the surrounding area, but for obvious reasons the numbers prepared to stay overnight were dwindling. We decided to try to get a bigger crowd there the second weekend, in a final push for what Mrs Thatcher would later call, quite accurately, the oxygen of publicity. Although we were now stuck on our patch of grass with no telephones (we are in pre-mobile, pre-Internet times here), hardly any cars, no means of communication other than psychic, we managed to summon friends and supporters thanks in part to increasing help from local Newbury sympathisers. A group from Oxford brought along the white dummy 'Cruise' missile they had made for a demonstration in Oxford that Saturday afternoon. They were very proud of their handiwork, having turned a cardboard roll used inside a carpet into a realistic-looking 'Cruise' missile, which they carried on their shoulders like a large cigar while they were clad in white boiler suits with silver skull face-masks, obtained from a carnival supplies shop.

As it happened, their afternoon arrival coincided with that of a photographer from the *Observer* newspaper. This arresting image was the most eye-catching thing on the front page the next morning, with the headline, 'Women at Greenham Common.'

The Sun and the rainbow

While the numbers of people who now knew there were women protesting about 'Cruise' missiles camped at the gate of Greenham jumped overnight from a few hundred to a few thousand, the numbers outside the base itself were not noticeably increasing. It was still just us, the marchers. We held a meeting that Sunday to discuss what to do.

Karmen, Liney and Lynne had been on a visit to Fleet Street, then the place where all the main newspapers had their offices. Continuing our naïvely direct approach, they had literally knocked on the plate-glass doors and asked to speak to a reporter. Not one news editor would deign to send anyone down to Greenham, until in despair they decided as a last resort to make a call upon Britain's most famously trivialising tabloid, the *Sun*. Here at last, a young male reporter was dispatched to speak to them in the lobby.

'You see,' he said kindly, when he heard their story, 'I know you've done all these things, walked miles, chained yourselves up, but it's just not news, ladies. It's just another little protest, there's lots of them all the time, tiny discontented minorities, these things always fizzle out.' But he was friendly.

'All right,' said Lynne. 'What do we have to do to make it news for you guys?' He thought for a minute. 'Stay there' he said. 'Then it will start to be news.'

The weather had finally broken after almost a month of sunshine and squally showers sent us scurrying after belongings carelessly left out. We sat in the biggest tent, an old white square thing belonging to the boyfriend of one of the marchers from the Amman valley, while rain drummed on the sides and thunder rolled dramatically. Laughing, the three of them reported back from Fleet Street. 'The *Sun* says we've got to stay here.' We knew it had come to this, but many of us had to admit we were not prepared to stay for longer. However some of the older women, such as Barbara Doris, Helen John and Jean Pike, who had come on the march, said they now felt they wanted to stay on and would do so provided we all worked like mad to get in the support they would need. Marjorie Lewis from Cardiff and Eunice from Ystradgynlais said they were prepared to spend a lot of time there so long as they could get away to clean up and have a proper bed sometimes. We agreed then that some would stay and others would work on gathering support and encouraging more women to come and take turns at staying. Someone produced the paper with the picture on the front page. It announced we were there, because of 'Cruise'. For the moment, that was enough.

This is when the double rainbow appeared. It was a classic cold-front day of the kind that brings rainbows chasing each other amid high-contrast clouds in a hard cobalt sky, and we emerged from the tent with our new-found sense of clarity and direction into the lovely brightness of a clear double rainbow. It was tempting to see this as a sign from Mr and Mrs God that we were doing the right thing. Tempting, until one remembers that many dictators, and criminally foolish leaders such as the then-in-power Ronald Reagan, and plenty of other nasty pieces of human work besides, have all been cheered along in the belief that the gods were on their side. God, being notoriously vague and fickle about the giving out of signs and portents, no doubt positively showered these people with enough rainbows, meteorites and suchlike to firm up their resolve.

This particular meteorological event has been moved around

and given to other decisive moments, other turning points, such as the decision a few months later to expel the men, but those of us who were there that afternoon saw it then, and in its corny old way it did indeed cheer us up.

October 1981 – The forgotten march

The first few weeks were grim. The rain fell, the wind lashed. The boys strummed their guitars and attracted undesirables from the town. The mud invaded and local hostility began. Helen remained indomitably cheerful, but some of the others fell out with her and went home. She had an intense dislike of work rotas and would destroy these as fast as anyone arriving, and trying to create domestic order out of the surrounding chaos, would devise them. She regarded people who talked about 'taking decisions democratically' as fuss-pots who would never get anything done. The CND rally that October was expected to be vast in size, a quarter-of-a-million-people-in-Hyde Park affair. We asked if we could have a speaker's slot. It was the only way to get the support we now desperately needed, before the real onset of winter.

CND was a democratically-run, therefore committee-led, outfit. They were good at just doggedly carrying on carrying on, but didn't particularly like new ideas. It's not so much a question of dislike (after all, how can a committee have individual feelings) as a matter of simply not noticing. They just didn't think that a bunch of women camped outside Greenham Common airbase, protesting at the notion of 'Cruise' missiles, was at all interesting or note-worthy. But our unofficial sponsor within CND, John Cox, knew we really were something different. He suggested we should undergo a further exercise in martyrdom, and then we would be more likely to be allowed a two minute slot to make a speech from the platform in Hyde Park. We should walk from the 'Peace-camp' (as I had casually christened it six weeks earlier, noting that a collection of tents without a collective identity was really on a hiding to nothing) to London. Idiotically, some of us agreed to do this during the school October half term. There wasn't enough time to organise it properly and Karmen and I had to drag our little kids along this time. The weather was bad, the whole exercise seemed unnecessary and that is why this little episode is called by those who had the misfortune to participate in it, 'the forgotten march' because we all tried to forget about it as fast as we could.

Most of the time I looked at the wet pavements of Slough and Uxbridge and memorised what I wanted to say – I was determined to make the maximum possible impact and this meant speaking without notes. When people speak using notes or words written down in any place other than on the inside back of their skulls, their voices don't have the edge that comes from a brain that knows it can't afford to make a mistake. Whatever I said, it had to stand out and be memorable in comparison to all the other speeches by sympathetic film stars and politicians and churchmen and leading campaign figures from other countries.

Witness

I felt in an agony of responsibility by now – I was expecting of others what I wasn't prepared to do myself for longer than a few nights at the most – stay at Greenham Common. The only solution was to persuade enough other women to make a rolling, ongoing sort of rota (that word again) of volunteers, to spread the responsibility and minimise the disruption to lives. Also, I wasn't even sure if sitting by a fire of damp sticks outside Greenham Common airbase was the best way to arouse public opinion to reject 'Cruise' missiles.

In some despair, I talked to a Catholic priest who had offered his hospitality to some of us on this miserable little march. His name was Andrew King, and since I first recorded these words of his as I remember them, I have received notice of his death, for many years have passed between then and now. In tribute to his insight, I will highlight his words lest they be overlooked.

'It's a witness,' he said, with simple finality, when I admitted I questioned the point of the whole exercise. 'It's quite irrelevant how many of you there are there doing it.'

'The point is that 'Cruise' is a potential first-strike weapon of enormous destructive capability. It would cause massive and unpredictable global consequences. A nuclear bomb is designed to cause massive suffering to civilians, by burns, blast and radiation. Anyone planning to use these things must know this. What is planned for Greenham is the deployment of weapons of an evil nature. An act of great evil is planned for that place, and it is better to stand before it simply as a silent witness, even if there is only one person there, than to walk away and pretend not to know. To witness an evil act is to act responsibly, even though you may be unable to prevent it happening.'

This concept made sense to me, and placed our actions back into the clear moral context from which they had sprung. So although I still kick myself for agreeing to walk from Greenham Common to Hyde Park for the sake of a two minute speech, there maybe was some point to it after all. We were witnesses.

So how did that speaking slot go? Well, I spoke for considerably longer than two minutes. And I did succeed in getting everyone's attention to begin with. Right down below me, in front of the platform, there were a hundred or so young lads heckling every speaker, shouting and swearing and putting some of them right off their stride. I could see this because you had to sort of wait your turn in the wings of the big platform construction. They annoyed me. As someone began adjusting the microphone down to my height, I looked down at the spiky hair-do's and open mouths as they chanted 'Class war...' and 'Anarchy...' and I shouted as loud as I could, 'Are you lot going to fucking shut up? Because I've got something to say and I want everyone to hear it.'

What I didn't know was that the microphone system had just been switched on, so my novel opening was heard all over Hyde Park. Not only the punks at the front, but the whole vast crowd, extending as far as the eye could see, fell into a shocked pin-drop silence. Speaking into this absorbant, spongy, sudden moment of attention, I told them about the march and the unique spirit we had created. I explained the reason why this was a protest by women. Since it seemed to be men who played such a leading role in nuclear weapons development and planned use, it seemed only right that women should play a leading role in opposition to such things. I told them we had set up a camp at Greenham Common with the aim to disrupt the 'Cruise' programme; I said we needed their help, we needed women, with the support of their families and communities, to visit and maybe stay for a day, a week, it didn't matter so long as they just went there. I suggested it would be nice in time, after the winter, to see more such camps set up outside the other American bases, there were plenty to choose from, 108 in fact, all over the British Isles. I used the image of the mint plant, which disappears in the winter but spreads its roots and stems underground, sending up shoots all over the place in the spring. Then I met Barry and the kids and went home. Home to the cow, the pigs, the chickens, the rain-sodden garden, the washing, the playgroup run, the whole pent-up frustrating mish-mash. Someone told me afterwards that they had overheard someone talking on the tube saying, 'Hey, did you hear that woman from Greenham Common?'

Letters

The October CND demonstration in Hyde Park had been very large indeed, involving an estimated quarter of a million people. But still, for about two weeks afterwards, Helen was still, at times, the only person at Greenham Common fully committed to staying there.

I drove on my own down the M4 at the beginning of November, still racked by doubts, thinking to persuade Helen to make some kind of dignified tactical retreat before the winter weather set in. It would be better to hold a demonstration, block all the gates to the base, and then leave, than take on more than we could sustain and let things fizzle out ignominiously. I had in my mind the image of General Khutuzov in Tolstoy's *War and Peace*, sitting in his tent as Napoleon advances towards Moscow across the vast swampy plain of Byelorus and muttering about Generals January and February. Given our desperately limited resources, there seemed no more we could do to get women there. But just because we couldn't sustain a permanent presence it didn't mean we couldn't demonstrate in other ways against 'Cruise'.

I was surprised, as I turned off at the short entrance road to the main gate, to see a PortaKabin, and thought that perhaps the Americans had decided to make things difficult by installing these things all over the small area of available space. There were a few unfamiliar faces about, too. There was a tent with quite a lot of food in it, and a stack of firewood, obviously from a building site somewhere. Helen bounced up.

'Good isn't it,' she said, waving at the PortaKabin. 'It just arrived. Some CND group in Southampton are paying for it. Now we can keep all the paperwork dry.'

Paperwork? What paperwork? I thought and started on my carefully composed little 'retreat with dignity' speech. Helen cut me short with a snort – she was good at this – and gestured towards the PortaKabin. 'Leave? Don't be stupid, woman,' she said. 'Go in there and read the letters.'

Letters? I thought. 'What letters?' I mounted the couple of steps and pushed open the door. It was big inside, dry, and fairly empty apart from a few sleeping bags. At the far end were several black plastic sacks. They were indeed full of letters, letters of support from all over the country and some also from Europe. Many of them were from pensioners. They applauded our stand and told us we had to stay there. They talked about the war – World War II, and some also about World War I and what they had fought for, and about the immorality of the mass slaughter of nuclear weapons, which some called a holocaust-in-waiting. They related to what we had done in a simple, straightforward way. They enclosed fivers. They said how cheered they felt by us. Waves of emotion poured from the hand-written pages – of anger, disgust and despair at the blind stupidity of governments. Again and again the word 'hope' popped up. We had given them hope. We must not give up, we had to stay, they would support us in every way they could, we spoke for them. I sat in a crumpled little heap among the plastic sacks surrounded by opened and unopened letters, hundreds of them, crying.

Helen stood in the doorway, chuckling.

'This isn't the end,' she said. 'This is just the beginning.'

Chapter 15

Embrace the Base, December 12ᵗʰ, 1982

The single event that catapulted the Greenham Common Peace-camp into fame was the demonstration known as 'Embrace the Base'. By the end of that terrible year, 1982, anybody who had a TV or saw cinema newsreels (this applied, for instance, to almost the entire population of the USSR) would have heard of the Greenham Women. There was nothing ordained about this nor was it an inevitable result of what had already happened. This story continues to be one of particular women doing particular things at particular times and places. None of this history happened all by itself. Greenham Women everywhere, they made it happen, out of the maelstrom of their lives. They made the times, the places, and the decisions.

Six months after we had arrived from Cardiff, the Peace-camp was a lively, busy place, heaving with people and daily visitors. It was also drowning in paperwork, since every visiting peace group wanted to leave their newsletters and leaflets; they spared little thought for the unpleasant effects of rain on paper, plus mud.

In the winter cold of December 1981, the first 'blockade' was held at the gate that was hidden in the woods, which was where most of the building work for the silos to house the 'Cruise' warheads was starting. Later, this would be called 'Green Gate'. Many of the women from the march had returned to sit down in front of the gates where the lorries went in and out. They had to be carried away and taken off and arrested. This all took plenty of time. The 'blockade' would soon become an effective way to delay things. The Americans carried on inexorably preparing the base to receive 'Cruise' missiles, digging trenches to accommodate the expected increase in sewerage from the increased personnel, pouring concrete, reinforcing the perimeter fence, continuing to make sensible preparations for Armageddon. Equally inexorably, their efforts were dogged and stymied at every step by simple, effective delaying tactics cunningly devised by women who were by now coming from all over Britain, and who could pop up out of the surrounding woods at any time, any place, in any number.

They got dropped off at the main gate by husbands, mothers, daughters, friends, boyfriends, and found a muddy site with many tents and other structures. There were at least two PortaKabins, and round the edges of the site were pieces of polythene stretched over saplings and weighted down with stones to make them waterproof. These were called 'benders' and were surprisingly dry and comfortable; the fire, still in the same place, was now the centre of a huge open-sided Berber-style tent, with a kind of crow's nest structure at the top which was meant to be a look-out, as surely an attempt at eviction would soon come.

The minority of men who had accompanied the march, a couple of whom (the two lads from Cardiff) had stayed on into the first winter, were now a thing of the past. It was a women's protest and presence, and perhaps we should have been clearer and harder about that right from the beginning. At some point a vote was taken and the remaining men were asked to leave. I wasn't there, but from what I was told, the men seemed to have outstayed their welcome, and had not endeared themselves by attracting more young men from the town, and by showing the usual aversion to housework, albeit open-air housework. But the atmosphere in this first heady year of buoyant chaos was still one of cheerful tolerance.

It was impossible to classify or stereotype the women who would greet a new arrival. Everyone would be wearing warm woolly clothing – long tubes worn by ballet dancers, apparently, to stop their legs getting cramp after their *pas-de-deux* and standing on their points, called legwarmers, were hugely fashionable and nearly everyone wore these in bright stripes over their jeans or woolly tights. Of course everyone also had to wear waterproofs of some kind, and boots or wellies, so from the outside there was a certain uniformity of appearance, but on the inside there was as much grey hair as any other colour poking out from the woolly hats, accents from the shires as much as from London or Liverpool or Devon. No one was in charge, although Helen and whoever was around that had been there the longest, tended to talk to the media, or go off responding to the constant requests for speakers from every CND group or peace group in Britain.

Although there were few women who left children in order to live at Greenham, Helen's decision to sacrifice her home-life became emblematic for the Peace-camp; she would often declare that whereas men left home for war, women were leaving their homes for peace.

The idea for 'Embrace the Base' took a while in the growing. Easter-time 1982 saw the first ever demonstration at which someone thought of using the entire perimeter of the base. Caroline Taylor had come to live just three miles from me, at a smallholding called Bwlchyddwyrhos (to a mind steeped in deepest Anglo-Saxon, these names are like eating a mango for the first time) and it seemed but a few days after I had told her all about Greenham, she had promptly gone to live at the Peace-camp. She had tremendous energy, and decided to organise an arts festival, with different events happening at each of the seven gates. At some point during the winter, women had discovered that there were exactly seven road entrances into the sausage-shaped base, conveniently lending themselves to be named after the seven colours of the rainbow. Caroline worked for months enthusing people with her ideas; thousands of people – men and women, for these were still young, pre-hard-line, days came to hear music and choirs, see the chain-link fence transformed into an art gallery, take part in live theatre, watch films and puppet shows, dance and eat and sing.

Caroline 's vision made all of us connected with Greenham

think more creatively. We began to see the potential of that nine-mile fence, began to see what the place would look like from the air. Already, women had begun setting up camps outside the other gates, having explored the perimeter whilst organising the Easter gathering. This new multiplied Peace-camp conveniently allowed for the emerging different styles – women who liked to commune with all sorts of sprites and spirits could retreat deep into the mature woodland of Green Gate, a group of older women from Wales made Orange Gate their base (this was where you had the best chance of a cup of tea and a piece of cake), while Blue Gate became the territory of a big noisy group of younger lesbian women. The old main gate was given the strictly non-hierarchical nomenclature of Yellow Gate.

But Caroline died, two years later, in a road accident. She was breast-feeding her new baby in the cab of her partner's truck, parked in a layby, when another lorry with faulty brakes skidded off the road straight into them. She died having thrown herself over the body of her child, who now walks the world somewhere as an adult who never knew his beautiful, creative, brave and intelligent mother. There were three Greenham Women that I know of who died as a result of road accidents. Caroline was the first. After the Easter gathering, she had set up a camp outside Aldermaston, and after that had an idea for going on a walk thousands of miles, perhaps to Russia, I can't remember because I lost touch with her then, it was the mad time of trying to respond to everyone and everything and milk the cow, in the life I was lucky enough to be still living.

I went to CND Cymru (Wales CND) meetings, which were awful, and loads of other meetings, with no means of distinguishing between those that might be productive and those that were a complete waste of time. I kept thinking 'I must sort out a career for myself'. I never would. I wrote endless letters and articles, some of which got published, lots of which didn't. I went to Greenham when I could, which wasn't that often, because I was having to visit Colin more and more often in the home in Sussex where he was living.

In the autumn of 1982 a group of women from Porth in the Rhondda valley went to Greenham Common for a while. They brought a fresh energy and a certain daring to bear on the place. With Helen they carried out the first occupation inside the base, locking themselves into the small sentry-box just inside the main gate. They remained undetected for about half an hour, until they answered the telephone when it rang, to the horror of the American military person on the other end. Arrested in due course and carted off, they were imprisoned, after their November trial, as an example... In future the authorities would deal with such pranks more seriously. As it happened, the newspaper and television coverage of this first prison sentence brought public attention to the Greenham protest just when it was most urgently needed. The most ambitious demonstration yet, to attract enough women to entirely encircle the nine-mile perimeter fence of the base, was due to happen on December 12th that year – 'Embrace the Base'.

It was Barbara Doris, one of those who had marched from Cardiff, who brought the idea for 'Embrace the Base' to Greenham from America. Barbara Doris, with wiry grey curls, from the Wirral, down-to-earth and straight-talking with a scouse accent, had a distinguished record. She had taken part in the 1950s 'mass trespass' for public rights of way on Kinder Scout. This is a big, bare mountain in the Peak District, itself part of the chain of weather-worn mountains that clamber bang up the middle of the island of Britain and are called the Pennines. Standing on the Pennines, you are in the landscape of the Brontës, in particular of Wuthering Heights. You are on Heathcliff and Cathy's golden moor, with nothing but the lapwing and the curlew for miles, and you are there thanks to unconventional spirits like Barbara who disobeyed the laws about private property and took upon themselves one day the right to walk over those great wide uplands, hitherto the sole domain of Lord Thingummy-Whatsit and his grouse-shooting chums. Nowadays we might have to share this incomparable place with thousands of other anorak-clad figures, because that daring action, in which the landowners tried brute force and even guns against the walkers, gave to our country, eventually, the long distance footpath known as the Pennine Way.

Barbara had heard that women in America were going to surround the Pentagon in a new kind of direct action. With help from some of the donations that were coming in to the Peace-camp, she and another woman went to this event.

They returned with eyes a-gleam. I went down to the Peace-camp to meet Barbara and we sat around the camp fire while they talked about it, and about the American Indian shamanic ideas it had embodied, of surrounding an evil thing with love – would you believe – of the way the women had used balls of wool, thrown between them, to surround the place with a multicoloured 'web'. December 12th was the anniversary of the decision to site 'Cruise' in Britain, and it was a Sunday. Why shouldn't we do what had been done with the Pentagon, and get enough women to Greenham to surround the whole base? We could call it 'Embrace the Base'. We would surround it with love, a spiritual negation of its murderous purpose. We would bring gifts to it, things which would represent the things we valued about our lives, the loves of our lives.

In a single conversation the little fire of this stunning idea was breathed into life. Now all we had to do was actually do it. How many miles was the perimeter fence? Nine miles, according to the Ordnance Survey map someone produced. How many yards was that? How many women would be needed? Well, what did one stretched-out woman measure, finger-tip to finger-tip? Did anyone have a tape measure? Did anyone have a calculator? It would take, we worked out, 12,000 women. Could we get that many? What if we got everyone to bring scarves and belts and things so that if there weren't enough, we could bridge the gaps?

The idea was on, then off – we couldn't possibly get that many women to come – then on again, with barely two months to organise it. It was publicised by chain letter. You were asked to make ten copies, but women just made as many as would go round all their friends. You were asked to bring something to give the base, a gift to leave behind on the fence. Such a bizarre concept fired the imagination. The publicity was given unexpected boosts such as that jailing of the Porth women, which produced interviews in which we could, if it was live, do just what you weren't meant to do and look straight at the camera and say (with a producer drawing fingers across his throat across the studio), 'We want women to come to Greenham on December 12th, we're going to surround it, it's called "Embrace the Base", if you agree with us, just come!'

December 12th, 1982

And they did. On December 12th, 1982, at 10am the car park at the Severn Bridge services on the M4 was completely full up with coaches from South Wales and the West country. As we approached Newbury, our coach from west Wales was stuck in gridlock even before we left the motorway. Every vehicle, every coach was full of laughing, waving women. The weather map of Britain for that day showed heavy rain all over the southeast. But it didn't rain in Newbury. It was white and still and cold, like a blank canvas, for all our colours.

It was an eerily quiet demonstration. There were no loud-hailers or marshals or shouting or people telling anyone what to do. There were banners a-plenty, but no chants or even slogans. There was no marching up and down, and no one to confront. Only the clattering of police and press helicopters broke into the midwinter stillness. The women were dropped off from their coaches at various points within reach of the perimeter, much of which is miles off the narrow Berkshire roads, in the birch woods, and they worked out all by themselves that all they had to do was walk until they came to an empty bit of fence, and stand there. The aerial views taken from the press helicopters showed that by early afternoon the whole nine-mile perimeter was surrounded by crowds of women, thick along the roads, thin in the back-of-beyond woods.

There was much industry going on, as women wove dead,

golden grasses and tawny bracken and lengths of wool into the fence, leaving behind intricate tapestries spelling the message in myriad ways. Every square foot of the fence seemed to have something attached to it, for mile after mile. There were innumerable photographs of homes, families, and babies, babies, babies. There were photographs of partners and husbands. There were cakes. This was a demonstration by women who belonged to their local WI, who would have avowed, if asked, that they did not care two hoots for feminism or politics. There were sanitary towels, red with menstrual blood, and nappies, yellow with shit. This was a demonstration by political, feminist women who were bold, unconventional and angry and who were saying, 'This beloved mess is life, as she is truly lived – how dare you military men devote your lives to life's destruction?' There were paintings and sculptures, flowers and toys and teapots and wedding dresses – yes, wedding dresses – and in one spot, an entire beautiful dinner service in bone china, carefully attached and left there. Everything was left there, until the good citizens of Newbury demanded the council come along and bin everything that hadn't rotted. If there are still any daffodils around the old boundary line, they were planted by me that day, as my gift. I bought them from a farm on Dinas, in Pembrokeshire.

The fence plunged down giddily into muddy gullies in the woods and reared up again to surmount dry, heathery heights. Inside the British and American soldiers stood uneasily watching. Outside were women, several deep in many places, fixing, embroidering, weaving, greeting friends, joking. At 3pm when everyone had finally managed to get there through the traffic, we turned inwards to face the Tarmac and vehicles and building sites of the base, linked arms and sang the 'Spirit Song'.

> You can't kill the spi-i--i-rit,
> She is like a mou-ou-ountain,
> Old and strong, she goes on
> and on and on, you can't kill the spi-i-i-rit

(Years later, I got a postcard out of the blue yonder, telling me that the origin of the 'Spirit Song' was a North American West coast Indian woman.) Well, it was a good song. Nobody was quite sure how long we were meant to go on singing it and holding hands. You could still hear it being sung as the light died, from across the other side of the base, a good half mile away. A lot of us were crying as we sang. As it got dark, we lit candles. You could see them, too, from where I stood along the back fence, thousands of pin-pricks of light along the other side.

'Embrace the Base' had been organised on a shoestring, with the simplest of modern technology: the telephone, the photocopier, and the postal system. It took place not in the centre of a great city, but in the depths of the English countryside. It was completely unique in the history of protest, and uniquely effective. It ambushed the British psyche.

The next day many thousands of us returned, to lie down in the road in a serious attempt to stop the base functioning as normal that Monday morning. It was scary because the drivers of the buses carrying people in to work were nervous and it seemed highly possible that whoever was in the front line could get crushed under a wheel. That day Greenham Women and 'Cruise' missiles and nuclear weapons were at last in every living room that had a television. It didn't even matter what people said about us or what they then thought, if they were actually thinking about these things for the first time. The thought was out there, and when it came to the arms race, people could work things out for themselves. It wasn't that difficult.

In my personal life, however, the very day of 'Embrace the Base', was the weekend things really started to become difficult. On the 11th December, as I was frantically trying to organise babysitters for the next day's demonstration and for the Monday morning 'Close the Base' action, I heard that my father could no longer stay where he was living.

The problem had been looming over me, for four years. Solange, my brave, forthright and loving mother, had died in

1978, her damp-damaged heart and factory-dust-damaged lungs conspiring to give her a shortened life-span. Colin was completely devastated by grief and never recovered. The community place where he was living, run by the Quakers, wasn't an 'old people's home' but a large house where people of all ages lived, who for one reason or another had no home of their own. My father was homeless because my parents had sold their house in England, gone to live in France, decided this was a mistake, returned to live in England and were staying with friends when my mother, Solange, fell ill and died.

I visited him as often as I could, but it was a long journey and it meant (for he was in no state to enjoy small children) leaving our two little boys with my partner, Barry, yet again. In September of that year, 1982, (Helen and the Porth women are entering the base for the first time, and being arrested and put on trial – soon to be sent to Holloway prison) the local geriatrician wrote to me to say that my father had Parkinson's disease. He was rapidly losing his memory and ability to walk, and was becoming incontinent. I could not envisage putting him in a home, but we still had no proper bathroom, no central heating, and no carpets on the cold, quarry tiled floors – we couldn't afford them.

Nonetheless, he would just have to come and live with us, at Gwastod Bach. The week after the 'Embrace the Base' demonstration, I drove down to Surrey to bring Colin back to our house. It was my last chance to attend anything at Greenham for some time. But these constraints were not unusual – I was probably typical. Most women there had made a difficult moral choice about leaving their responsibilities, whether to work, family or both, to spend a Monday morning in terror of being crushed, certainly likely to get some nasty bruising from being picked up and thrown to the side of the road by the police, who were getting impatient, all in a seemingly impossible cause: stopping the unstoppable, the arms race between the superpowers.

For even as we seemed to have achieved everything we had set out to do, little in fact seemed to have changed. In 1982 the Falklands war boosted Mrs Thatcher's popularity, polarised the country, and distracted many people from noticing the efficient demolition job she was performing on British manufacturing. Greenham was getting increasing support, CND membership was still growing, but out there in the country, most people still mistrusted us for being unrealistic, naïve, woolly-minded pacifists, who would leave us open to a Soviet invasion and might even welcome it. The world had reached a kind of impasse, and the arms race was still lumbering towards its inevitable conclusion, sincerely regretted by all political leaders but considered unavoidable – a nuclear war.

Karmen and I were very taken up with being mothers, but we still kept meeting each other and some of the women from the 'first march'. We had a new project – we wanted to visit the USSR, and for the past five months we had been thinking about little else.

1. The fence, Greenham Common (Rupert Hopkins).

2. Not quite as idyllic as it sounds: Gwastod Bach as we found it in 1977.

3. 'Cruise' in erectile mode, ready to fire at the 'enemy' (Ministry of Defence).

4. With the Red Army Ensemble and other 'red' friends and family, London 1955. I am in the middle in the school blazer.

5. In milkmaid costume with Dolly the Cow, Gwastod Bach.

6. The march – the back banner made by Thalia Campbell and daughters on the first night in Newport.

7. Women for Life on Earth, somewhere in Wiltshire. Who the hell do we think we are?

8. A rare image of one of the Greenham men – Steve, from Cardiff, childminding at Greenham Common.

9. Liney Seward, 5th September 1981 at the gate.

10. Karmen on left, and Lynne, at the gate. Behind them the chain we bought in Marlborough, attached to Helen or Eunice.

11. Women blocking the gate to Greenham Common and singing, December 13th 1982 (Olivia Elliott).

12. Solange with Marie, Tourcoing; Solange and Colin, Tourcoing; Solange and Ann in Ulverston.

13. Colin in Moscow, 1937.

14. Colin risks a stint in the Gulag to photograph this bridge, the Kremlin and the Spassky Tower – Moscow 1937.

15. Ann with son Harri at Greenham Common, winter 1983 (David Hoffmann).

16. Jean, Karmen and Ann collect signatures for 'Natasha's Toast' on peace poster, on the same bridge as in 14, Moscow 1983 (*The Times*).

17. Moscow Group for Trust, June 1982. Volodya Brodsky, far right; Yuri Medvedkov, bottom left; Olga Medvedkova, bottom right with their son Mischa.

Part iii
The Duck of Peace Flies East

The sagging, feminised fence, Greenham Common 1984

Chapter 16

June 4ᵗʰ 1982, in Maenclochog

It was while we were walking to Brawdy, back in the late spring of 1982, that the idea of going to Russia suddenly occurred to me. Brawdy is the name of another US base in Britain. It is situated right out on the cliffs of Pembrokeshire, looking out across the sweep of St Bride's Bay, wild islands at each corner. From there, underwater cables extend out into the Atlantic, to listen out for Soviet submarines. It, too, is 120 miles from Cardiff, only instead of walking east to get there, you walk west.

We humans are far too keen on repetition. As soon as we do something new, which achieves any kind of success, we immediately start making copies. So, no sooner was the Peace-camp clearly generating its own support, independent of those of us who had walked there, than there was talk of another march. The urge proved irresistible. Linnie Baldwin, one of the original marchers, who lived near Karmen, threw herself into organising mode.

As with any Hollywood blockbuster sequel, on march no. 2 improvements would be incorporated and essential features retained. Thus we would hold evening 'everybody talk in turn' meetings, while ensuring far greater participation of local people in the reception and hospitality side.

Occasions rich in irony ensued. Some of the women who came on this march did so because they regretted not coming on the first one; some came expecting some sort of magic to transform this arduous plod along roads into an event that would spectacularly inspire others; some were looking for something which would transform their lives. One small rotund American apparently was hoping to get sun-tanned tits. She was a big hit with the strict non-conformist chapel members and miners' club and Labour people from the Welsh valleys. These second march women were on the whole a more politically educated lot, and knew which foods to eat and what to say. They talked a lot about 'empowerment' at the evening meetings. The vegans among them complained to us, the organisers, when the Socialist Women's group of the Rhondda valley provided pasty and chips for the evening meal, with a vegetarian but not a vegan option. The women of various chapels along the route did what they always do, baked lots of Welsh cakes and made tea, while the male preachers made polite welcome speeches about peace.

But amidst the swampy mass of recycled clichés, which this women's activism was already generating, some tiny shoots of real growth were stirring. I was beginning to feel fed up, when something happened that for me, made sense of the whole exercise… June 4th 1982, was a strangely memorable day. March no. 2, which had begun in Cardiff, was nearing its objective out on the edge of the Atlantic.

Maenclochog is a tiny village, a hamlet of a settlement, with its back to the sweeping heathery tops of the Preseli mountains. Grey bouldery outcrops mark the summits, but not as many rocks as there once were because a long time ago some were taken and moved, by means which remain a mystery, to be re-erected on a chalky plain some three hundred miles away, as the justification for the existence of the Stonehenge Visitor Centre. Our lunch that day was in the village hall of this little idyll, and we were to be addressed by the Mayor of Cardigan, a woman.

The march seemed to be buzzing with ideas of making East-West contacts that morning, of breaking down the barriers of the Cold War that made the populations of East and West mutually ignorant of each other and so easily manipulated into supporting policies governed by fear and mistrust. All the conversations seemed to be revolving around one or other aspect of this communication gap. The Americans knew nothing of how we felt, likely as we were to die in a 'European Theatre of War'. There was talk of raising funds to pay for some women to go to America, to speak and meet with people there. (From that discussion, there would indeed issue a visit to America, and a court case against 'Cruise'.)

The short speech that the lady Mayor of Cardigan gave that day seemed to chime very well with this theme of building human bridges across the Cold War gulf. Janet Dubé is a poet who lives in west Wales. She went on the march, and she remembers June 4th as its best day, and the simple eloquent way the the Mayoress gave voice to our thoughts. The poem she wrote about that speech, part of a long, very moving sequence describing the way she and so many of us felt in 1982, is the only one which bears a specific date:

To the leaders of nations and sellers of weapons from Maenclochog Village Hall, June 4th, 1982.

> gentlemen, this is the mayor of Cardigan
> her hair is white
> her figure slight
> her tongue is a dove
> plain as a pigeon;
>
> since you cannot hear
> or maybe understand
> what she is saying
> I will translate;
>
> she says
> war is over
> if *you* want it.

Janet Dubé, from 1982: a lament

That afternoon I was on 'crèche rota', keeping an eye on the several small children we had with us. They played outside the hall in the sunshine. It was a perfect early summer's day of rising billowy clouds. The whole landscape seemed to be streaming past in the wind, the ears of barley in a field, the little flocks of finches feeding among the scraggy yellow gorse, the mane and tail of a white horse cropping the grass below the mountain, which rose like a gently curved recumbent breast, topped by a rocky nipple. The countryside thereabouts is ragged with small trees and woods, whitish stony walls and thorny hedges around odd-shaped fields, all indicators that one is out on a limb somewhere.

The sea is not seen but felt as a surrounding presence. An extraordinary flow seemed to engulf everything. In the midst of all the rustling movement, of flicking cows' ears and bending grasses, my eye came to rest on a single standing stone in the middle distance, a grey point of stillness around which field, farm, rock and mountain seemed to swirl. Ancient signifiers of long-lost meanings, the whole area is littered with them, many used as gateposts. Like a finger, it denied the steady waves of the westerly wind. The beauty of it all was making me dissolve. The strange conversation I had been having earlier with a friend, Annie Tunnicliffe, about whether there was any way out of the arms race impasse, had left us both in tears.

'I don't want to go to America,' came a thought into my head, 'I want to go to Russia.'

How easy it is to miss the obvious

It seemed so undeniably obvious, I felt stupefied that I hadn't thought of it before, nor felt until that moment the slightest curiosity about the way the world looked from that side of the Iron Curtain. I was kicking myself. So many times along the road to Greenham people had leant out of their cars, vans, lorries, shouting, 'Why don't you go to Russia?' Why on earth hadn't we listened to them properly? Why hadn't we heard the message?

How right they were! Why didn't we just go there, and find out how the dilemma appeared from the 'other side'? Could we do it?

I said nothing to anybody about this, just letting the new thought kick its ball against the back of my skull by itself for a while, but about a week after we got back from the march, Karmen suddenly said to me, 'I've been thinking – I think we should go to Russia.' The same thought was banging away noisily in both our heads, keeping us awake at night, so that meant we would have to take it seriously. I knew then the idea was out there somewhere, and we had caught it, like a virus.

We knew we didn't want to go as 'peace tourists', to look at art treasures, and express our sympathies with the poor old Russian bear, forced into an arms race not of its making by the evil empire of the West. Nor, by any remote stretch of the imagination, did we particularly want to risk being put on trial in Moscow for 'anti-Soviet activities', e.g. a Peace-camp outside some Soviet base or other. We were not martyrs, nor 'self-sacrificers'. We were still, in the midst of constant meetings and letter-writing and marching, trying to carry on as normal with our lives. Our limited knowledge did not indicate that there might be much land on which to place our little feet in between Scilla and Charybdis, either you were pro- or anti-Soviet, it seemed, to the dim vision of the Soviet bear. Nonetheless, we shared an unspoken conviction – similar to the one we had shared about going to Greenham Common in the first place – that some reason existed for us to go there. We had no idea what the reason was, but to find it we would have to follow our curiosity.

We didn't really know where to start, and as before we had no money and, outside of looking after our families, little time that wasn't taken up with campaigning, encouraging support for the growing Peace-camp, speaking at meetings, visiting all the new groups that were springing up like mushrooms in August.

However, the idea still rummaged around in the back of our minds, restlessly. We gave it a name-tag – 'The Duck of Peace'. We had already had enough of doves.

I started reading everything I could about the Soviet Union, and developed special, invisible, extra-large, 'news from the USSR' ears, like a desert fox. Meanwhile, once Colin came to live with us in December 1982, I changed a lot of sheets, and became familiar with the various types of nappies made for adults, and learned how to manoeuvre an old-fashioned heavy wheel-chair around a town with high kerbs everywhere. I learned my way around the underworld, which exists as a sort of parallel universe, of day centres and geriatric services and places where kindness exists, and places where it doesn't.

Colin couldn't really help me very much. The mind that had mastered Latin, Greek, and large amounts of what the Romans and Greeks wrote, that had learnt how to build radios and telephones that worked in battlefield mud, that was fluent and literate in five European languages and three alphabets, was now in pieces as Parkinson's overtook grief. Only traces remained, like the summits of underwater reefs... Such as the story of an old woman in Moscow who had stopped before him in the street: 'Moscow is so big, young man!' she had sighed, putting down her heavy bags. The legs that had walked over the *Mer de Glace* on Mont Blanc, and all over Germany's forests and the Austrian Alps, could now barely stand for shaking, and would crumple beneath their owner halfway down the stairs, or hanging onto the washbasin in the bathroom.

It sounds a lot grimmer than it was. For a start, we weren't coping alone with Colin. Incredibly, even from the depths of his grief, after the death of Solange, he had still succeeded in making friends and a young man called Thor left his home and job to come and help with the Colin-care at Gwastod Bach. Thor did this as an act of pure goodness, because he had grown fond of Colin. He gave us loads of help, too, with the Russia business over the coming months.

And then, there is a strange kind of farcical hilarity that can accompany the business of caring for someone who is old and marble-less. When there is reason enough to be miserable, people can actually become more generous-minded, and more cheerful.

It is when life dangerously approaches perfection, with the dream home, dream kitchen, dream job, new car, perfect holidays, ideal children, that anybody with their wits still connected should be getting nervous, and may wonder why somebody up there seems to have switched the lights off. Imperfection, inconvenience, the awkwardnesses and discomforts of life have their saving graces. In the midst of them, we can feel good. It is in the unforeseen deviations from the plan that the best moments occur, the moments that make a life worth living. In a society obsessed with insurance against the unforeseen, the value of adaptability is missed.

White duck sits on news

The fat white duck we kept had managed to hatch several ducklings, but she kept treading on them. Added to that, everything that is dog or cat, loves a squidgy duckling. Soon there were just two little fluffy quacking things left. They had to be kept in the house, where they made a dreadful mess, splashing in the bowl inside their box on the window-ledge. I had to tear up prodigious quantities of newspaper to put in with them. Naturally, it is in precisely such situations that items of great importance invariably catch the eye. Thus it was, in the early autumn of 1982, that I noticed a one-paragraph report of the Scandinavian women, the same lot whose walking activities had set me off to Greenham, trying to make contact with an 'independent' Russian group called the 'Moscow Group for Trust'.

Now this was news, something genuinely new. But where to find out more? Nobody seemed to know. I tried talking to journalists who were sympathetic to Greenham and wrote objectively about the Soviet Union – of which there were not many. Eventually I found one woman journalist who had actually been with the Swedish women in Moscow when they had tried to reach the Trust Group. Karmen and I went to meet her. She thought the group had seemed genuine enough, but like everyone else, reckoned their chances of survival as a campaigning, independent body of people within the existing USSR was about the same as that of a mouse in a sealed roomful of hungry cats. All that was really known about them was that they were a small group of citizens who claimed to be a sort of Russian CND, a peace group independent of the state apparatus of the USSR, acting on their own initiative. This claim was implausible, because political groups truly independent of the state did not exist unless they accepted the role of 'dissident', in which case they were swiftly imprisoned, sent to Siberia or else to a psychiatric hospital. Every effort was made to conceal their existence from anyone, inside or outside the USSR.

All experts on the USSR in the West, university lecturers, Kremlinologists etc. were in agreement that the dissident movement had been successfully eliminated by the KGB, the secret police, by the end of the Seventies. Their most outspoken and internationally eminent figure, Andrei Sakharov, had 'disappeared' amid rumours of his death at the hands of the notorious State terror machine. No one else, as one expert put it, was going to show their head above the parapet. This group made statements that carefully avoided any direct criticism of the Soviet state, which would have earned them the status 'dissident'. Yet they had, according to the few reports there were of their activities, already been subjected to a 'low to medium level' degree of persecution by the KGB.

Autumn descended towards winter; we killed the pig and salted it for ham, and brought the cow in at night. When we milked her inside the stable she would rise, unfolding her hind legs first from the midden upon which she slept, steaming in the cold mornings. The demonstration 'Embrace the Base' was being planned. Every day fresh copies of the 'chain letter' arrived in the post. The East–West communication virus was at work too. Since that day in Maenclochog, I had been trying to find out what I could about the whole area of contacts between the peace movement in the West and the Soviet Union. Soon I realised that there was quite a lot of to-ing and fro-ing, what with the Quakers, various

American groups, doctors who were trying to get together with Soviet doctors, scientists who met up as a group called 'Pugwash' and, of course, CND. The buzz-word was 'counterparts', everyone was trying to find their counterparts it seemed. CND and the Quakers seemed to accept that their 'counterparts' were to be found in the Communist Party-run 'Soviet Peace Committee', which immediately struck me as odd.

In February 1983, six weeks into our new domestic regime looking after Colin, I went up to London to a 'Soviet Women's Day' of 'workshops'. It was organised jointly by CND and European Nuclear Disarmament (END), a group founded by the historian E.P. Thompson. END had brought something new into the nuclear disarmament movement: a fresh perspective on the Cold War.

This view suggested that changes would have to happen within the Iron Curtain countries, particularly those former European countries now part of the Soviet Bloc, the 'Warsaw Pact' countries. The vision proposed a 'dissolving of the blocs', by promoting once again a free flow of personal contacts throughout Europe. Peace campaigners should support their true counterparts – the 'dissidents' who were campaigning for human rights from behind the Iron Curtain. These were the people in Poland, Hungary, Czechoslovakia, East Germany and Rumania who followed their consciences, always to the detriment of their own material wellbeing. And there were more and more of them.

Impossible though it seemed, given the implacable resistance of the USSR to any change, this was the only direction that might lead to an escape route from the endless impasse of the Cold War and the arms race. Somewhere in the future there was a tiny opening, still hidden, the proverbial window of opportunity, through which the pent-up waters of frustrated history would pour. Like the electron that is neither wave nor particle, yet simultaneously both, this was as much a feeling as an idea. Many people were starting to move in this direction and it occurred to me that this was what might motivate the Moscow Trust Group – whoever they were.

Our idea of going to Russia was squirming and kicking like a foetus. I went to this London event on the off-chance that I might learn something that would give me a clue, a hint, a direction to follow. Somebody told me that the only other person in Britain to have met the Trust Group since the previous summer, a young American student at Oxford called Jean McOllister, was expected to speak there.

Jean McOllister

I stood in the back of a crowded room in a rambling Community Centre in Archway, North London. At the front a tall young woman with a long neck and curly brown hair started talking about Moscow Group for Trust. Almost immediately it became impossible to hear what she was saying. Her face registered shock and dismay as a group of women in the front started barracking, shouting at her, that the Trust group were a fraud and a creation of the CIA, that she was anti-Soviet, that this was a distraction from the purpose of the meeting. Other women present objected to this horrible, bullying behaviour, but the shouters succeeded in shutting Jean up and she just disappeared. Throughout the rest of the day I searched for her, trying to find her, but it seemed she had left the building and was nowhere to be found. But I had heard enough in those few brief moments to know that she was the person Karmen and I needed to talk to.

My next opportunity came a few weeks later, when I was asked to speak at a weekend of workshops on 'non-violent direct action', to be held at Bradford University. I accepted the invite, although I had no interest whatsoever in the theory of NVDA, and couldn't begin to understand how this subject could take up a whole weekend of so many intelligent people's time. As far as I was concerned NVDA was pretty simple, it meant sitting or lying down somewhere to cause an obstruction, and, if you wanted to make the process more comfortable, you took a thick newspaper to sit on and a Thermos and some sandwiches, so that low blood sugar wouldn't sap your morale and send you scurrying to the nearest café. Rather like long walks in winter, it really wasn't that complicated. No, my sole purpose in travelling to Bradford was to meet Jean. One of the organisers had heard of her, and said she thought she would be there and would be speaking at a meeting.

But by the time I arrived by train from west Wales, she had already spoken and I had missed her. I spent the rest of my time there, it seemed, just missing her. I went from canteen to discussion to seminar to bar to forum to workshop and back, only to hear on each occasion, 'She was here earlier – she must have just left…'

In a mood of frustration and despondency, I got onto the last train going south out of Bradford on Sunday, at 4 o'clock. Right up to the last moment I had been running round trying to find a woman called Jean McOllister. I sat down and leant my head in weariness against the dusty window. I had drawn a complete blank, and being able to get away, even for a day and a half, was so difficult and costly in personal time, because of the way my life was at home, that I felt a fool for having wasted it on such a fruitless effort. I looked at my watch. The train was a minute late leaving. The guard went along the empty platform, clacking the doors shut, and then blew the whistle. There was a shout. The train didn't move. I looked out of the window and saw a figure weighed down by a backpack, running down the platform. The person opened the door of my carriage, got in and, breathless from her run, came to sit down opposite me. The whistle blew again and the train began to move.

The young woman burrowed in her rucksack and took out a thick wad of typing, which she placed on the table between us. Reading upside-down, I came across the heading: 'Report of meeting with Moscow Trust Group, January 1983, by Cathy Fitzpatrick, Helsinki Watch'. I had already recognised the backpacker anyway. She glanced at me, smiled neutrally at this person staring at her with a strangely fish-like expression, and began to read. Reconnecting my jawbone with my skull, I put my hand on the typed paper. It sounds melodramatic, but I couldn't think what else to do.

'I don't want you to read this, I want you to talk to me,' I said. You won't know me but you are Jean McOllister and I've been looking for you all weekend and I've been trying to meet you for months.'

'Oh no,' she said when I told her my name, now doing her own impression of a fish blowing bubbles, 'it's the other way round. *I've* been looking for *you.*'

Bradford central to Didcot Junction – I find out about the USSR

Jean McOllister was a tall young woman with thick, shoulder length wavy brown hair, and round brown shining eyes. She was a remarkable linguist and could learn difficult languages and remember them, just like that. An American, she was a Rhodes Scholar at Oxford University, although at the time I had no idea that this put her among the academically brightest of her generation. She had studied Russian at university, could speak the language fluently, and was currently working on a PhD in Soviet Ecology – with some difficulty, since ecological problems had no official existence in the USSR of Leonid Brezhnev.

Jean was a genuine intellectual. She had an open-minded curiosity for that which was new and different to what she already knew. Encouraged by the liberal rationality of a comfortable upbringing in America's mid-west, she was completely fascinated by the sheer oddness, the smelliness and passion, the irrationality lurking beneath an over-ordered exterior, of Russia and its system. She regarded the Cold War as an alien might have done. It puzzled her, and she genuinely wanted to find out what it was really about. In this way, she was already thinking outside the Cold War and turning it, in her mind, into a historical phenomenon.

I didn't have to ask many questions, for each one produced a flowing seminar of such fascination, such erudition, displaying such a wealth of information presented by a mind with a fresh, completely non-aligned and dispassionate approach, that for the next four hours I did little but listen. She talked non-stop about the USSR, its awful paradoxes, its terrifying history, its horrifying habit of devouring its own children – even about the potential for good embodied in its great socialist experiment. She had read and digested *The Gulag Archipelago*, Solzhenitsyn's detailed account of Stalin's prison camps, where an estimated twenty million died, and were still dying, as we sat in a train heading south across mild, Atlantic-influenced, chequered-fielded England. She had read everything there was to read, and gave me a long reading list. Many of the more interesting books were those written by various western correspondents after they finished their stint of several years reporting for the newspapers. The constraints of working from within a totalitarian state operating strict censorship, and believing every foreigner to be a spy, coupled with the demands of a right-wing British or US press, which wanted to have its own notions of Soviet life confirmed, meant that the real stories, the truth, could only be told later.

Jean had her own stories. As a student of Russian at an American University, she had done a stint on a Soviet fisheries research ship, and had also participated in a student 'Pugwash' conference in the Siberian city of Novosibirsk, one of those 'meet the counterparts' occasions I had heard of. She painted a picture of a country grinding towards gridlock, if not already there, caused by years of neglect and postponement of enormous problems, inexorably increasing by minute increments.

There were ruthlessly suppressed national feelings in the countries that had been swallowed up by the Russian empire, leading to simmering resentment. There were suppressed religions waiting to burst forth, particularly amongst the Muslim countries of Soviet central Asia. There was an agricultural system that barely functioned, and that could not deliver fresh food across the country. There was an economy starved of investment by the prioritisation of the military, so that consumer goods scarcely existed, and were badly made anyway. There were, for instance, no Tampax equivalents and no contraceptives, yet the birth rate was extremely low, thanks to an average of eight abortions per

169

woman. These operations took place, without anaesthetic, in hospitals chronically short of the most basic drugs and equipment. There was the daily misery caused by a Byzantine bureaucracy, in a country where 'shopping' was a sort of hunter-gatherer business to be carried out by those living an urban industrialised lifestyle. It was a land where even travel within the country required official permission to be granted, and rewards for complete conformity included meat distributed to loyal Party members via work-places. No real decisions, above all no innovation, could be made without reference to higher authority, all the way up to the Politburo. The whole system was in a state of atrophy. Nothing new could happen, because to suggest change implied criticism and nobody dared criticise openly. Meanwhile, in that place in the human psyche from whence new things always start, the whole Communist-Socialist-People's-This-and-People's-That she-bang was widely regarded, albeit in strictest secrecy, as nothing more than one enormous joke.

Even when the Soviet leader, Leonid Brezhnev, died, nothing changed — it couldn't. The USSR was stuck fast in the success of its own repression of the new, of any ideas, any initiatives from anyone anywhere within its vast landmass, which the state now controlled completely.

Change, Jean concluded, at the close of her overview of the current state of the society, could only come from the top, from within the higher echelons of the Party itself.

Doveriye — Russian for 'trust'

There was of course another level to this society — the kitchen tables of tiny, cramped but at least heated, flats. This was a society within which people needed strong ties with each other — where goods and ideas flowed along the labyrinthine veins and arteries of an extraordinarily complex system of interconnecting personal and private debts and credits, a dense, fibrous mesh of favours and obligations. You hear about a consignment of bananas, you spot a queue for lettuces, or somebody hands you a manuscript. You tell your friends and family about the bananas, so that they may share in this find, you stand in the lettuce queue not just for yourself but also for your cousin, who queued for fresh tomatoes for you both last week, you pass on the manuscript to someone you know who will appreciate it and won't blab about where it came from.

Beneath a frozen, bland surface of official facts, which existed in complete denial of virtually every aspect of contemporary Soviet life, life flowed along human channels of communication, a life full of warmth, humanity and humour. People passed on the myriad irreverent jokes ('We pretend to work, and they pretend to pay us.') around tables laden with home-made pickles, with home-made jam, with goods diverted from here, there and everywhere. There were connections to be made. There were people to be met. There were vast, tangled and interconnected information grapevines.

Jean had viewed the Cold War – from her vantage point as an American student learning more and more about the enemy, the Russians at first hand – with increasing concern. The belligerent rhetoric of the West, with its paranoid assumption of a super-efficient enemy, armed to the teeth and poised to strike at the West pre-emptively, seemed oddly innappropriate when placed beside the shambolic inefficiencies she was beginning to realise characterised the contemporary, late-Stalinist-era, USSR under Leonid Breznhev, a man who ruled not by terror so much as by sheer boredom, with always the hint of terror.

She had found her own way, once she became a student at Oxford, to the British peace movement, but had been disturbed to find the movement rather dominated, in meetings, by people who seemed to be if not pro-Soviet, at least naïve about the USSR. They ignored the active role played by the Soviet State in the nuclear arms race, and seemed blithely unconcerned about the fundamental question of human rights and freedoms within the Soviet empire. The only suggestion for a way forward out of the present fruitless situation appeared to be that the West should start making unilateral cuts in its weaponry. This was clearly unrealistic.

Then she had heard about the emergence of a new life-form, the Moscow Group for Trust, from a friend, Cathy Fitzpatrick of the New York based human rights group, Helsinki Watch. She felt intrigued. Being an independent-minded and resourceful person, and by now a fluent Russian-speaker, Jean decided to visit the group herself. She had spent a week with them, in November 1982, five months after the public announcement of their existence and their open invite to people from the West to come and visit them in Moscow.

She, like Cathy, felt convinced they were genuine people. After her visit, she knew that without active support from the peace movement in the West the group could not hold out against KGB intimidation for very long – months, probably, rather than years. And support meant persuading somebody to accompany her on a second visit, to raise awareness of the group's existence and to convince the public of their genuineness. She had started trying to interest the British peace movement in the fortunes of the group.

She tried going to END meetings, and found them sympathetic but far too busy with their agenda of meetings and contacts in Eastern Europe to be of much practical help. She tried CND – to be received with scepticism and even hostility, since the CND committee that dealt with Soviet contacts was, predictably enough, packed with pro-Soviet members of the Communist Party and their sympathisers. In February 1983, she went, hoping for a breakthrough in this increasingly frustrating business, to a 'Soviet Women's Seminar' day, in a rambling building in North London, organised by CND, END and others. This was the meeting I had witnessed, when she was shouted down by the Stalinist faction of the British Communist Party.

Finding herself enmeshed in the complex, often nasty politics of British left-wing life in the early Eighties, she had concluded that the people she really needed to contact were the Greenham Women. But here, too, her search had proved fruitless. She had tried visiting the Peace-camp, but found little interest among the women there, on whatever day she dropped by, in an obscure, dubious group of people in the Soviet Union.

In January 1983, Cathy Fitzpatrick had made a second visit to the group. By then the group's founder, Sergei Batovrin, had been arrested for 'schizophrenia', incarcerated in a psychiatric hospital and drugged by the KGB (this was by now the standard initial procedure for dealing with 'dissidents'). Cathy had been smuggled in by other group members on a visit to the psychiatric hospital in Moscow, where she had managed to have a brief, bizarre conversation with Batovrin. Cathy's report of that visit now lay, unread, on the table between us.

Jean had along the way heard of the women who had organised the march to Greenham. Increasingly blocked in her search for support for the desperately fragile Moscow group, she had decided her only remaining hope was to find some of these women and tell them her story. Someone had given her my name. She had indeed been searching for me with as much eagerness as I had been searching for her.

Two weekends later she came to meet Karmen and myself in Wales.

Chapter 17

June 4ᵗʰ, 1982, in Moscow

On a March day in 1983, a day of early, starry yellow celandines, Jean arrived at Gwastod Bach and began talking about the Moscow Group for Trust.

'June 4ᵗʰ 1982, is a very significant date for the group,' she began, 'because that is when they held their first open, public launch meeting in Sergei Batovrin's flat in Moscow.' (I never really know what to make of the several apparent coincidences which punctuated the events of that time. We could not help but be cheered and encouraged by them. I think that when human beings are engaged collectively in a great effort to change our world, thoughts can indeed fly and communicate in ways which will always remain elusive... I remembered that day nine months earlier, that was the day the whole group I was with had seemed obsessed by the notion of East-West relations between people, and that was the afternoon I had lingered by a flowery bank at Maenclochog, thinking for the first time, a thought that had struck me with a kind of revelatory force, about going to Russia.)

Jean continued, oblivious to the fact that I looked as though a ghost had just strolled into the room, 'The meeting was different to previous meetings between Soviet dissidents and the West's correspondents, because those were always highly secret. The Trust group went for openness, as if to call the Soviet State's bluff given that official state policy states that it is the duty of every citizen to 'struggle for peace'. These guys decked out the flat with paintings and drawings by their founder, Sergei Batovrin, and dished out the tea and biscuits as if holding an open 'press launch' was something just anyone could do! They invited members of their own press, *Pravda* and *Izvestia*, as well as the Western press, and they sent a letter to the official Peace Committee asking if they could meet them to discuss their proposals. Of course, only the Western press went along – any Soviet journalist would have lost their job for covering something like that.'

Their manner of operation was innovative, to say the least. They had behaved exactly as if they were a little citizen's action group somewhere in western Europe or the USA. They acted like visitors from a future in which the wildest optimist would have difficulty believing.

'Most of the group are "*refuseniks*"', she said.

'What's that?' I said.

'That's the word for a Jewish person who has applied for a visa to leave the USSR, and who's been refused, as they always are. But for them it makes the point, it's a kind of ritual. But it means they are already flouting convention, they've already marked themselves out as not your one hundred per cent patriotic citizen – so, they have less to lose.'

'Might they not be just hoping to get kicked out if they make enough of a nuisance of themselves?'

'Well, I guess it's a possibility, except that a much bigger possibility is that they'll just get sent to prison, and into the Gulag. Things there haven't really changed since Stalin's day – these people are taking a big risk. Being *refuseniks* means it's not the first risk they're taking, is all.'

I thought about it. The peace movement, Greenham – we were hardly drawn from the ranks of the respectable and conventional, either. Most of the women camping out at Greenham Common were now lesbian, cheerfully flouting rules in more ways than one. Weren't we always seen as outsiders, unrepresentative – and perhaps that's what we were?

The group, of about a dozen men and women, most of them highly qualified academics, working as physics or geography lecturers or else hospital doctors, had read out, to the few intrigued and sceptical western journalists who'd attended, their 'First Proposal' in which they called for a 'Four-way dialogue':

'Between ordinary citizens of East and West;

'between ordinary citizens of East and West and their respective governments, on the subjects of the Cold War and the nuclear arms race;

'between the citizens of East and West and their 'enemy' governments; (Soviet citizens should be able to write, petition etc. the White house, etc. as should Mr and Mrs Jones of Pontypridd be able to address the Politburo on the subject of European nuclear war.)

'between the governments of the nuclear states of East and West.'

This was the way to build trust, through dialogue and communication, they argued, and without trust, there could be no process of disarmament. That was why they called themselves '*Doveriye*', the group for building trust.

It was a simple, brilliant, proposal, one which invited everyone, from powerless individuals to heads of state, to participate in the tricky process of making a huge change. It was obvious. Anybody who could write a letter or buy a plane ticket could take part in this new international dance form: trust-building. It looked innocent enough. In fact, it was very clever. Its target was not the Soviet State, it made no criticism of the Soviet system. There was not one shred of illegality in the Trust group's proposal. Instead, it targeted by implication the one truly vulnerable, and absolutely crucial, aspect of that system: the Iron Curtain.

Soon after that first meeting, the Scandinavian women had held a peace-march in Moscow with the full cooperation of the state-run Soviet Peace Committee. The tiny newspaper report I had saved from being trampled by ducklings had been about this event. The Trust group had tried to contact the Swedish women, but when just two of the peace visitors tried to visit the group, they found their way barred by large, unidentified, leather-jacketed men. They had conducted a shouted interview at the door of the flat.

During the march, none of the Trust Group could leave their flats. They couldn't get past the men who stood in their doorways. Batovrin was taken to a psychiatric hospital for the duration of the 'international peace events'. Most of the western peace-marchers either didn't know any of this, or else didn't protest for fear of upsetting their official hosts.

The KGB then called in Group members for 'chats'. They made it clear that their shenanigans would not be tolerated for long. The western journalists thought they might survive as a group for six months at the outside. But then people from the West began to visit the group. They did not come in what you might call droves. The first was Cathy Fitzpatrick, from Helsinki Watch in New York. Then there had been Jean, and just a handful of others from western European countries.

What we should do was now clear. The three of us, Karmen Jean and myself, would meet the Trust group, and we would meet the Soviet Peace Committee. We couldn't let the Trust Group know we were coming, (mail sent to them was intercepted) but we could write to the Soviet Peace Committee. We would seek both official and unofficial cooperation for our proposal for a visit by a larger group of women. We would have to raise the funds for our air fares. We would have to ask for some of the Greenham funds for this, and pass the hat around the peace movement (which in practice boiled down to passing the hat around the good, stalwart Quakers).

This, with the usual difficulties, is what we did. We asked to use some of the money from the Greenham funds towards our travel expenses, and had difficulty over this because Helen, shortly after the start of the Peace-camp, had put herself in sole control over the account, and did not support our aim to meet with 'peace dissidents'. At a public meeting, a more democratic form of control was established over donations, and the meeting voted to support our trip. We were beginning to realise how divided the peace movement was on the question of the USSR.

Colin dies

The next time I collected Jean from Carmarthen train station, for a last meeting before we left to catch the plane to Moscow, I stopped the car beside a bank in the village of Llanpumsaint to pick a big bunch of the wild white bluebells that grew profusely in that spot. It was May 13th, a day of blinding bursts of May sun from behind big indigo clouds. The greens were luminous, the white stitchwort and juicy bluebells were all out along the high banks of the hill.

An hour earlier, I had gone upstairs with a cup of tea for Colin, who seemed unwell, he had a cold and Thor had given him a bath and helped him into bed. Mozart's 'Magic Flute' was playing on the radio.

His chin was on his chest, his face the colour of old ivory piano keys. His head was cold but his body was still pink and warm. The ivory colour was slowly spreading down from his neck. I kissed him – why should we not touch and kiss and hug our dead? Why not? They do in other countries, they do everywhere else. They are still ours, still there somehow. That's how I felt anyway. I flew down the stairs then, and went and grabbed my two sons by the hand.

The two little boys were playing outside under the enormous high arch of our neighbour's big black corrugated iron hay-barn. They burrowed in the hay, climbed about on the old tractor out there and pretended to drive it, and took their toy cars out there, and made complicated roads and landscapes in the dust beside the hay bales, in which they made hidey-holes in the winter. They rode around on their toy plastic cars, and squabbled, and rushed in for drinks and biscuits, and rushed out again. This was why I had wanted to have my children in the countryside – so that they could do this.

We ran up the stairs to the bedroom and I showed them their dead grandfather. They didn't react much, because he had only ever been a grumpy old man with them, and they had never known the man who had walked across the mountains of Europe, the man who had grown out of the frightened, lonely, bullied child to find courage and resolution, the man who, it seems to me now, had really lived the life of a true Christian without allowing himself the comfort of a belief in a God or an afterlife.

They knew nothing of the man who tried to stop the Cold War happening at all, right at the beginning of it all, in the chaos and human lava-flows of Berlin, 1945 and 1946.

Berlin, 1946 – Colin attempts, and fails, to strangle the infant Cold War

My father had the foresight to take a camera with him when he was sent to Germany with the Signals Corps in the aftermath of war… There is Colin's friend and ideological sparring-partner, Vic Jones, in his khaki uniform, standing in the snow somewhere in Northern Germany. The caption to the photograph says 'Winter 1945'. Colin took snapshots of half-timbered houses, the river Weser flooding the streets of Minden, of the ruins of Hamburg, of a child in *lederhosen* on a street in Gottingen, of dappled sunlight in the Harz mountains. Finally, Berlin, framed by a black rectangle. The rectangle is the blown-out entrance to Hitler's bunker. Colin stands with various friends in front of, beside, the blackened blown-out doorway. Everybody looked forward to getting home after this incredible time, the end of World War Two, to the start of real justice and real socialist values, real humanity, a health service for all, the main industries, the railways, the public utilities, owned and run by the state in the best interests of the whole population, no more grinding poverty, in their own country.

The next picture shows him arm in arm with some Russian soldiers. They are children, barely out of their teens, and they are beaming. One of the British soldiers in these photographs was a man called John Marshall.

This friend John Marshall was the same John who had posed the sceptical questions at those meetings when true comrades were not meant to oppose Hitler, while Stalin still believed Hitler wouldn't invade Russia. The dutiful, loyal chairman of the branch and the awkward bugger who'd come along to meetings but never actually joined the Party, had found each other again, in Berlin, in 1946. It was John who told me the stories I have told here about my father, about the Party meetings, the pub discussions, the efforts at friendship in the ruins of Berlin, when I visited him one day in 1985.

Colin, John recalled, was constantly moving about between the 'Western' and 'Eastern' sectors into which Berlin was already divided. As one of the few British who spoke German, Russian and French, he was often called upon as an official interpreter, but soon started making friends in the Eastern Sector. When trains travelling from the West entered the East, the doors would be locked. This meant that my father climbed out of the window, much to the horror of the other British Army officer passengers.

As I tried to find people who were starting to create personal contacts with those in the Soviet Bloc countries, I heard from John stories my father had never told me, of how he had tried to create human contact in an atmosphere of suspicion and prejudice. The climax of these efforts to smother the infant Cold War came with an impromptu dinner party in the Winston Club, Kurfurstendamn, in Berlin, in early spring 1946.

Four Red Army soldiers were hanging around, shyly, outside the door of this temple of delights, promising food and warmth, which was the British Army Officers' Club. They had the extraordinary luck to encounter, on his way in with his friend Sergeant Johnny, my father, who was the only British officer who could speak Russian. Colin, in defiance of protocol, invited them in for a meal and a drink. A stunned silence of disapproval greeted them – the Germans may have been beastly, but at least they were Anglo-Saxon, but the Russians – weren't they smelly, and did they know about cutlery? The Russians didn't smell, and were familiar with cutlery. Furthermore, they came from all over the Soviet Empire, from Georgia, Siberia, Uzbekistan, the Black Sea, yet seemed to get along famously, each describing his homeland with happy nostalgia. There really did seem to be a genuinely fraternal unity of spirit and purpose to the Red Army.

The Russians, once inside, took charge. They opened the proceedings with an order for fifty beers (for six people), soon to be repeated, and an equal number of stodgy large white rolls, filled with margarine and a gruesomely tasteless processed cheese, which all present had to consume, further moistened with illicit vodka. It was a Soviet style of entertainment that would remain constant for the next forty years.

The Russians had heard news of Churchill's latest speech. They were puzzled and hurt by it. They regarded him as the great hero of the war, yet he had, just three days earlier, used for the first time the words 'Iron Curtain' to describe what was happening to eastern Europe. As the party staggered down the street much later, largely leaving its stomach contents in the toilets, they sang a popular song, 'If tomorrow never comes'. They had unwittingly enjoyed a brief interlude, and the possibilities for such spontaneous human occasions would disappear within weeks. Tomorrow, would begin the paraphernalia of the Cold War: the fences, the prohibitions on travel, the mistrust.

Curtains of Iron

Why should our simple, innocent intention to meet people in the USSR be so controversial? Why should the Trust group's proposal, to which we so keenly desired to respond, arouse such flurries of alarm in a state that might, by now, have allowed itself a little self-confidence?

The Soviet state since its inception had exercised control over the individual in the name of the good of the many. This went beyond simple law enforcement. It controlled information particularly. If everybody were able to travel freely in and out, visiting aunties and cousins in Canada and Britain and so on, they would then be able to compare their impressions of life under a welfare capitalist system, with life in their own, existing-socialist-developing-into-communist system. This would not have been a good idea, from the point of view of those running the USSR, who, like most people who have a lot of power, were convinced they knew best. They knew, for instance, that the wonderful world of fully mature communism would take some time to develop, and that in the meantime, sacrifices would be needed, though it would all be worth it in the end. They knew the gaudy array of consumer goodies which, they had heard, greeted travellers to the West, was but a façade behind which the working class still lived in Dickensian squalor, but they also knew how easily the common people might be taken in by such a façade. So, the first fact to digest about the old USSR is that nobody could leave. Soldiers on war duties were an exception, but they weren't supposed to get friendly with people from capitalist countries. Those four musketeers who collided with Colin outside the Winston Club in Berlin 37 years earlier had no idea the ice was so thin, nor the waters beneath so deep and so cold.

It followed from the closed-off nature of this society that talking to anyone from outside was regarded as unpatriotic, or suspicious. After all, how else would the spies that most foreigners were assumed to be, gather their information?

Tourists were controlled. Their sole purpose from the State's point of view was to contribute foreign currency, so they were charged ludicrously high prices and paid an exchange rate hilariously at odds with the 'real' street exchange rate. They were processed in groups by carefully selected Intourist 'guides' who shepherded them between monuments, pouring a steady stream of statistics into their ears that effectively drowned out any irrelevant noises of everyday life. If Western vistors 'met' Soviet people then they did so as a 'delegation' under the unspoken rules governing visiting delegations: lots of banquets with long welcome speeches, one bottle of vodka per person per day to be consumed by each member, no aimless wandering (unless to be sick in the loo) and no random unsupervised chatting.

The effect of the mutual ignorance of each others' lived reality, Western and Soviet, was to bolster support on each side for the continuing arms race. The arms race did not run on rocket fuel:

it ran on ignorance, paranoia and blind patriotism.

So simply meeting people at random and aimlessly chatting to them was, in the circumstances, a pretty subversive, daring, new and interesting kind of thing to want to do.

Chapter 18

Welcome to the USSR

Let's fly to Moscow on a perfect Spring morning in the early 1980s. It's a cloudless blue day, we can see the carpet of northern Europe spread below. The rectilinear pattern of brown ploughed fields, green pasture and greenish-yellow arable fields becomes more disordered the further east we go. Irregular dark green patches get bigger and the white threads of the roads, rarer. Then quite abruptly, all below is dark bottle green with only the occasional brown patch below, completely irregular in shape and size, and apparently unconnected with other brown or pale green blobs. Down there in the USSR, they don't seem to be doing a lot with all that rich chocolaty earth, black with the leaf-mulch of millennia. What wouldn't I give for that earth in my garden where I have toiled on clay over shale!

This kind of flying is easy, you just sit on your backside, there are no arm movements at all and in the twinkle of an eye the drinks trolley is gone and you're closer to the rising sun, and you're so close to landing you can see that the dark green is actually Christmas trees, interspaced with tall spindly white birch trunks. At ground level, we shall find the air is warm and thick with the floating seed-heads of dandelions, billions of them, the simple tenacious weed of waste ground.

'We' being me, Ann, still sticking with Karmen through thick and thin, plus Jean, our brilliantly fluent, ace Russian speaker. We are on a mission of course, no happy-go-lucky holiday this, we've been laboriously fundraising for three months to cover our air fares and we're responsible to a lot of CND local groups and Quaker meetings and friends and individuals who've supported us so that we can be on this plane...

Publicity in the western media was crucial to the success of our idea; however, this was an exploratory trip, and the wrong sort of news coverage could create difficulties. Already 'Greenham Women' had become a stereotype, part of the British political furniture. This means that already our ability to make people think was waning. In the eyes of the British public, the big weakness of the peace movement was its perceived bias in favour of the 'other side', the USSR. Those truckies who had shouted, 'Why don't you go to Russia?' might as well have added, 'Cause that's where you belong, don't you?' It was like a razor-sharp mountain-top ridge walk, with big drops on either side on a windy day. So we hadn't contacted any newspapers about our visit, fearing the 'Greenham Women welcomed in USSR' treatment, with all its assumptions. We needed journalists who were prepared to sit down and listen, for at least an hour, carefully, to what it was we were trying to do. So, for the first time we were not seeking publicity, for we were feeling our way forward as if blindfolded, we didn't know what we would find, what our real purpose would turn out to be.

Soon another passenger on the BA flight to Moscow, a dapper young man, overheard our conversation, and introduced himself as the Moscow correspondent for the London *Times*. He brought over his two friends, the *New York Times* correspondent, and another American correspondent. He expressed intelligent and well-informed interest in our intentions. This was luck indeed. We had a three-and-a-half hour flight before us, just about enough time to explain what it was we were trying to do and to pick their brains too.

These journalists corroborated what we had already been told by all the other experts on the Soviet Union, about the publicity given to 'Greenham Women' by the Soviet media. For 'Greenham Women', we were assured, were 'big' in the USSR. So big, that most of the newsreels preceding all films in cinemas (perhaps the most popular form of public entertainment) would show the latest footage of these anti-American-imperialist heroines, bravely defying winter cold and police brutality (the cameras would close in on arrested women being dragged off into vans), being assaulted, as now they often were, by the police, women shivering in the cold, and all to stop American missiles from being placed on British soil. Whereas we were scrabbling after every bit of coverage we could get to put across our point of view to our own press (and then as often as not the story would concentrate on some trivia of the lives of the women, how awful they looked in their muddy clothes, how messy the camp was, what their husbands thought), in the USSR 'Greenham Women' were taken seriously, frequently making headline material or the lead story in the papers. *Or so it seemed.*

So there was no way we would have been able to slip incognito into the USSR, be free to make our own contacts with anyone we met, independent of state interference. We had contacted the relevant Party Committees, those for 'Peace' and 'Women', and asked them to arrange a meeting with us hadn't we? So, we would be swamped by official hospitality, which we would have to use a mix of cunning, guile and immense determination to avoid. We would probably be greeted off the plane by flag-waving young '*Komsomolski*', patriotic tiny tots, who would be lined up on the tarmac singing peace songs. We would be swept into an official car, straight off to the first of many banquets that we would be made to feel churlish to refuse. We would be plied with endless vodka until we sank into a stupor. Above all, our movements would be directed by our 'guide' who would ensure that no unsupervised contacts with anybody, and certainly not with any Trust group members, took place. And if we did 'escape', we would be followed, by little old ladies looking like Kruschev's wife, all headscarves and bulging shopping-bags, who would in fact be KGB agents.

If meeting the Moscow Group for Trust, about whom little had been heard for several months, was our priority, then second on our agenda was something we anticipated no difficulty in achieving: the 'official' Soviet Peace Committee could safely be assumed to be falling over themselves to meet some real 'Greenham Women' at long last. Of course they knew we were coming: we had explained that we were two of the original women who had organised the march, which developed into, etc. etc., in letters and telegrams that we knew they had received because they replied to them. They just told us to telephone to arrange a meeting when we arrived in Moscow. It did seem a bit casual, but that was fine by us. Capture by 'the program' was our biggest dread.

The SPC, to abbreviate its title, was, like all the other 'Committees', run by the Communist Party. The Communist Party ran the State also. That's how it worked. 'Peace' had a special meaning in the USSR. It meant patriotism. The Peace Committee existed in order to generate support for the Soviet half of the nuclear arms race. It did this by constantly organising 'mass rallies' and 'marches' of millions of people, in favour of 'peace' and protesting against whatever new weapons system the West was currently introducing. As a visitor, you could confidently expect to be shown lots of photographs of these occasions, many featuring children waving home-made 'peace' placards. Any new Soviet weapons systems were merely a deeply reluctant response on the part of this manifestly peace-loving nation ('See the photographs! Ten million across the USSR! 200,000 marched in Pyatigorst alone!') to the new threat. Another purpose for this Committee was to meet with visiting Western peace delegations. The committee members would, naturally, try to glean from their polite, well-behaved and diplomatic visitors any genuinely useful information on, say, the likelihood of a Labour government with a unilateralist agenda for nuclear disarmament coming to power (a snowflake's chance in hell, any truth-teller should have told them, but that wasn't generally what they were told by these all-too-nice visitors who often regarded the USSR as very much the wronged victim of the situation) – in other words, they were a useful kind of low-level-spying, and information-gathering, organisation of the state.

But, having met these Peace Committee people both in Moscow and, a year later, in London, I came to another conclusion as to their true purpose: most of the men and women who got to be on this Committee, who spent hours listing all the Soviet disarmament proposals, all the 'peace initiatives', all the competitions for the best 'peace poster' by all the millions of school-children, in fact were there for the shopping. This was an arm of the Party that met with Western organisations, and whose members, if they were lucky enough to be chosen, could expect to be invited back for return hospitality. This was the way, occasionally, very loyal Party members, could get to visit Paris, or London, or New York: as part of an invited delegation from the USSR. And this way – and this was for anyone below top diplomat level - was the only way they could get to go to the shops, with their allowance of Western currency. The true purpose of all the Peace Committees in the USSR and all the Warsaw Pact countries, was that their members got to the shops: they wanted to visit Marks and Spencer.

There was competition to be on this committee; it and the other committee we had arranged to see, the Women's Committee were popular activities among the wives of Politburo members.

So, you must be saying, why bother when it's all such a sham? Well, we had an idea to put to them, a little proposal. We wanted to bring over a group of women, about thirty say – not too big, not too small, like a bowl of porridge – and we wanted this group, split into smaller groups, to go on a 'wander-about-and-meet-people-at-random' visit of about two weeks' duration, taking in both cities and rural areas. We had a TV documentary programme interested in the idea, should it happen. For this we needed the active cooperation of the State, paradoxically, whilst wanting them also to allow us personal contact of an unsupervised and unorchestrated nature, simply because without official sanction, all the participants could have been arrested as spies. We thought just asking for such a visit, discussing its purpose with those who spoke for the State, would be an interesting exercise. If people could start coming over to Moscow and just meeting ordinary people, as citizens with fears and hopes in common, then some of the support for hawkish policies, which ultimately depended on a willingness to consider mass annihilation of the innocent inhabitants of the 'enemy state', could begin, in however small and humble a way, to erode

Karmen and I were there, on a plane now losing height above Moscow, because ten months earlier, the time it takes a foetus to grow from four cells to full-blown baby, we had become obsessed with the idea of going to Russia.

We were entering a zone of hunger – for information, for ideas, for nice things. Where we lived, the most meagre village Post Office was a cornucopia of forbidden fruits. We had shopped for gifts. Jean, innocently reckless as ever, had brought proscribed books with her, including Karl Popper's book *The Open Society and its Enemies*, to pass on to people she had met on her previous visit. I, ever the 'improver', had brought the most objective information about the arms race I could find, from the Stockholm Peace Research Institute. Karmen, canny as ever, had brought lipstick and Tampax.

So, shall we land our aircraft? On this tarmac, which looks in dire need of repair?

Young pioneers fail to welcome arriving Peace champions

The airport, a fraction of the size of Heathrow, was not busy. The only hold-up was occasioned by the passport check. A pimply teenager in some sort of military uniform subjected each entrant to the Worker's State now entering its final phase – that of true Communism after the preceeding 64 years of planned Socialist development – to a full three minutes of stony scrutiny. The three journalists were met by courteous chauffeurs beckoning towards comfortable, waiting cars. The football team were whisked off by coach. If there were any other tourists, they were in groups and they, too, were soon insulated from the hoi-polloi in their own transport.

That left us, and the Russians, with their peculiar packages that were done up with an outer casing of hessian sacking and string, a bit like something very cool and designer, only it wasn't, it meant they had been visiting client countries in Africa. Far from being overwhelmed by an embarrassing surfeit of attention as befits heroines who feature on newsreels from Minsk to Vladivostok, we were the only travellers from the West who were *not* met from the plane.

An enquiry at the Intourist desk met with a dismissive wave of the hand and the three words, 'Intourist bus – finish!' After this instructive introduction to Soviet service culture, we realised we were in for an immediate, rather than comfortably delayed, dunking in local realities. To get to Moscow, we would have to do whatever the Russians did. So we stood in what seemed to be a developing queue outside the building. When I say 'developing' I mean an arrested form of development, whereby a very old, battered-looking taxi with a wheezing engine and spluttering exhaust would arrive about every ten or fifteen minutes, and people would get into it from either end of the queue irrespective of how many minutes they had already been waiting. It took us some time to appreciate these new rules. Eventually, after about an hour of fruitless politesse, we used the run-shove-shout method ourselves to good effect, climbing into the taxi with an indignant Russian couple who made little scandalised noises all the way into the city centre.

We travelled through miles of faded yellow plastered flats, and arrived at a large building the colour of fresh liver – the Hotel Metropole. Beyond its façade, a vast space opened up, also liverish, with strangely familiar twirly domes – Red Square. There didn't seem to be any of the usual milling of other western tourists there in the hotel lobby, in fact there were none at all. The Metropole, we later discovered, was not a hotel normally assigned to Westerners. I have no idea why the small travel company with whom we booked put us in there, but we were lucky they did, for the surveillance of inmates here was traditional, in other words lax, rather than rigorously modern.

The woman behind the desk in the dimly-lit foyer played the

part assigned her by the right-wing capitalist-imperialist press superbly. She pretended to ignore our arrival, only motioning us towards a hard leatherette settee with a dismissive wave of the hand when we went up and tried to speak to her. She then devoted her full attention to her fingernails and to another woman beside her, a woman whose blonde bouffant hair-do and very red lipstick recalled the glory days of the Sixties. Every so often we half-rose from our seats, parched after the long journey begun very early that morning and hoping for some refreshment, but before any query could penetrate her shellac she quelled us with another imperious hand gesture and made an unpleasant Russian sound at us which sounded as though she was spitting cabbage soup across the room – 'Ssschass!' Looking at us disapprovingly, she would return to her manicure and her conversation, also conducted in unpleasant-sounding tones. *She did this for one and a half hours.*

There was little other movement in the large, semi-dark, high-ceilinged lobby. There were imposing double doors leading into an adjoining room with the word 'restaurant' written in beautiful Cyrillic lettering, but it was evidently shut. We tried to take an interest in our surroundings, but hunger and thirst were impeding our appreciation of the art-nouveau decor of this famous building, once the home of correspondents who had covered the Russian front in the Great Patriotic War, 1941-1945. The vastness of the innumerable achievements, beside which we were as three ants in the Gobi desert, began to settle on us, like dust, like fallout. We sank into ourselves, into history, into the repellant surface of the banquette. Oh for America, for have-a-nice-day and eggs-sunnyside-up, for smiles and cheeriness and efficiency all round, come back all is forgiven, you win, you win, you win hands-down!

Without warning or other stimulus or change of circumstances, the woman behind the desk beckoned us to follow her up a wide staircase whose red carpet, like the rest of the surroundings, had seen better days.

Our Soviet bombs are for peace only

People were not allowed to roam freely and unobserved in this hotel, which was inhabited largely by mysterious 'delegations' from eastern European countries and the Soviet republics, and was run along the lines of a pre-war boarding school. Each floor had a large desk opposite the only exit, the staircase and lift, and behind the desk sat another woman with a bouffant hairdo, long carmine nails, an intense dislike of hotel guests and a big book. Upon leaving you had to 'sign out', and had to sign back in when you returned. However, she too was subject to the inertia of vastness, of achievement beyond imagining, she too was apt to nod off, or simply disappear at times. In search of a simple cup of tea, (room service was clearly out of the question) we tip-toed, unobserved, past her inert body and down to the end of the corridor, where we found the service staircase. Following the distant sound of clashing crockery we descended the grubby stairwell into the labyrinthine depths of the huge, complicated building. Soon we tracked down the tell-tale sounds of washing-up to a small door, upon which we knocked.

Inside were three very big women in dirty white overalls. Surprisingly, they welcomed us in unhesitatingly, with floods of Russian, laughter and big hand-shakes. They sat us down in their tiny cubby-hole of a kitchen, and made us tea. 'Milk?' ... 'Ah no,' they threw out their hands. 'No fresh milk – no refrigeration.' Their cupboard housed a motley collection of mismatched, chipped, once-white cups and saucers. Their bare legs were marbled with blue, bulging varicose veins.

Jean explained the purpose of our visit to their country, our mission.

'Ah,' said one, throwing out her arms, 'our Soviet bombs are for peace only.'

A torn poster

Fortified, we set off forthwith to try to contact the Trust group.

During her previous visit, Jean had spent most of her time with one of the most active of them, a cardiologist called Volodya Brodsky. Brodsky lived in an old part of Moscow – the cracked yellow ochre plaster zone of ten-storey flats – reasonably accessible by public transport, and she could remember which bus to catch, and the way from the bus stop. The streets of central Moscow were warm in the May evening, and crowded with people. Many appeared hurried, and were clutching small children. Almost all carried shopping bags. As we stood on a street corner waiting for a bus, wearing our 'Nyet bomba!' badges and being stared at by people who looked away as though they hadn't meant to look at us, we noticed nearly every woman that passed glanced at us, then looked briefly downwards at our shoes. Their shoes were often cracked, old, and ugly.

One reason we were looking forward to visiting Brodsky was that Jean had received a good impression of his hospitality and general skills as a host, and she assured us that we would certainly be given something to eat. The Hotel Metopole restaurant remained as enigmatically closed to would-be diners as ever, and by now we were very hungry and very thirsty.

But when we followed Jean down a dusky street heavy with trees, things were not as we expected. The building was derelict. The windows were all broken, the stairs to the flat, where we had hoped to find a delighted host, were full of rubbish. It was ten o'clock at night and in the warm dusk, we could see through the birch trees, which grew thickly around the waste ground at the back of the block, a group of men who were filling a small truck with big pieces of wood that must have come from the floors, doors and windows of the building. Jean came down, dismayed and upset. 'I don't understand,' she said. 'This is definitely the flat – look, I found one of their posters. This is a photo of Sasha Rosenoer, who's been "arrested". She was holding a dusty, torn piece of A4 size cardboard with a young man's bearded, concrete-spattered face on it announcing something. 'He even left the kitchen table – Have they all been arrested, or what?'

We followed her up the rubbly concrete staircase to where

the entrance door to a first floor flat swung on its hinges. A thick line of trees would have blocked most of the light reaching the window. Broken glass lay strewn on the floor.

'I sat here three months ago. We talked for hours. They were such lovely flats – so cosy, so Russian.'

'Well, we'll just have to try the other address tomorrow,' said Karmen briskly. 'Come on – we've got to try to get something to eat. It's so long since I've eaten I can't think properly.'

During our ten-day stay in Moscow and Leningrad, we made a careful, highly-motivated study of food and its availability. To be assured of eating in the USSR, one had to belong to a defined category – worker, Party member, delegation, tourist group. Being simply human was insufficient. The conclusion we drew was that the only edible food that was reliably and openly offered for public sale was ice-cream. Bread-shops sold stale bread, even in the early morning; there were no other food-shops. Some apparent food-shops displayed huge pyramids of tinned fish, beneath thick layers of dust, but no one ever seemed to buy any of these. People everywhere carried bulky bags, which bulged suspiciously with what might have been food items. These were not the now ubiquitous black or logo-ed plastic bag. They were what our mothers used to call shopping bags, made from canvas or other strong material, sometimes reinforced with vinyl or plastic. Often they were string bags, with the bulging shapes wrapped up in brown paper.

The restaurant, on our return to our hotel, was open. A band was playing sluggishly and there were many empty tables. Diners were dining. Waiters were present in large numbers, waiting but not at tables. True to the sarcastic images painted by biased Western observers, they stood in a row, motionless, against the walls of the room, chatting smoking and ignoring the diners. We went in and sat down. They ignored us. We went up and spoke to them and they said we could not have food. We asked why and they said there wasn't any, which was clearly a lie, as food was visibly being consumed on all sides. We had received some very good advice about overcoming obstacles in the Soviet Union –

brandish hard currency and/or create a '*skandal*' (stamping your feet, waving your arms and alternately shouting and bursting into tears). In this instance both Western currency and a minor '*skandal*' – just one or two foot-stamps and raised voices – were needed to produce three ham sandwiches with no butter and three beers in a city centre restaurant of the world's other super-power, at eleven o'clock at night.

Chapter 19

Welcome to the Moscow Group for Trust

The next morning we discovered that breakfast was quite substantial, but could only be had if you first queued up separately for a ticket. However, this tiny piece of wafer-thin paper would prove to have another useful application.

Our itinerary, like that of most tourist trips to the USSR, had been created around the need for Intourist to fill its quotas for train seats on particular days, rather than around any wishes we may have had, let alone our convenience as visitors. Accordingly, we were booked to leave for Leningrad on the overnight train which left at 10 pm, returning after three days to Moscow for our final four days. We therefore had to leave our hotel room by ten in the morning, but didn't want to carry our heavy bags around with us all day. There was no officially-sanctioned provision for this kind of problem, but we were already developing a feel for how to approach these matters. In another part of the hotel lobby, out of sight of the bouffant hair-do harpies behind the 'reception desk', we found an elderly man who seemed to be in charge of a broom cupboard. His response to our entreaties was genuinely sympathetic, but he was concerned that we had no official permit from any government ministry to deposit baggage in the hotel.

He urged us to search our pockets and bags for permits, *laissez-passers*, dockets, signed letters from members of Party Committees, anything. We produced our breakfast tickets, which he seized triumphantly. These would cover him, were anyone to ask any questions. Carefully he stowed our bags away behind him in his cupboard, vowing to guard them faithfully against whole regiments of Cossacks, cunningly fashioning a disguise with a nonchalant swathe of grey string floorcloth. As we left thanking him, he grinned toothlessly, winking as he patted his pocket containing the precious breakfast tickets, giving us an encouraging thumbs-up.

We lost no time in setting off on a renewed search for the Trust group. The landscape was one of vast streets, the size of fourteen-lane motorways, and equally wide pavements. Set back from the streets were high-rise blocks of flats, some grey, many yellow, almost all faded-looking. The ground in between was covered in unmown grass and thick, young trees, mostly birch. Dirt tracks wound their way through the grass. Many people trudged along these tracks, and little boys fished in muddy ponds. The city centre landscape featured beds of orange tulips which were being pulled up, to make way for the next floral display we supposed, by women for whom the only appropriate collective noun would be 'squad' or 'detachment', since all were wearing identical grey overalls and white head-scarves. The centres of these beds, and many of the building façades, featured display stands showing black-and-white photographs, rows of mugshots. They were of local and national dignitaries, Soviet deputies and the like, nearly all middle-aged men, and they all had a similarly soft, air-brushed look about them which gave them an ageless, botoxed appearance. Once past this display of civic pride, the long grass, dust and dandelions took over, giving an unkempt air overall.

The taxi-driver drove hither and thither, stopping to ask for directions, for the blocks of flats set far apart in this landscape, which reduced humans to Lilliputians, seemed to have no distinguishing features, no numbers or marks, no actual address as such. Eventually he set us down before one such block and drove off. The next problem was – how to get inside? We couldn't ring in advance – the Medvedkov's phones had been cut off. The front access door was firmly locked and there was no means of attracting the attention of a resident. Somebody, however, had thoughtfully provided a solution to this dilemma by breaking out the large pane of glass in the window to the side of the door, and neatly clearing the waist-high exposed edge of razor-sharp glass debris. Hauling ourselves carefully up and over, we stood in the lobby. There was a small lift, and up we went to the eighteenth floor. The flats were numbered. We rang the bell.

Yuri and Olga Medvedkov, academic hooligans

A fuzzy blur ran past the door then returned. Someone fiddled with a key and answered to our knock. A thin boy of about ten stood there. His parents were out, he explained, but would be back shortly. Jean spoke reassuringly to him, and we entered a spacious, bright space with bookshelves and a big settee and sat down. A few minutes later a man and woman walked in − Olga and Yuri Medvedkov. Olga was small with thick wavy dark hair, big bright eyes and a neat appearance. Yuri was older, with a slightly tired look about him, a large man with greying hair and a kind, intelligent, quizzical face. He had the slightly crumpled look of the classic academic, an intellectual who had never lavished much thought on his appearance. If he wasn't wearing corduroy trousers he should have been. The boy who had opened the door to us was their only child, Mikhail. They told him off for opening the door, but were too pleased to see us to be really cross.

They recognised Jean and the kettle went on. Jean introduced us and explained our purpose. A pan of water for sausages went on. Yuri was an academic, a lecturer in human geography at Moscow University. So was Olga. Yuri, looking dreamily into the middle distance, launched into what sounded like a set-piece speech detailing the Trust group's latest proposals for disarmament. Olga, giggling, told Jean she was phoning someone − Volodya Brodsky. Jean told her about our visit to the ruined flat. 'He's moved!' said Olga. 'Rehoused! Those old buildings are being pulled down − he's only fifteen minutes away!' Winking at us, she left to phone from the box at the foot of the stairwell – their own phone had been cut off by 'them'. She would say that Yuri had had a heart attack and required a doctor immediately. 'He will be here at four,' she said.

All our meetings with people in the Trust group over the next eight days would have contradictory elements: we would sit around tables drinking black tea, eating black bread, cheese and pickled cucumbers, and discussing the pros and cons of high-rise buildings, or sharing our information about the arms race, and hearing about how, despite the known risks, more and more people were wanting to sign the Trust group's document, or were forming their own groups, in other towns and cities. People would seem remarkably up-beat and positive. Then, inevitably, talk of 'the repressions' would surface and someone would talk about the latest arrest, and the latest rumoured arrest, and were the authorities playing games or did they really mean to eventually arrest, charge and condemn the whole group to prison-camp, and if not the whole group then which ones, and when. As we sat there drinking our tea and eating gristly sausages, Yuri – both he and Olga spoke very good English – told us that Batovrin, the young artist who had inspired the group into existence, who had been told he was a 'schizophrenic' and stuck into psychiatric hospital, had been given an exit visa, and had left his country for ever the day before, on a flight to Vienna. 'When one is let out, they jail another,' said Yuri philosophically, trying to find some form of logic in the behaviour of the KGB.

In the eleven months since the group's first meeting, they had had sufficient contact with visitors from western peace movements to realise that people such as us found it almost impossible to fully understand what life was like for them inside a full-blown one-party, totalitarian state. They had recently spent a long two hours patiently explaining to some visiting Americans, the authorities' response to their initiative: house arrests, being taken away for interrogation by men who tell you to 'bring warm clothes – you'll need them where you're going' and telling the family 'say goodbye – you won't be seeing him again', being given long and tedious work such as making an inventory of all the nuts and bolts in a laboratory, being told you will be demoted from university professor to part-time caretaker. They finally thought they were getting somewhere, when one of the Americans piped up, 'Yes, we understand now. It must be extremely difficult for you. But why don't you go to your lawyers for protection?'

They were in a quandary. If they tried to really explain things, that was all that ever got talked about or reported. News of arrests, curtailment of jobs, interrogations, beatings and threats gave the impression that here were a group of people who could not possibly survive, and whose experience showed that the Soviet state was so repressive that the West needed all the arms it could muster, to defend itself against any possible aggression by such a cruel and irrational regime. So, drawing attention to their plight could so easily be twisted into support for our own dear Cold Warriors... 'What did we tell you? You can't have a Peace-camp there!'

If organisations which were anti-Soviet anyway tried to champion their cause, it would only undermine them: 'See who your friends are – the aggressive Capitalist-Imperialists – those who wish to see the downfall of our Soviet State – what did we tell you!' their KGB tormentors would crow.

The only people who could possibly help were people like us, non-aligned people from within the peace movement, people who were not naïve about the USSR, but who were motivated by the same horror of a nuclear conflagration as they were. The only way we could make any difference was by bringing western publicity to bear upon their fate, and so possibly embarrassing the Soviet leadership into treating the Trust group with uncharacteristic leniancy. The Medvedkovs had been Party members: like drowning creatures clinging to the proverbial straw in a river in spate, they hung on to a minute amount of hope that this unlikely fate, of simply being allowed to quietly continue advocating human dialogue across the Iron Curtain, could be theirs.

Meanwhile, as support, spread by word of mouth, for their ideas had grown in other parts of the USSR, two forestry workers collecting signatures for the 'Appeal to Governments and Publics' had been arrested in Tyumen, a city in Siberia.

'Authorities can do what they like there, is no world to see, is no Western press, is no way to discover fate of these people,' they said in their perfect but definite-article-free English. The Tyumen two had gone on hunger-strike, causing murmurs of disapproval – martyrdom was not an aim. Just meeting in their flats and talking was already quite enough to produce a range of reactions from the State.

The stories began. The Medvedkovs' status as academics meant they possessed a car. Unbeknown to them, 'someone' had loosened the wheel nuts. The wheel nut business had produced something of an own goal: the moment when a wheel had chosen to part from the Medvedkov's car had coincided with a drive-past of Leonid Brezhnev's motorcade. Brezhnev was the then first secretary of the Communist Party of the USSR, the man who occupied the position simultaneously of Prime Minister, President, and monarch – in other words, the head of state. The car belonging to the fly-in-the-ointment peaceniks had careered towards the centre of the line of speeding black stretch limos – the model in favour at the time was a classic looker called a Zil – narrowly missing the Leader himself, before harmlessly scraping into the side of the Leninski Prospect highway. The shocked Medvedkovs had the satisfaction of seeing the KGB, in their accompanying cars, horrified at the near-miss, and took great delight in complaining to the police that 'hooligans' had tampered with their car, causing this near-fatal accident.

'Hooligans' were the cover for many of the pranks played by the secret police on individuals who had signed the Trust group's appeal. Not all these incidents, designed to un-nerve, had happy endings. Another member, a physics lecturer, had experienced cars full of leering men knocking him off his bicycle once whilst he was carrying his son on the back. The ten-year-old son of another couple had been killed, incredibly, in what had been passed off as a playground brawl – but there was no investigation and so it appeared it hadn't just been a terrible accident. This was such a strictly ordered, hooligan-free society that they had every reason to see the hand of KGB thugs at work in these disturbing events. But it was also becoming easy to see how a genuine paranoia, a state of fear for which rational grounds do not necessarily exist, could be aroused by just this kind of tactic and could then be left to destroy the cohesion of a group of people from within.

The young man whose face had been on the poster we'd collected from Volodya's old flat, Oleg Radzinski, had been arrested and was currently in Lefortovo prison. He had proposed a co-ordinated ten-minute silence on January 1st, 1982. The group urged all peace activists all over the world to join them in prayer, silence and universal reflection on peace, disarmament and the removal of mistrust among nations. Their appeal put a stress on the responsibility of the individual. This would have been considered highly provocative: 'Today, when 25 million people are in military uniform, and when the stockpiles of nuclear arms can turn the world into radioactive ruins, no one can hope that the world will survive by itself or due to someone else's efforts. Everyone shares responsibility. Neither geographical borders, nor political contradictions should be a handicap in realising this responsibility.'

Shortly before our arrival Leonid Brezhnev had died. Hopes that a change of leadership might mean a change of attitude were swiflty dashed. In the first official statement on the group, a senior commentator, Yuri Kornilov, had denounced the group as 'anti-Sovieteers, renegades and criminals' and had described their activities as 'an act of provocation of Western secret services.' For good measure he had also thrown in that they were 'a handful of swindlers who do not represent anyone.'

The Medvedkovs speculated that Oleg had been picked on because he was young – only twenty-five years old – and because his family, who were highly conformist, were scandalised by his action and could put pressure on him to save himself by denouncing the group, and also because he had a long-term illness. If he received the expected jail sentence, straightforward neglect on the part of the authorities could turn prison into a death sentence for him.

We had little time, and soon began to talk about a time and place for some sort of action together when we returned – something of the kind of low-level, barely public nature as would not possibly be considered 'provocative' or 'anti-Soviet', something like a nice little harmless 'peace picnic'. Fingers were pointed upwards at the ceiling and rotated in circles. It wasn't melodramatic to assume the flat was bugged – the KGB had visited the neighbours to install the equipment. Paper and pencil were produced for the details to be written down, conveyed, memorised and destroyed. There was a burst of sound and laughter. Volodya had arrived.

Brodsky

Russian is a language rich in plosive sounds. Volodya spoke little English (we would in the coming days become used to hearing that little: 'I gentleman!' he would roar as he zoomed past to open a door or pick up a bag). Now he was giving vent to the full range of those 'Sch! Cha! Schsha! Kak! Tak! Fschtakak! Zhak! Zapat! Pzaschakak!' noises in his delighted shock at the sight of us all. I looked at Jean. She wore a pale blue, rather old-fashioned, girly, cotton dress with short sleeves and a slightly gathered waist, and her long neck and astonished look gave her a strong resemblence to Teniel's drawing of Alice in Wonderland, straight after she has drunk from the second little 'drink me' bottle in the hopes of counteracting abnormal shrinkage, and has suddenly shot up in height. The room now hosted emotions best expressed by a full string orchestra.

Volodya Brodsky was a tall horse-faced man, with hair swept back from a high forehead. He was wearing cords, and a woollen jumper, and they suited him down to the ground. He carried an old-fashioned bulbous pipe and a tobacco pouch from which he constantly filled the pipe. His mouth was made for sardonic humour and his eyes flashed like a Georgian. He was clearly a born iconoclast, a non-conformist, a rebel. He stared at Jean, shaking his head, as if she were an apparition about to disappear. He looked at us and the large peace badges in the Russian language we wore, which we had made ourselves. We had T-shirts too, featuring East-West hand-holding and the like. He loved these. Soon 'pacifisti of the world unite' adorned his jumper. He produced a little greyish scrap of paper with some typing on it and a signature.

'Here!' he exclaimed. 'This is how you lose your job, here!'

He was a heart surgeon, and one of a handful of people in Moscow who could work a defibrillator machine for people who were taken to hospital in the course of a heart attack. He specialised in emergency and trauma surgery of all kinds, a highly trained person with skills that were valued by his patients, who rewarded him with various kinds of '*defitsinye*' – valued goods in short supply, whose nature varied with the season. That day at work he had been handed this notice that he was to be investigated for negligence of medical records – a sign that the KGB were taking up more serious and systematic methods of intimidation. They were taking the first steps towards depriving all the active group members of their professional jobs.

Events seemed to be moving swiftly in an ominous direction – Batovrin thrown out, Brodsky about to be sacked, and rumour of another member, a physicist, also threatened with loss of his job. Should we even bother to go ahead with our planned meeting with the Peace Committee, which when questioned by visiting Westerners always denied all knowledge of the group anyway? By meeting them, weren't we just being manipulated?

Yuri, the diplomat, said that we should meet with the Peace Committee – 'the officials'.

'This is very important, that you meet with these people, and that you tell them you also have met us,' he said.

Brodsky waved the piece of Izal toilet-roll-like paper around scornfully. 'There are three categories of officials who will deal with us,' he said, smiling, 'KGB, militia and procurators'.

Black leather jackets

We had to leave. Jean had fixed up by telephone a meeting with another person, belonging to a circle of scientists studying the effects of nuclear weapons, and collectively known by the name of the distant suburb where they lived – the 'Dolgoprudniki'. Our contact had agreed to meet us at 5.30pm by the Mayakovski monument in central Moscow.

So far one thing was very clear to myself and Karmen: the Trust group was no put-up job. They behaved uncannily like our very own home-grown CND peace groups in Britain. They were a bit chaotic, they were worried, they disagreed among themselves, some of them were quite prepared to go to prison for their beliefs, others seemed to search for an answering spark of human intelligence in the ranks of the powerful, and believed that if they just argued patiently enough for long enough, something would surely change.

Volodya rabbitted on in the taxi into Moscow, with Jean breathlessly translating at top speed. He clearly belonged to the activist wing. Since, he argued volubly, everyone was likely as not going to end up with an insider's view of a watchtower and a perimeter fence, they might as well have something to show for it. 'They can fiddle around with their mathematical models of the arms race and make all the proposals they like – it's contact between people that counts, that's what we should be doing – that's action, not all this talk, talk. Like you people – you took action.'

'The driver says he likes this discussion, it's cool,' reported Jean as we swerved out of the way to give road-room to a convoy of fast-moving black stretch limos with curtained windows that came roaring down the middle, preceeded by a police loudhailer.

The Mayakovsky statue was crowded with young men and women walking up and down clutching bunches of flowers. It was a popular meeting place. Mind you, buying flowers seemed such a popular thing to do that on any day Moscow resembled

London on Valentine's Day. Beauty was in short supply, clothes were made of nasty materials, nylon and thin rayon, winter had abruptly ended, the sun shone and people couldn't get enough of flowers. We hung around, but our man didn't show. I said we should wait longer but Volodya suddenly said there was no point – the KGB had arrived, were watching us and would certainly have intercepted him. He pointed to a stubby man wearing a black leather jacket. This was a kind of uniform we would come to recognise – no one else could get hold of such a macho fashion item. The man walked up and down, shooting us a glance on every back-turn. Volodya said he recognised him, he was one of those who called in the more active group members for warning interrogations disguised as friendly 'chats'. These took place in a ground floor room at the back of the huge complex, which took up one whole block of central Moscow, known as the Lubyanka, the headquarters of the secret police, and according to report, ran along these lines:

'Why have you suddenly started to concern yourself with this question? We are trying to disarm the West. The Western pacifists are helping us disarm the West. And where do you fit in? You want to disarm us? We won't let you!'

'Why do you feel the need to make trouble like this?'

'Are you dissatisfied with your job? With your life? Is there some aspect of state provision you wish to criticise?'

'You are aware there are channels for you to voice your opinions if you have grumbles – why do you not bring up your problems with your local party committee?'

'Are you suggesting our country should not defend itself against the aggressor?'

'If you have peace proposals, you may submit these through the programme of the Peace Committee.'

'Our Soviet Peace Committees have many peace champions, who represent you, of course,' and so on.

The building, said Brodsky, had ten floors beneath the ground. Whether or not it was true, that was what was believed. And had we read the first chapter of *The First Circle*, by Solzhenitsyn? If you were finally arrested, that was what it was like, just the same.

We were hungry, again. There would be no food on the night train to Leningrad, due to leave at midnight. We collected our bags from our man in the hotel, rewarding him handsomely, and set off along the streets towards the station. Suddenly Volodya dived through what appeared to be an unmarked entrance. We were in some sort of cafeteria. Our exploration of Soviet public food culture was about to begin.

A pair of arms

'Formerly, in the days before the revolution, the diet of the people was poor and even famine was common. Now, workers and peasants enjoy the highest standards of cuisine that once were the preserve of the elite few. Delicacies, hygienically prepared in large, modern well-equipped kitchens, are eaten in the clean surroundings of public cafeterias, the choicest cuts of meat appearing on every plate.'

From the 'Little Lenin Library',
Soviet propaganda, 1937.

These cafeterias, called *stolovayas*, seemed to have been designed as a cruel experiment in how hunger could increase people's tolerance of disgusting food. There were no seats, just high clattery zinc-topped round tables. There was a strong smell of rancid boiled meat, mingled with equally strong disinfectant. People queued for a choice of grey sausages in greasy water, or dyed shocking pink sausages in the same water. Or they could have the water on its own, as soup. They could eat this with a rock-hard bun. We joined the queue, which was stationary. They were evidently waiting for something else. With a crash, it arrived. A dumb-waiter descended, bearing on it a huge cauldron that surely had seen service in the war to repel Napoleon. From it came an even more sickening smell than that seeping from the ghastly-looking sausages – the smell of badly-burned rice. A woman behind the counter turned to pick up the cauldron, which was the size of a small arm-chair. Her arms were more than equal to the task. They were neither shapely nor apparently muscular. They were simply huge, and despite the muggy heat, the sight of them made me shiver. In those massive, pudgy arms I glimpsed, just for a second, a vastness of lives and geography, of flatness encircling with monotony almost the entire northern hemisphere, an unending endurance of unimaginable cold, an accumulation of expendable, dreary, unknown lives, and behind all that, the yawning menace of Siberia. Glaring bleakly at her clients, she began flinging lumps of sticky, congealed rice from a ladle onto the proffered plates, most of which showed grubby finger-prints.

The reason why I shuddered at the sight of an oversized pair of arms on a woman, a person like me, was because it reminded me, not of the achievements of Soviet female athletes, but of a detail that had stuck in my mind ever since I read *The Gulag Archepelago*. In the name of equality, the daily work quota for female prisoners working in the logging camps in Siberia was almost that of the men: it was five cubic metres of wood felled, cut and stacked. Has anyone living today in a western European city, or in urban America, the faintest notion what that actually means? Added to which you lived on half a loaf of bread a day, and some watery soup.

The KGB who did the arresting and rounding up and transporting of the millions of men and women who felled the trees and actually built the roads, railways, canals and huge factories of the industrial wonder that was the USSR, were honoured with a fine statue of their founder, dominating the big traffic roundabout in front of their building, the Lubyanka. Made from a giant column of dark basalt, the statue was a larger-than-life respresentation of Felix Dzerzhinski, the first head of the Cheka, the Soviet secret police set up by Lenin to root out spies, collaborators with the White Russian enemy, or with the western states whose armies tried to destroy the infant workers' state.

The Cheka morphed into the NKVD under Stalin, and were now the KGB – the 'kaygaybay.' He was wearing a cloak, giving him a Darth Vader-like appearance. What was really distinctive about this particular monument, however, was the fact that the ground it stood on consisted of short, neat mown grass.

This, and one other feature, made it unique among Moscow's statues. All the other statues stood amidst long unshaven grass. The other feature was that the other statues had wreaths and bouquets and even posies of wild flowers laid at their feet. This one was conspicuously bare. What if we found the Trust group had all been arrested when we returned from Leningrad, I was thinking – would we have the guts to stand there, under that statue, with placards reading, 'Where are our friends?'... 'We protest at prevention of peace contacts.' The thought made me shiver even more. The camps, hidden from everyone's view, were like background radiation, invisible, undetectable, yet everywhere present.

Recoiling from the meat balls floating in their greasy soup, Karmen announced her vegetarianism. Heads turned. Volodya laughed and said she was far too thin and should eat meat, lots of it. She found a plate containing hard-boiled eggs, blackened on the outside. Despite our keen hunger, we could find little that was at all palatable except for yogurty sour-milk, and pre-sweetened insipid coffee. We dunked the stale bread in this to soften it. Everyone else was standing at the zinc tops, throwing down the pink or grey sausages with neither enjoyment nor apparent ill-effects.

For pudding we repaired to another type of establishment, a champagne-and-ice-cream parlour. Since this was an under-standably popular place, the doorman had to be bribed with hard currency. Everybody, it seemed, except the large matronly ladies who waited at the tables, was swooningly drunk on sweet, very fizzy, Russian-made 'champagne' that cost about one pound a bottle. About half the men were in various military uniforms, but everyone had a look of soft-focus innocence.

Outside, the warm night had brought people into the parks.

Park benches were always crowded, and the parks themselves were drenched in the smell of lilac. The trees were huge with black, twisting trunks. It was eleven o'clock, time to catch our train for Leningrad.

Night train

Soviet-era trains were impressively large, standing high off the platform. The massive locos pulled not only carriages, but history, too. I couldn't help thinking of Lenin's famous arrival at the Finland station in the Russian city of Petrograd, sixty-six years earlier. What would have happened if, as he walked away from the welcome party inside the waiting room to address the small crowd waiting outside as 'Dear Comrades, soldiers, sailors and workers,' he had slipped on a patch of ice and broken a leg, entailing a lengthy spell in hospital? At that point, the Bolsheviks were the minority party in the new provisional government. To achieve power, they would have to grab it by force from the elected majority, the Mencheviks. Lenin was the man who convinced his own supporters, against their better judgment, to do this. So – Lenin trips up – would the twentieth century still have been shaped by the Russian revolution and reactions to it?

Since these train routes were of hefty global dimensions, they were well equipped as sleepers, with starched linen sheets and pillow-cases on the bunks and a samovar, a sort of Russian tea-urn, plus a samovar-lady, at the end of each carriage. The domed station from which trains departed for Leningrad and other cities such as Novgorod, had the usual features, boards announcing departures and arrivals, benches, kiosks selling ice-cream, a metro connection etc. but no recognisable ticket office. This intrigued me.

'Ask him, Jean – how would we buy tickets, if we didn't already have them? Could he buy a ticket, if he had the money?'

Volodya was edgy, his eyes darting everywhere.

'He says it's a problem.'

210

'What sort of a problem?'

We were looking for an empty bench. Eventually we just sat by the platform on our luggage.

'He says everything like that is a problem.'

A bunch of young teenage boys with ill-fitting clothes and shaven heads, sidled past staring at us. They were evidently sharp, and took in the little differences that indicated we were foreign. Jean asked a question.

'They get put in institutions, but a lot of them escape, he says,' she said. I was still pursuing the ticket question.

'I don't understand – how does an ordinary person catch a train?'

'Look,' he says, 'you have to show a reason for the journey. Tickets long-distance aren't sold, they're allocated: to Intourist, to unions, Party people – you have to approach somebody, you can't just buy a ticket.'

We boarded the train. It seemed full of men in suits, and with none of the usual clutter of families. With a minute to go, Jean got off to say goodbye. The train began its imperceptible glide out of the station. We could see Volodya with his arms raised in farewell at the end of the platform, but no Jean. After a nerve-wracking few minutes, she appeared. 'He thinks he will be picked up the minute we're out of sight,' she said. 'He said, if anything happens to me while you're gone, you know, an accident, a catastrophe, they always pass it off as suicide – it won't be, you know what it will be.' We had no way of knowing whether his fears were melodramatic, exaggerated, or not. We would only be away in Leningrad for three days, but we all wondered whether we would see him again.

Lulled by the seductive delayed-action sway and lurch of a long train, I climbed into the top bunk, pulled off my trousers and slept a couple of hours. But my head was full of Volodya and the Medvedkovs, and how we could possibly give them some sort of protection, from what seemed like an inevitable fate? It was their very nervousness, their evident tendency towards panic, their lack of stern heroic resolve, that I found the most compelling. I awoke to a grey dawn. I pressed my nose against the window and looked out at the Russian landscape.

There was a swamp, and a star of electric light somewhere a long way off in the mist. Then there was forest – dark conifers and spindly white birches, with bushy young growth in the many gaps. There were lacy rivers gleaming white, and shimmering lakes, and more forest and more swamp. Suddenly there was the most beautiful house, built entirely from wood, with a neat pile of logs beside it. Presently there were more dark brown wooden houses, with dark pitched roofs. Some had little dormer windows, some rose to two storeys. All had another wooden hut beside them. They were set apart from one another, and all were sunk in the ubiquitous soft greenery of bushes and trees in new growth. There were irregular patches of chocolate earth, some fenced in beside the houses and some just open, beside the railway line. They bore ridges for potatoes and cabbages, newly planted. These patches of cultivation had an air of frailty in their seeming randomness, a brown bit in the middle of an open field, or skewed across a bank. There were no signs of any animals to graze the long, lush grass.

Roads were unmade, buff-pink with water gleaming in the ruts. Occasional larger villages or small towns sported a station name and a scattering of yellow stucco or grey concrete block buildings, but still unmade roads. Sometimes the houses were painted, usually blue, and many had hearts carved into shutters, curly gable ends, and scalloped window frames.

The forest went on and on, punctuated at long intervals by scattered settlements. As I stared, through eyes prickly with tiredness, I began to sense I was seeing something I already knew, as if I had visited this place already. Soon I realised why. Of course it was familiar, this endless forest, these wooden houses, this appearance of imminent engulfment by dense undergrowth, unchecked by modern machinery. This was not just primal woodland, an ecosystem that had stretched half-way round the world since the ending of the last ice-age; this landscape was the setting for the whole of northern European folklore and fairytale;

212

out of this sinister and life-giving wood had sprung the stories which had entranced me as a child. This was the land of the wood-cutter and his daughter, of the innocent who were despatched down wells by the wicked only to find another world at the bottom; of robber brides and of magic knapsacks, of the wolf, the bear, and the witch. This was where I really lived when I was a child, not in Ilford or Kent or Surrey but here, in the midst of the wild-wood that was the setting for the stories I devoured, into which sons ventured to seek their fortune and where children got lost and met with enchanted beasts.

Any minute now I expected to catch a glimpse of three giants just disappearing into the trees, or perhaps a little girl in a red hood carrying a basket. Abruptly, a concrete wall signalled the outskirts of Leningrad, the city built on a swamp by the modernising, Europe-oriented, Tsar, Peter the Great. The Cyrillic letters spelled themselves out so slowly as we glided past, dead on time, that I could make myself read them.

Chapter 20

Leningrad – Natasha's red gingham kitchen

In Moscow, we met the people who had constructed the theory that direct human contact was the way forward. The talk centred round the theory, and the likely fate of those propounding it. In Leningrad, the people we met just plunged in gaily, and talked about everything.

Our three days in the city where Lenin had arrived sixty-six years earlier, to kick off the process called the Russian Revolution, were an interlude of pure relief from the fears, real and imagined, of Moscow. The architecture, which hundreds of thousands had died to construct, was classical, gracious and airy. There was no neon, no advertising, very few signs and notices of any kind beyond the standard rows of air-brushed photographs of local apparatchiks. This absence of the usual street clutter of the West meant that you could actually see the buildings, which is an irrelevance if the buildings are the kind of ugly blocks hastily thrown up all over British towns in the 1960s, but a distinct advantage if they are worth looking at. The trees, moreover, were sensibly confined to the many parks, not striving to gain entry by the third-floor windows of apartment blocks, as in Moscow. The many parks were full of statues, which had been housed in wooden shuttering to protect them from the ravages of winter temperatures. These were being taken down, revealing numerous gods and goddesses, and the whole city had an air of sudden summer liberation. Moscow had been thick with blowing dandelion-seeds. Here they were in full bloom and little girls walked about wearing tiaras made daisy-chain fashion from yellow dandelions on their heads.

Furthermore, there was food, good and plentiful, available in our hotel, whose ground floor sported a kind of Russian breakfast buffet which stretched across lunch. After that you had to be part of a 'delegation' to get anything to eat, we would later discover, but still – incredibly, this temple of delights seemed to be open to the public. The lady on the reception desk smiled, and even gave us a key to the bathroom.

We spent much of our time in the city in the company of a woman Jean had met when posted here as a student. Natasha liked meeting Westerners because it livened up her life. She was not in the least bit inclined towards the serious risks involved in making an open political point about what Batovrin, the Trust group founder, called the 'humanisation of East–West relations'. But she was a woman of spirit, with a certain amount of independence gained from her work: she was a businesswoman, a clever entrepreneur. She was a self-employed dress-maker, working from within one of the two main rooms assigned to her in a communal flat.

She herself was a perky, roly-poly person with round black eyes, creating an impression of energetic bustle that was a far cry from the languid emaciation of the Parisian cat-walks, whence originated the impulse that brought the women of Leningrad up five flights of stairs to be measured for that which could not be supplied by the Soviet system – fashion and elegance. Using Finnish dress materials smuggled in across the border and with designs inspired by western magazines likewise smuggled across that same border, Natasha created outfits tailor-made to suit and, just as important, to fit her clients. Her enterprise was legitimate, but to make it work effectively she had to be a wheeler-dealer. Her first husband had been imprisoned for currency dealing; prison conditions, she said, were very bad, very bad indeed.

Natasha welcomed us with enthusiasm and promptly rearranged her life so that every moment could be spent with us, mostly sitting around the table in her kitchen talking, drinking Turkish coffee and eating with her, her husband, brother-in-law, and friends.

She had a simple explanation for the noticeable difference in atmosphere between Moscow and Leningrad.

'Leningrad,' she explained,'Is European. Moscow,' she continued, with undisguised contempt,'is Russian.'

Gingham, the cheerful check fabric of the 1950s, had reached Leningrad. Natasha's kitchen was all red-and-white. Here we were able to talk and listen for hours on end about any and every aspect of life, for they were as consumed by curiosity about our everyday existences, as we were by theirs. Her brother-in-law Misha, was a sociologist. The universal ideological control affected people in different ways. Conformists could have an easy life, with modest rewards placing them on small, but crucial, ladder rungs above their fellow citizens. But people with a spark of curiosity or creativity became eager seekers after the holy grail of objective truth. Misha wanted us to bring, on our next visit, modern sociology books. What he wanted most of all, was a truthful account of the Russian Revolution. Stalin, he reckoned, had hijacked Lenin's good idea, killing off a whole generation of creative, clever, gifted and intellectual people.

The difference between survivors, like himself and Natasha, and idealistic risk-takers like the Trust group people, was one of a seemingly crazy belief in real change, and the innate pessimism of those who think of themselves as 'realists'. The Medvedkovs and their circle were banking on change happening in time to save their bacon. Misha and Natasha, and husband Genya, firmly poo-pooed any idea of radical change to the basic repressive nature of the system. Instead, they carved out little spaces of private freedom for themselves within it. Yet they did seem to sense a loosening somewhere. 'There will always be a prohibition on meeting with foreigners,' they said, yet the precautions they took – unplugging the phone, not talking English in taxis, seemed merely token, and they were quite happy to walk around with us with Jean translating at ten to the dozen into loud English. Whatever risks they considered they were taking, they clearly thought it a price worth paying for some jazz tapes, Russian books selected by Jean from London, fashion magazines, and most of all our company.

This was the great paradox: information and ideas were the greatest *defitsinye* – scarce goods – of all. They were eagerly sought and sitting up late at night having the most intense and soul-searching discussions about not humdrum things, but airy-fairy and arty-farty ideas, was a top-of-the-tree, favoured leisure activity. Not one hint of any of this fevered free-thinking, these heady free-wheeling passionate discussions, cracked the surface layer of official publications, such as the glossy, unbelievably turgid, pamphlet-format tomes churned out by the Peace Committees on 'contemporary problems'.

Misha imagined that with all the great pantheon of philosophies and ideas available to us in books and newspapers and magazines reflecting a giddy plurality of world-views, we too, the Western public, would be up all night discussing with passion the rights and wrongs of this or that sociological theory, interpretation of history, or the function of art. Had we been able to spirit him back with us to our land of open-access to the world of ideas, he may have found the usual quality of human conversation rather dull. The price of leisure-wear in this or that discount store, or the inevitability that a game of football would end with a win, a lose, or a draw, didn't really match up.

On one of our walks through the city we passed a strange sight. A number of men were standing around outside a large building of many windows, whose inmates seemed to be lowering baskets to the men on the ground. Natasha explained: this was a hospital, and for the women in the maternity ward this was the only way they could get some decent food, a change of clothing, or pass messages. Like many Russian women, Natasha had no children. The thought of giving birth in a hospital (a home birth was not an option) clearly terrified her. Husbands and partners were strictly disallowed. When you entered, you were at the mercy of whoever attended you. If they were kind, you were lucky. Anaesthetics and pain-killing drugs were in short supply. Babies were removed at birth, tightly swaddled, and mothers were not allowed to see their newborns for at least twenty-four hours.

This kind of 'strictness' and mistrust of mothers was similar to the punitive regimes administered in British hospitals before women began, in the late Sixties, to protest and campaign for humane treatment. Here in the USSR, women seemed to be passively resisting by simply not having babies.

We were plunged into twenty-four-hour living, for this was the first of the 'white nights', the two months straddling the summer solstice when darkness would never come, and in the milky midnight twilight the people of the city thronged the quays and watersides to see the bridges on the wide river Neva rise one by one to let the ships through. They would continue on their journey up to the Arctic ocean along the White sea canal, built under Stalin by slave labour. Contemporary accounts from 1933, corroborated by photographs, describe and show women – 'political prisoners' – digging out the subsoil into wooden wheelbarrows, which they would then have to push up the steep sides of the excavation. Few reading this book will ever have pushed a loaded modern, light metal wheelbarrow up even a slight slope, let alone a wooden one up a steep gradient of sticky mud. The work was unimaginably hard, and most of them died by the hundred thousand, of exhaustion and starvation after no more than a few months, some only lasting a week or two. When the canal was opened, leading Soviet writers such as Maxim Gorky were taken for river cruises along it to admire and record the achievements of Soviet technology. The price paid for it was never mentioned, just as we do not generally connect the Atlantic slave trade with our own industrial wealth, nor, in addition to slavery, the genocide of the native Americans with the rise to supremacy of the USA.

Even at 3 am the streets were crowded with people simply strolling about. Couples canoodled, youths strummed guitars. 'When do Leningraders sleep?' we asked. 'When we are at work,' came the reply.

Around midnight we set off to visit a friend, Lena, another

woman in her forties like Natasha, who lived alone. Natasha wanted to take us to meet her because she'd never met anyone from outside the USSR. The conversation continued once Lena, like Natasha, had pulled out the telephone connection. This was widely believed to be an effective precaution against the possibility that the KGB might be listening in to the conversations in the room. To me it seemed absurd – technically impossible anyway – and if they really had every single room in every home in the USSR bugged, how on earth could they process the information? But no, you couldn't be too sure, they nodded sagely, before proceeding with the real business of the evening – the telling of one anti-Soviet system joke after another, many long and triple or quadruple-staged, all so funny we were laughing until our sides ached. This was the enormous saving grace of the system – its apparent attempt at perfect logicality produced the exact opposite, so it functioned as an immense ironic joke production line. Tragically, as soon as the Soviet system collapsed – something which seemed quite inconceivable in 1983 – and everyone could get on with the serious business of being proper consumers, life just stopped being funny. The river of jokes dried up.

The scientist in need of a photocopier

We had more insights into the way unconventional thinkers functioned within the one party state when we briefly met with a would-be Russian ecologist. Jean had met the young scientist on a previous visit, during her language student days, and had brought with her, in answer to his request, a copy of Karl Popper's book *The Open Society and its Enemies*. We went at his invitation to his flat, where he lived with his wife, new baby, and ten-year-old son. The boy was doing his homework, and was rapidly covering sheets of paper in what looked like perfect hand-writing. The sheer volume and presentation would have been impressive in a British school, but his mother was utterly dismissive and denounced the Soviet curriculum as empty lies. Sasha preferred to talk outside, so we sat on a park bench.

He was young and good-looking with curly black hair and a black beard and moustache. When Jean gave him the requested book his eyes lit up. This book, he said, was available in the main library in Leningrad, but in the 'closed stacks' along with all other philosophy that was not written by Lenin, Stalin, or approved leading members of the Communist Party. To have access to this dangerous stuff you would have to apply from within an academic institution, and so draw attention to yourself. Obviously there had been no shortage of those willing to take this risk, since he went on to say that the one copy in the library was barely legible, so thumbed were its pages and so heavily annotated its margins. He was on the Trust Group grapevine, but he was wary of what he saw as their risky and high profile strategy. He was digging away in libraries trying to find things out, all the things those in power try to conceal, working quietly and behind the scenes, one of innumerable Soviet academics who talked to each other, very slowly discovered who they could trust, and shared information. They called it the 'Free University of Leningrad'. Just as sceptical peaceniks in the West suspected their own government propaganda, designed as it was to maximise the impression of an evil, threatening enemy, and therefore, like trees bracing themselves against a powerful wind, tended to believe the opposite – so Sasha was trying to see wood through propaganda trees.

Speaking in a low voice, in good English, he said exactly what people in the Western peace movement didn't want to hear.

'Russia has 'Cruise' missile technology already, we may even be ahead of the West. Size of military budget is…' He quoted what sounded like enough roubles to fill Lake Baikal, until you remembered that it would probably take enough roubles to fill Lake Baikal just to make a dent that might be noticed in the American military budget.

'Here, slogan "The Party is the People" is not just empty slogan. Is sociological phenomenon,' he hissed. 'Here can be no public opinion, no one can call for halt to Soviet side of arms race, no one can suggest this – or you will be accused of anti-Sovietism. So, is up to you – is job of Western peace movement, to make demands on both superpowers.' We flinched slightly as this not inconsiderable burden was tossed upon us. But it was, of course, unavoidably true.

'Our leadership wishes to weaken western Europe, decouple it from America, gain influence through your political parties,' he continued. 'People here are only concerned with day-to-day problems – they have no idea what is going on with military, with Afghanistan – no, is just where to get nice food, buy nice things, how to get a car – it occupies all their time when they are not working.'

He seemed to think his society was uniquely handicapped in this respect. We tried to tell him, but he simply could not believe that in the West, where he knew everyday life to be free of all these problems – where attractive, well-made goods could be exchanged for money in functioning shops, where cars could be bought, where the telephones of intellectuals were not cut off, where fresh and refrigerated food was freely available, as he had heard on his news gathering forays – people were just as obsessed with acquisition, with day-to-day living to the exclusion of higher things, just as insecure, as they were in Leningrad.

He did not, however, think that the Soviet military-industrial complex was in attack mode. 'Don't worry about us,' he said. 'They are very inefficient. They have to be. Is inefficient structure – it has to be.'

'How can we help you?' we asked. He handed over a piece of writing, a scientific paper about the possible extent of pollution-induced disasters in the Soviet Union. We were to try to take it out with us in our luggage. 'We move very slowly, we are not a group as such, we make no great public protest – those people in Moscow – their lives will become very difficult. We want to survive.' Brightening, he said, in all seriousness, 'When you come back, could you bring us a photocopier?'

How, you may ask, did we manage to spend three days in Leningrad and not visit the memorial to the twenty million dead of the siege of the city during 1942-1943, and how did we also manage to miss out on the glories of the Hermitage, one of Europe's greatest art galleries? This is how: The Russians – sorry, I mean the Leningraders – wouldn't stop talking and asking us questions, and when we did manage to get away, we rushed back to the hotel and slept for a couple of hours.

Walking towards Finland

It was Sunday and Natasha had planned an outing for us.

This was the plan: we would catch a bus and then we would go on a walk to a place where we would get something to eat. We were going to walk through the woods that bordered the Baltic Sea, towards Finland. This sounded wonderful to me – walking, woods, eating, yes, yes, yes. No, this is not the prelude to a story of dashed expectations told with that rueful irony we British are so good at. No, it was a good day; not one of whose every shining aspect could have been reproduced in any other society at any other season, or at any other moment in time. It could only have belonged to that teetering threshold, to those magical, seductive moments of ambiguity just before the USSR really began to change and the Cold War began to slither into the history books.

The bus ride was long, and took a good hour. The bus was full, and we were clearly the only Westerners on it. Visitors to the USSR were not meant to be swanning about here, there and everywhere on outings to places not on the Intourist list of statistic-saturated 'sights'. Foreigners were, supposedly, strictly prohibited from travelling more than twelve kilometres outside of the centre of any city. Soon we had blithely passed the 'Leningrad thirty kilometres' sign, which even I, with my slow-learner's Cyrillic, could decipher. No one seemed bothered, least of all Natasha, who radiated a quiet pride at being our chaperone.

The bus seemed to reach some sort of terminus in the middle of nowhere – well, in the middle of the woods, which was very much somewhere for the squirrels and their friends I would imagine, and everyone, everyone being mostly parties of youth, piled out. We set off at a brisk trot along an asphalt path which wound through the straight trunks of pines and birches, parallel with the road. A sign proclaimed that the next place of any significance was Vyborg, close to the Finnish border. After that, Helsinki, the Finnish capital. So this really was the main road to the border. It was quiet beyond belief. The occasional car was supplemented by the occasional tank, trundling along at the same leisurely pace. Soon we could glimpse through the trees a great light emptiness.

The Baltic was more like a lake than a sea, the beach an unending expanse of flat, forest-backed pinkish sand. Jean played Bob Marley on a portable tape recorder. Tiny scummy waves lapped almost soundlessly. Above the high tide line wooden *chaise-longues* for sun-bathing were set at intervals. These were sun-bleached to a greyish-white, and were obviously put there for public use. Like the wooden climbing frames and equipment in the children's playgrounds that could be seen in the courtyard of every block of flats, they were not vandalised. This beach, a bus ride from a huge city, had another strange, non-western aspect to it: there was no litter. No snack-bar wrappings, no cans, no plastic, nothing but the odd glass bottle the sea would one day, if it ever got up enough fury, pound back into sand.

I doubt very much if this was due, as I daresay admirers of the USSR would have claimed, to an innate love of a tidy environment on the part of the Soviet public. Nor, as the detractors would have suggested, was it because the population was too terrified of retribution to besmirch the flowery banks with discarded packaging. This popular outdoor beauty spot was surely as clean as Disneyworld is reputed to be, and more or less as nature had designed it, which Disneyworld is certainly not, simply because the planned economy of the USSR did not have much of a packaging industry. The poor, deprived citizens just didn't have cling-film, plastic carrier bags, foil-wrapped confectionary, expanded polystyrene fast-food trays, cotton buds, aluminium drink cans, press-moulded packaging for screws, toothbrushes, and pencil-sharpeners, in fact, they didn't seem to have much made out of plastic at all. They had wood and paper, which rot or burn, and iron, which rusts, instead.

In the clearings and dunes at the back of the beach sat many groups of people: families, friends, teenagers, all drinking and eating picnics, cloths spread on the ground. They greeted us cheerily. We were surrounded by an atmosphere of bucolic abandonment to the sun's warmth and the luminous greenery on the trees newly burst into leaf. We walked on, and the path continued past wooden houses – the dachas, the holiday houses, of the Leningrad lucky. They all seemed pretty dilapidated, surrounded by collapsing wooden fence palings. We noted the absence of high security fences, alarms, 'Beware of the Dog' signs and high walls topped with glass shards, all the usual paraphernalia that we were accustomed to see protecting the houses of the better-off from the rest. Sure, these were obviously pretty low-grade properties, hardly the rural retreats of Party high-flyers, but their sheer vulnerability contributed to the general feeling of security. Some of them were being opened up for the summer by their owners who were happily unloading forks and spades from car boots, others already sported freshly turned, enviably black, soil. Then these habitations stopped, and we wondered where on earth Natasha was taking us. Periodically out of the endless procession of tree-trunks we would see a group of people coming the other way, talking and laughing, carrying big bunches of wild flowers.

'This is really weird,' said Karmen. Here we are, in what feels like a pretty isolated spot, but quite near a big city, it could be Epping Forest. But we don't feel that tension we would back home, coming on a big group of men in a place like this – ordinary people don't seem as threatening as they are potentially with us, and all the mistrust that goes with it. So I feel quite safe. But,' and she pointed to the empty road we could still see through gaps in the trees, 'a big black car could come down that road with a bunch of guys in black leather jackets, and they could just order us into the car and that could be it – we could just disappear off the face of the earth. Questions might be asked about us, but Natasha? You can't ask to speak to your solicitor can you?'

We walked on, in a state beyond exhaustion after four days with hardly any sleep. No black cars materialised. The forest of pines and white-trunked birches enveloped and soothed us, and we fell silent, content with our thoughts. We were immersed in the enchanted landscape I had seen from the train. The air was full of many smells – damp earth, and moss, sweet violets and lily of the valley. Thrushes and other less familiar birds translated the sprightly roundness of new leaves into sound, while the forest floor and the sides of the path were thickly strewn with the white stars of fragile stitchwort. In places where the path ran close to the road, open tracks seemed to lead off from the other side, heading in an easterly direction. I became lost in speculation as to what would happen if, compass in hand to keep me on the exact latitude (60 degrees N.), and back-pack with enough for my needs, I were to start walking down one of those long, glimmering glades. Would I carry on walking through forest and taiga almost unbroken, through the northern part of the Ural mountains, right across the centre of Siberia, crossing somehow all those huge rivers, the Ob, the Yenisei, until, years later, I would stumble, fit, aged and gibbering, my nails become claws and my hair matted down to my waist, upon the shores of the Sea of Okhotsk, in the Soviet far east, somewhere to the northeast of China?

I crashed into my three companions, who had stopped and were looking at something at their feet. The four of us stared in incredulity at the women's peace symbol adopted by the Greenham Peace-camps, drawn in chalk on the path. We explained what it meant to Natasha, who had never seen it before. Who on earth had drawn it here? Sometime later, in the middle of the afternoon, we arrived at our goal – an unmarked wooden shack that functioned as a restaurant.

Natasha's toast

The place was crowded with diners. Nearly every table was taken. A small vase of wild flowers – starry white stitchwort, again, decorated each one. There was no menu, and no need of any. This was a shashlik restaurant, serving meat barbequed on skewers with fresh bread and tomato salad. Russian champagne, beer and wine were available to drink. We ordered and the food arrived. No wonder the place was full. The meat was the real thing, tasty chunks of solid muscle, slightly charred but not overcooked, originating from which animal I could not guess – it could even have been reindeer, and the tomatoes, sprinkled with salt and parsley and with extra helpings for Karmen, had the delicious flavour that has long-since vanished from our Western all-year-round, uniformly ripened, pesticide-coated product. The bread was good too, flecked with rye. One glass of 'champagne' had nearly knocked us off our chairs, we were so tired. Now we felt instantly revived physically and mentally. We refilled our glasses. Natasha raised hers and proposed a toast, a long Russian toast.

'If people all over the world could achieve the same kind of contact as we have today, without even the benefit of a common language, there would be no need for bombs or missiles or war, and the people of the world could teach their children about love, life, people and art.'

We had brought with us a poster showing the original pink march banner bearing the 'Women for Life on Earth' heading above the tree and the CND sign. We found a biro and Jean wrote 'Natasha's toast' on it in Russian, then we all signed it.

Shashlik with Elvis

Some kind of Soviet-era 'muzak' was playing loudly but listlessly on a tape recorder from behind the bar. You heard this stuff everywhere and it was a kind of derivative pastiche of Western pop styles with no discernable identity. I had brought with me, as a random gift, a tape recording of early, classic Elvis Presley – the 'Sun Studio' recordings he made in Memphis when he was only nineteen, and it was still in my bag. I took it up to the bar and handed it over. Nothing happened for about five minutes. Then the musical goo stopped. Moments later the unmistakable raw, primal sound of the king of rock 'n' roll shook the place. The first track was 'Hound Dog'.

'You ain't nuttin' but a hound dog, cryin' all the time.'

The effect on the assembled diners was electrifying. Everything stopped: all eating, all conversation. Forks, arrested in mid-air, clattered onto plates. They listened in shock for all of four bars, looking at each other with eyebrows raised. Then, clearly determined not to waste the opportunity, a couple rose to their feet. Within seconds, the rest followed. Tables and chairs were pushed aside. As one body the erstwhile diners threw themselves into frenzied dancing, arms flailing, feet kicking, overweight bodies gyrating, hearts throbbing. Elvis, poor dab, never knew it, but he was made for this moment, for these people who hungered and thirsted for a sound and a rhythm which had begun its long journey into our lives a good three hundred years earlier, in the dark puke and shit-stinking holds of the slave-ships crossing the Atlantic.

Western-style inhibitions abandoned, we all danced and boogied wildly through 'Blue Suede Shoes', 'Blue Moon', 'That's all Right', and 'You're a Heartbreaker'.

Elvis started singing 'I forgot to remember to forget,' and an East German giant in army uniform clicked his heels in front of Karmen and asked her to dance. Her head reached his waist. On it went – 'Jailhouse Rock', 'Don't Be Cruel', 'Good Rockin' Tonight' and the haunting, incomparable 'Mystery Train', the dancers refreshing themselves with more 'champagne' before returning with gusto to the fray. The food turned cold on the plates. Suddenly, in mid-track the tape was switched off and replaced by safe Soviet muzak. Shrugging their shoulders, people returned to their seats and consoled themselves with fresh rounds of shashlik, more tomatoes, and more alcohol. It was brief and brilliant, it came from nowhere, it was an utter mystery but they knew better than to ask questions.

A thunderstorm turned the summer sky violet with constant lightning the whole of the night's journey back to Moscow. Elvis's 'Mystery Train' played itself over and over again in my head. We had entered the looking-glass world, and the forest of fable now appeared as Alice's giant chessboard. The worlds of East and West now seemed more than ever like interlocking pieces, societies moulded by a mutual antagonism and distorted so that their opposing, jigsaw shapes formed a hidden whole.

Regimes on each side exaggerated the threat from the other in order to justify increases in military spending and particularly 'modernisations' of nuclear weapons. Leaders of both sides said identical things and thought identical thoughts about the aggressive intentions of the other. Free-thinking sceptics on both sides also behaved like mirror images, doubting the propaganda of their own regimes, but inclining towards belief in the other side's propaganda. We could demonstrate and wave placards, write to the papers, wear badges as much as we liked – we would always be sidelined and ultimately ignored. But on this side of the looking-glass, one person wearing a home-made badge created a talking-point that would reverberate on and on, while four people giving out leaflets on a street would have to be bundled off swiftly, for fear of creating too much of an effect throughout society. Lewis Carroll's surreal story kept playing through our minds. Workmen seemed to be repainting roses, while in the far distance a voice could just be heard faintly bawling, 'Off with their heads!'

The train arrived in Moscow at 8 am, dead on time, again. As I walked past the engine, I was seized by the irrational desire to practise my Russian and say 'Hello,' to the driver. I looked up. There were three of them, high up in the huge cab. They caught my glance and grinned back.

Chapter 21

Moscow – 1) Apparatchiks

We had arrived in Moscow apprehensive and, as ever, very hungry. Would the Medvedkovs still be in their flat, would Brodsky have been arrested? We went to our hotel, found our baggage, still in its cupboard, gratefully devoured the dry bread, fried eggs and pickles that were breakfast, found our room and fell into an exhausted cat-nap.

I awoke to hear Jean speaking on the telephone in English to somebody at the Peace Committee, to arrange our meeting with them, and sounding disappointed.

'Oh – only half an hour? That's not very long,' she was saying. We needed to talk to them about our 'minder-free visit' proposal, and about the Trust group. We were being fobbed off. I felt very angry all of a sudden. Before I could think or stop myself, I had grabbed the telephone from her and was shouting down it.

'Do you realise who we are? We know you have heard of the Greenham Common protests, they are on all your newsreels. Well we are the founders of that movement and we have come a long way at great expense to meet with you and we need to speak with your chairman.'

'You wish only to discuss matter of delegation no? Why you need so much time? An hour is enough, no?' He sounded vague and wary.

'No! No!' I shouted back. An uncontrollable flood of crypto-communist prose, fed by the melt-waters of the *Daily Worker*s of my childhood years, flowed out of my mouth: 'We have new and important proposals to make regarding a visit. We wish to discuss many questions with you, East-West relations, détente, arms control, Geneva talks, the nuclear arsenals of the superpowers, the political situation in Britain, the Greenham Common movement... We need to speak with someone in the highest authority. We need a long meeting – we intend to spend a whole afternoon with you.'

'Oh,' said the voice. 'One moment please.' He came back shortly. We could meet them for as long as we liked, the following afternoon at 2 pm.

Before we could satisfy our curiosity about the people we had met, we had to attend a pre-arranged meeting with the Moscow Women's Committee. The positions on this Communist Party Committee were rumoured to be filled by the wives of Politburo members. The Politburo was the small secretive committee that ran the USSR.

This stilted event gave us a foretaste of the likely progress of our meeting with the Soviet Peace Committee. Stiff smiles, which turned on and off like fairy lights, repetition of the USSR's peaceful intentions towards the West and its role as blameless victim of the arms race, and a set menu of answers to our more awkward questions about the fate of political dissidents, had given us a frustrating sense of trying to shout through a thick glass wall, at people who not only sounded like automata but even moved as if under remote control. We were treated to platitudes about the heroism of the Greenham Women, and the need for us all to unite for peace. When we had mentioned the Trust group and their proposals, the fixed smiles vanished and the mood changed sharply. 'Who? Who have you met? What are their names? Who? What people? It's impossible!' The interpreter's eyes swivelled like a chameleon's, unsure of whether she should even utter the name. 'We have never even heard of these people,' the answer had come, followed by the statement: 'Unlike our committee, which represents millions, they represent no one.'

2) Picnickers

To our relief we found the Medvedkovs at home and expecting to see us. In our absence, they had been organising. More people turned up, including a couple called the Fleishgakkers, Mark Reitman and his wife, and Volodya Brodsky, who said he had been interrogated for two hours after he had seen us off on the train for Leningrad.

Eventually, late in the afternoon, we all straggled off and arrived, by bus and metro (a journey in the course of which more than four of the party could not manage to keep together at any one time), in a park bordering the Moscow River. This was called the Lenin Hills, although where the hills were to be found I couldn't tell you. Bathers ignored the 'no bathing' signs and numerous groups lay around under the trees, enjoying the warm afternoon. The picnic – a large, very flat, chocolate cake – was produced and tea was poured from a Thermos. I could see little that distinguished our group's picnic, a 'peace picnic', from those of the other people sitting around under the trees, so I took from my bag some of the posters given to us by the Women's Committee that morning.

These were of doves, impressions of atomic mushroom explosions coupled with anti-American slogans, and mothers cradling babies beneath the word 'Peace' and were produced by and for the various peace committees as part of their never-ending quest for proof of the involvement of the Soviet public in peace issues. Aha! I had also cunningly brought with me from the imperialist West, for just such an eventuality, a pack of blu-tack, which I now fished out from the bottom of my bag. I showed the group what I wanted to do. They all nodded.

I strolled over to the nearest tree and attached a poster. Then I went around all the other trees around us, doing likewise. The group watched in silence. Passers-by began to look at the posters, reading them with interest. Judging by their reactions, the material obviously hadn't been produced for domestic consumption. I sat down again and was warmly commended for my bravery. Their reaction seemed a bit excessive – all I had done was put up a few innocuous and officially-sanctioned posters.

'What?' I thought. 'It's not me that's brave,' I said. 'It's all of you. This is easy for us, hard for you.'

Marc Reitman stood up and began to read a satirical anti-militarist story, methodically translated by Yuri Medvedkov. The early evening air was deliciously warm. I fell asleep for a good hour. When I awoke I could see a knot of policemen standing a short distance away. On a rather more disturbing note, several men in KGB signature apparel, black leather jackets, seemed to be trying to hide behind the trees in the middle distance, some speaking into radios.

'They've been gathering while you've been asleep,' said Karmen. 'I don't know what's with this lot, either,' gesturing towards the group who were talking in low voices. 'They're discussing something, but not all together. They're very agitated. They keep going into huddles, then someone from one huddle talks to the other. It's really strange.' Jean was flat out asleep on the grass. I realised that although the posters I had put up were from an 'official' source, the fact that a person had put them there on her own initiative was the problem now occupying the attentions of the organs of internal security. I put the tree fairies out of their brain-scrambling misery by going from one tree to another, taking the posters down.

Then we discovered what these Russian peaceniks were talking about. Jean woke up and Volodya said something to her.

'OK, I don't know what you guys are gonna think of this,' she said. 'He's saying, "When you see the Peace Committee tomorrow, will you take one of us – a woman – in with you?"'

After a short discussion we agreed to this suggestion. We were not hypocrites. We knew by now that these people were genuine, and if they were prepared to accept the significant risks of such an action, we had to support them. There was little point to this visit to the USSR, if we weren't prepared to do more than just politely raise the question of the fate of the group, in the course of a meeting with the very people who were trying to shut them up. There was little point to a discussion of how to achieve more personal East-West contacts, if the people advocating this approach were to be marginalised and repressed by their own state. There was little point accepting the status of 'champions of peace' accorded us, if we were not to use it to defend those people who really were taking risks for peace. But it was no wonder they were agitated.

As we walked away from the park, a big black car cruised by, very slowly, its inmates staring at us malevolently through tinted windows. I remember looking at Masha Reitman, who was seven months' pregnant. Wearing a thin brown shift dress, she stared ahead and pointedly ignored the deliberate menace. It was Masha who had volunteered to go with us to the meeting.

Bolshoi salad and 'Greenham Common' – a KGB production

We were whisked off by Brodsky by taxi to his flat where he had prepared for us a real, four-square meal. Every taxi ride was an exercise in 'vox-pop' impromptu interviews, conducted for our educational benefit. The Russians had, not long before, invaded Afghanistan.

'Do you know people who have been wounded in Afghanistan? What's your opinion of that? Is it a mistake we are making, meddling and sacrificing Soviet lives?' the driver was asked.

'No,' he replied. 'We should be bringing order to that country. Before, it was chaos, nothing but warlords fighting. We helped them advance away from all that.' Then he added, 'There are two kinds of politics – peace-loving and aggressive. We are peace-loving, the imperialists are the aggressors. With these two politics, there will always be wars.'

Volodya cooked in ancient heavy aluminium pots that had surely been in use since the demise of the Tsar – and why not, since they still functioned perfectly? We had a rich chicken broth, followed by a meaty stew. He threw a great bagful of vegetables on the wooden kitchen table, stressing what trouble he'd had to go to to find them, somebody was repaying him a favour with things from their garden, and we began to chop these to make a salad. We started thinly slicing an outdoor cucumber, knobbly and snappy with freshness, and cutting huge tomatoes into dainty bits. He intervened.

'No! No!' he shouted. 'Bolshoi!' demonstrating the Russian word for 'big' meanwhile by hefting great chunks with a skull-yellow-handled knife and throwing them into a bowl together with whole spring onions the size of golf balls.

When the food was ready Volodya began to talk to us about Greenham Common and the way it was presented to the Russian people. Somehow images were selected that made it look as stage-managed as the formal demonstrations of patriotism that constituted 'peace marches' in the USSR. Only anti-American slogans or posters were shown. Most people seeing the ubiquitous newsreels were probably puzzled, while those of a sceptical frame of mind were utterly convinced that it was all simply a KGB fabrication, a production created for Soviet consumption using Russian actors in a studio somewhere in the woods outside Moscow. Some even knew exactly where the sylvan film-set was located, and knew some of the set designers, actors and extras.

'As a matter of fact,' he said, 'that's what I thought, at first. I didn't know who you were. When Jean said you were from Greenham Common, how can that be?' I thought. 'Only a fool would think the place actually exists, that those women really do camp there. In the winter, in those flimsy tents, when the temperature's minus forty? Come off it! Everyone knows all that's just propaganda. I never really trusted you, right up until you put those posters up on the trees, right under the noses of all those KGB guys watching you – then I knew you were for real.'

According to Volodya, the KGB had been hanging around from the moment we arrived in the park, but I, not possessing the right antennae, hadn't noticed them until much later. My action had not been brave, merely ignorant.

Chomping away on Bolshoi salad, we could only relish, along with the onions, this equally massive dollop of irony – Greenham

Common was believed to be a slick KGB production, and yet most people we'd spoken to in the British peace movement seemed to think the Moscow Group for Trust had to be a CIA put-up job. They couldn't possibly be for real, either.

More stories were told of the 'Peace Committee' and its role in Soviet life. A friend of Trust group member Valery Gdyak had tried to join his local Peace Committee. He had introduced himself to the woman sitting at the desk, and told her that he had become very concerned about issues of peace and disarmament. He feared for the future, the way things were going, and wanted to know what he could do, as an ordinary citizen, how he could play his part and contribute to his government's efforts towards disarmament. The woman had stared at him in disbelief before finally blurting out, 'Are you crazy?'

Visitors from the West were told, of course, that any Soviet citizen was free, indeed welcome, to contribute to the 'struggle for peace'.

We slept the night on a settee in the living-room of Trust Group members Valery and Olga Gdyak, no doubt to the consternation of the *dezayurnaya* – the watchdog – on our hotel floor.

It was bright gold sunshine when we awoke. The group, much to our relief, had sensibly decided that Olga Medvedkova would accompany us, instead of Masha Reitman who, in addition to the obvious vulnerability due to her pregnancy, spoke no English. Olga, although highly academically qualified, had begun to receive suggestions from her superiors that her Trust group activities would result in a sacking. But this hadn't intimidated her. Instead, it had made her defiant. She really wanted to confront the official hypocrisies and lies that blocked the possibilities for change. She wasn't reckless, she was simply angry with her government, an anger which gave her courage.

The usefulness of being late, sometimes

We were well aware of the high-risk strategy chosen by the

Trust group, which would ensure that our meeting with the functionaries of the State would be unpredictable, throwing us all into uncharted waters. The usual line given about the group, repeated to us by the Women's Committee, that they didn't exist, wouldn't work. If we managed to get Olga in with us, we would take them by surprise and they would have to improvise before receiving direction from above. On the other hand, maybe with all the super-efficient bugging everyone seemed to assume was going on, 'they' had got wind of our plans already, and we would be intercepted en route.

But in the best Greenham fashion, things didn't go according to plan. To begin with, we were late, through no fault of our own. That's how she got in with us, simply because we were late. There was nothing we could have done to prevent it.

Olga met us at the Gdyak's flat and we discussed tactics outside, in the shade, in the children's playground. Children could play outside safely in the USSR, an unremarked by-product of life in a totalitarian state. 'Okay,' she said, 'you lend me a T-shirt, they'll think I'm one of your lot. They don't know what I look like.'

'What if they bar our way?'

'We'll argue, and play it by ear.'

This seemed the most likely, that Olga would be identified at the door and they would refuse to let her in. We had arranged to meet Masha at Metro Sportiva. The city looked calmly beautiful, like a Monet painting, with every other person carrying flowers as usual, people moving about in dappled shade between buildings, dark tree trunks and big orange poppies, beds of lupins just coming out, the grey-and-white overalled gardeners gardening and no advertisements. We felt a rising knot of tension in our stomachs. We waited in silence by the entrance to Metro Sportiva for Masha, who had evidently been delayed. When she still didn't turn up after some minutes of waiting, we started to think this was ominous. Then Jean suggested brightly that she might be at the other entrance, which could only be easily reached, because of building works, by buying a five-kopek ticket and going underground – through the station along the platform and up again.

Moscow undergound stations have very long escalators, which plunge vertiginously down in a single long chute, illuminated by round lamps. First Jean disappeared into the station, to look for Masha at the other end, then after a long five minutes, Karmen to look for Jean. After another ten minutes had elapsed, Olga looked at me, winked and said, 'If I go, will only be you left.' I made it plain that I thought this would be a very bad idea indeed. Clinging firmly together, we went down, along the very long platform and up at the other end before passing Jean and Karmen going down. Scrambling round to follow them a quarter-of-an-escalator mile later, whilst half way down we passed Masha going up. Back on the side we had started from, we then passed Jean and Karmen going down to meet us at the other end, having misinterpreted each other's hand signals, while no one knew whether Masha had seen any of us at all. After another round of waving across escalators and scrambling through dense crowds on the immensely long platform, the unseen director of this impromptu Feydeau farce suddenly released us from our roles and quite by chance we found ourselves all proceeding smoothly upwards in the same direction, to arrive at the same entrance, having exhausted the possible mathematical combinations of people and escalators.

'Well,' said Olga, 'if KGB were following us before, I think that now, they are not.'

We proceeded back to the Medvedkov's flat, to eat. It was a humble and highly memorable meal: mashed potato, pickled onions, red peppers and omelette, cooked by Olga's father who had a lined, kindly face.

Nothing could be said about where we had been or where we were going, so we crammed round the tiny table making loud small-talk, communicating the serious business with gestures, sign language and the magic eraser pad from a kid's 'spy' set that someone had given the Medvedkovs. Olga got dressed in her T-shirt and badges, then decided that she looked too neat and tidy, so she messed up her hair.

We were still on schedule, time-wise, provided there were no more hiccups. Jean, Karmen, Olga and I went down in the lift, walked across the scrubby land to the main road, Leninski Prospekt, and hailed a taxi. Masha would follow on and wait for us outside the building. It took about fifteen minutes to reach central Moscow.

As we approached the roundabout of Dzerzhinski Square in the taxi, the wretched engine spluttered, groaned terminally, produced a few fits and starts, and stopped. Traffic hurtled by on all sides, flowing round us like water round a rock. The driver, unperturbed, got out and lifted the bonnet. We couldn't even safely open a door. He tried to start the car, to no effect, so then he tried to coast backwards into the side, across two lanes of fast-moving lorries, buses, Ladas and Volgas. I looked behind in growing alarm (the dodgems always scared me), to see a lorry looking set to crash right into us. Fearing our mission was about to be aborted by an unscheduled visit to a Soviet hospital, I yelled 'Stop!' and thumped the poor man unhelpfully on the back. After about seven minutes he succeeded in getting the poor car into the side and we managed to get out, run across the road, and attempt to get another taxi. However, at that moment an efficient Moscow street-cleaner went by, with high-pressure jets of water spraying out and brushes twirling. We were unable to escape, trapped in the roadway by high barriers. Our nether regions brushed and sprayed, we fell out of taxi number two outside yet another vast façade in the Stalinist neo-classical style, the Peace Committee building on Prospekt Mira.

We were a good twenty minutes late. The building was very glassy, and felt like a bank or airline office. We announced ourselves to the desk. A young man with cropped hair appeared, shook our hands and without a second look, whisked us through a maze of corridors, stairs and rooms, through a door and into a room with three secretaries in it, all young and heavily made-up, all sitting at large empty desks. They stopped talking abruptly, as we passed through, resuming in whispers as we went through a door on the far side into a large room with a very long table, a king-sized empty desk, and seven men and women, all standing at one end, looking nervous. One of the men was as wide as he was tall. The rest of them made efforts at smiling, but he did not.

We shook hands, apologised and explained about the taxi. A woman in an Indian print kaftan said sharply, in English, 'We were expecting three. Now, you are four.'

'We are Women for Life on Earth,' I said throwing my arms out. 'We grow every day. This is our Moscow member. We're very proud to have her here.'

Chapter 22

The Tepid Tea Party

The Peace Committee looked at each other, eyebrows raised. We sat down at one end of the table, facing their silent stares. To my left, an interpreter with a bushy Stalin-style moustache, wearing a military uniform, took out a note-pad. A photographer appeared at the other end of the table and started snapping away. I could see the headlines now, 'Women of Greenham Common on first visit to USSR express solidarity with Soviet peace champions. Together they urge US to withdraw aggressive threat of new missiles and to agree to Soviet peace proposals.' And the next day in our own press, 'Greenham Women cosy up to Soviet officials'.

'Where's he from?' I asked the interpreter.

'Oh, he is not for us – we are not so important. No, he is for you – the important people here,' he replied, pretending to laugh.

'Dearie me,' I thought. 'And they won't be able to publish a single one, because of Olga sitting here in the middle. Unless they airbrush her out, of course…'

In front of us were a row of men and women all sharing a certain look, a certain impassivity of rounded features, a certain stiff guardedness arising from a lifetime of watching your back, your front, your speech and anything else you could possibly think of that might betray anything less than one hundred per cent loyalty to the state. As we had previously noticed with the Women's Committee, smiles in particular were expressions under control, to be switched on and then immediately off, as if subject to rationing. They began to introduce themselves. The man in front of me, Oleg Kharkhardin, was the biggest of all of them, his face a greyish mass of fleshy folds, his expression congealed suspicion. He was the vice-chairman of the committee and as a special honour, we were here in his personal office. He may well have been kind to animals and cuddled children in his time, and at some point in the distant, traumatised past must have been one himself, but he looked like an absolute brute. He didn't even pretend to smile, clearly having no need to. He just stared through small grey eyes, and they looked mostly at what Olga was writing. She was writing their names down – and they could see that she was writing in Russian.

Tea began to arrive, borne in by a young woman dressed from neck to knee in denim. They didn't make nicely cut little denim bomber jackets and skirts, the height of Western fashion even in those distant times in the USSR. The hidden purpose of the Peace Committee was being revealed. With a Brigitte Bardot pout, lashings of make-up and a mannequin walk which she had ample time to display, she minced up and down placing a full cup before each person at the table. My heart was starting to beat so hard I looked downwards, worried lest its vibrations, which felt as if they were about to burst through the enclosing ribcage, would show through my thin cotton dress. At the same time I was seriously concerned lest I, or any of us, should develop a fit of the giggles, which in the circumstances could possibly have been fatal. None of us dared catch each other's eye. Instead, I found myself eyeballing Kharkhardin, who eventually moved his cold hard gaze onto Karmen next to me. The man looking at us expected to inspire terror.

'That man,' she said afterwards, when we were safely outside, 'When he looked at me like that, I felt my guts just turn liquid. I don't know where he's been, but that man's eyes have seen things being done to people, things you or I don't want to imagine.'

Her presentiment turned out to be accurate. Later, we would find out he held the position of colonel in the KGB.

I didn't dare pick up my tea, because I couldn't be sure my hand wouldn't shake and spill the liquid. I looked down the table. No one else was touching their tea either – except for Olga, who was calmly sipping from her cup. The woman in the Indian frock, attempting a smile as she pointed towards him, was describing Oleg Kharkhardin as 'the boss – and we are merely his humble helpers.' At the far end of the table, sitting with the minion who had ushered us in, were two young men from the US-Canada Institute, a sort of Western society watching think-tank of academics who, like Western kremlinologists, tried to figure out what the hell was going on the other side of the looking glass. They looked alert and sardonic. They could already see that their afternoon might not be quite as deathly boring and predictable as they had assumed.

Kharkhardin, naturally, made the opening speech. It was a lengthy affair, translated phrase by ponderous phrase, about what heroines were Greenham Women for the Soviet people, who all knew of us through all the news coverage. The Western press tried to ignore us, they knew, but here, every day some fresh activity was reported. This was how seriously they took us. Their movement held our movement in the deepest respect. Our two movements were dedicated to peace and disarmament through the removal of destabilising American missiles. The Peace Committee were deeply honoured by our visit.

Then it was our turn. Karmen and I explained, very briefly, who we were and what we had done. We tried to describe an organisation that was not organised by anyone in authority, but was simply a group of individuals acting according to their own consciences. We pointed out that we did not therefore 'represent' Greenham Women, although, crucially, we had initiated the process which had produced the Greenham movement.

Jean introduced herself as our 'colleague, interpreter and guide' and talked about the importance of Americans and Russians gaining an understanding of each other's societies and cultures. She embarked on a long, serious speech about how much Russians, who had suffered such losses in two world wars, had to teach

Americans, and about the meetings she had had in Irkutsk, and how she had dedicated her life to the business of establishing contacts and promoting understanding between East and West, but they were no longer listening. They were watching, with growing horror, Olga and the unmistakable Russian handwriting that now covered considerable portions of the pad in front of her.

We had skipped over her, and now it was her turn to introduce herself. There was a deathly silence.

As she began to speak in Russian, the interpreter who was scribbling notes in transcript and interpreting large chunks, began scratching an angry line under each phrase with such force that the pen bit through several thicknesses of paper, and finally put it down. I hissed at him, 'Write it down – what she's saying. I want you to interpret this for me – write it down!' The poor man looked in terror at Kharkhardin whose expression betrayed not a flicker of reaction, then back to me in bewilderment. Jerkily he resumed writing, and then broke off again, unable to bring himself to say her words out loud in English.

Instead Jean did so, stepping in as translator. Kharkhardin was simply staring at Olga, who defiantly looked straight at him with her head up as she said in Russian, 'My name is Olga Medvedkova and I am a member of the Soviet Academy of Sciences and a geographer.'

Fidgeting began.

'I came here with these women because they are my friends and we have similar ideas.'

They began tapping and rattling matchboxes, rising to a crescendo as she continued .

'I am also a member of the Independent Group to establish Trust.'

She was now scarcely audible, a chorus of voices, fingers drumming on the table, stamping of feet, was drowning her out, 'I am glad finally to have an opportunity to sit at the same table and talk with—'

Kharkhardin broke into the din, which quelled instantly. 'I will not allow her to speak. I am the host here. This is my office. I make the rules. I decide who can speak and who cannot. I will not allow her to speak.'

Now I know shouting is not supposed to be a very nice thing to do, but there are times when it does have its uses. You might shout, 'Watch out!' or 'Stop!' for instance, at a carload of occupants about to be driven over a cliff. This I remind you, is more or less where we thought the human race was heading, and this strange sense of urgency was influencing our behaviour. Eyes all down the table widened in shocked disbelief as we shouted back at him.

'Yes – you must let her speak! Why can't you listen to her? She is part of our group – how on earth can she be a threat to you? We're here because of their ideas – don't you see – it's the same idea. We're part of the same movement – how can you say we're heroines and not listen to her. She's with us! We want you to hear what she has to say – let her speak!'

This produced a brief, stunned silence. Olga continued by saying that the Trust group had tried on several occasions to contact the Peace Committee. This was too much for them. Not only was she, a member of a group that wasn't supposed to even exist, actually sitting there, but she was being allowed also to speak, to address them. The rattling of matchboxes, the indignant noises, the foot-tapping, the drumming of hands on the table resumed. Desperately they looked sideways at the impassive bulk of Kharkhardin to see what he would do. But he betrayed no reaction whatsoever. Olga stopped trying to speak. The two young men at the far end observed with interest the demonstration of scandalised outrage. Olga continued to sip her tea and calmly took out a cigarette and lit it.

Kharkhardin decided matters had gone far enough. It was time to put his cohorts out of their misery. He rumbled into speech again, advancing over the hubbub like a tank. His sentences, delivered in slow, deliberate fashion, unrolled in stately procession. This time he would not be interrupted. He reinforced his points by glaring at each of us in turn, pointedly ignoring Olga.

'We are your hosts,' he began, 'you are guests in this country. We do not know how you conduct yourselves in your country, but when you are in this country you must respect its,' he paused, 'customs. We have given you our hospitality, and this is how you repay us. This, shall we say, initiative, of yours to bring along Madame Medvedkova does not strike us as very tactful, to put it mildly.'

He swivelled his glare momentarily onto Olga. 'If we have things to discuss with Madame Medvedkova, it will not be at *this* table.' This was clearly a threat, a reference to other tables, in other places. He paused to allow us all to digest it. Olga carried on smoking and drinking her tea as if she were sitting at her own kitchen table.

'We thought you came here to discuss your peace movement with us.' He focussed pointedly on Jean. Before him, she could see he had our names written down, with a paragraph beside hers. Exercising her ability to read Russian upside-down, she could see that it said, 'American. Knows Russian very well. The Women's Committee have the impression she is not part of the Greenham Common group.' He continued. 'We do not know whose idea this was, to bring in this,' he paused again, 'element, and we do not care to know. We consider it a provocation and an act of unfriendliness. Frankly, we are amazed.'

The reference to hospitality triggered something in me, and I suddenly felt I had had enough of this kind of thing. There was no point skirting round the issue or apologising. This was the mind-set that, matched by American mistrust, had caused years of negotiations to succeed in nothing more than mutually agreed, fresh rounds of weapons escalation.

They had thought to turn us into tools of their own propaganda, they had created a false, Sovietised image of Greenham to deceive their own population into believing the arms race was an entirely one-sided affair. But in so doing, they had unwittingly given us status, and with it, a certain amount (how much was a matter of trial-and-error) of immunity. We didn't have to be intimidated by these threats and lies. We didn't have to conform to their image of saintly, pliant victims of imperial aggression. We could say what we liked to them. Obviously, it hadn't occurred to them that one day some real Greenham Women might turn up. Judging by their dozy reaction to our efforts to communicate with them, they too probably thought Greenham Common was just another Potemkin village, created by the KGB in their studio-in-the-woods.

'Yes, we are women of initiative,' I replied. 'And if we weren't, you would have no Greenham Women to put on all your newsreels and proclaim as your heroines. If we had not acted on our own initiative, there would be no Peace-camp, which you say you admire so much. Yes, we have chosen to meet these people, the Moscow Group for Trust. They are our counterparts because they too have acted on their own initiative, like us. This is the point – we want people to start demanding something new from their governments, things can't just carry on with each side blaming the other. It's getting nowhere. There must be Women for Life on Earth in Moscow as well, or if things carry on the way they're going, there won't be any life on earth.' I was shaking, my voice breaking with anger.

'As for your hospitality,' I heard myself saying, 'if it hadn't been for the genuine, wonderful hospitality we've had from these people, we would have starved in your city. This is a superpower with a huge nuclear arsenal, it's supposed to be the worker's state, run for the benefit of the people, but you can't even organise the distribution of fresh food! We've had the greatest of difficulty finding anything to eat here at all!'

Out of the corner of my eye, I glimpsed the young man at the far end of the table throwing up his hands to cover his face in reaction to this final statement; he remained in that position for some time. Through the deadly tension in the fear-filled room, from time to time muffled squeaks emerged. He was undergoing a fit of the giggles that could cost him, at the very least, his job. If the proceedings had uncanny undertones of the Mad Hatter's Tea-Party, he would be a very good candidate for the dormouse. His companion was likewise making valiant efforts at self-control.

Kharkhardin's face had turned white. The rest of the committee were also pale with shock. Taking a slow, deep breath, watched in silence by us all, he resumed.

'Peace movement in Soviet Union,' he intoned, 'has two hundred and fifty million members,' (the entire population of the USSR at the last census). 'Yet, you choose to spend your time with a tiny, insignificant, worthless minority of people who only wish to slander our state. These imposters represent no one but seek only to interfere with visiting Western peace delegations in order to implant false and anti-Soviet impressions. They are disreputable, hooligans, people who do not represent the mainstream of our society. But of course they are very popular with the Western press.'

This was nonsense, in fact, as they had been virtually ignored by a sceptical Western press, and equally nonsensical were his final rhetorical flourishes. The threat, however, was not nonsense at all.

'Why do they not join in with our activities of the great mass of Soviet people? Why do they never invite us to their activities? They are nothing to do with our true peace movement. We will deal with them in whatever way we decide.'

Oh – so it's up to him, is it, to decide then, what happens to these people, I was thinking; to the Gdyaks and the Fleishgakkers, to the satirical Mark Reitman and his pregnant wife, to the thoughtful idealist Yuri Medvedkov, to the bold, sardonic, heart surgeon Volodya, who had already lost his job, and to Olga sitting here defiantly in front of him? So just who is this great bullfrog, I was thinking, with his idiotic claim that the Soviet peace movement is synonymous with the entire population? Who is this man, what does he do? Where does his authority come from, who sees fit first of all to try to flatter us, then to lecture and threaten us? From forcing terrified people to grovel and sign confessions perhaps, from signing execution warrants maybe? People like him, thinking the same way, in a general's uniform, would as happily lead us waltzing into a nuclear nightmare as would cowboy Reagan and mad Mrs Thatcher, out-doing each other in their loud protestations of innocence, as their pre-emptive-to-pre-empt-

247

the-pre-emptive missiles were launched – purely for defence, and purely, as the tea-ladies had said, for peace only.

Twenty-five years later, I am still thinking about that strange confrontation, for if he was just a bully, who were we? What were our real claims to distinction, from whence came our authority to speak so openly? We had none. We were complete nobodies, of course – that was the whole point. That we were in the room at all was the result, chiefly, of a strange amalgam of human resolve and imagination, and a large amount of sheer, delightful, accident. If the Trust group were insignificant individuals, so were we. But we nobodies, by combining, occupied the very hurricane's eye, the tiny centre of this vortex of ironic symmetries. Our government regarded us and the views we represented with the same contempt as Kharkhardin had just voiced towards Olga. We had demanded a public debate – and been similarly dismissed as a worthless, insignificant and disreputable minority. Yet, had the Trust group been able to travel, no doubt they would have been welcome to give evidence on the repressions they faced to the Foreign Office, and been invited to address a parliamentary committee. But they could not travel and we could. The only way either of us could get to speak to anyone anywhere near those in power was like this. So here we were.

I tried again. If he couldn't hear what we were saying, maybe someone in the room could.

'How can anything we do, in our country, make any difference, when you treat your true peace campaigners, people like us, in a far worse manner than we are treated? Can't you see how this just undermines everything we do, you are repressing people for simply giving out to the public the true information about nuclear war. You are behaving the way our capitalist press says you do, it just makes people fear you all the more. The Trust group – they're not attacking the Soviet State! You say they're insignificant – so what have you to fear from them? Why—' My voice was suddenly choking. I was incoherent. Tears of frustration were filling my eyes and starting to overflow. I stared at him in silent fury, speechless with rage and despair. There was a short, embarrassed silence.

'There's no need for all this emotion,' said one of the women opposite me, in perfect English.

'Oh, but it is an emotional issue,' said Karmen, suddenly leaning forward and speaking in a wonderfully calm, reasonable voice. 'Of course it is – so it should be. There's a lot at stake here, if you think about it for a minute. If neither side is prepared to back down, we could very well have a nuclear war. You don't seem to realise this, but America is serious – if they feel threatened enough, they will use their missiles. And you will respond. Or you might think they're about to strike, and you'll launch first, saying it's in self-defence. And you know, it's only because of the way you treat these people that the Western press focuses on them and not on your millions-strong peace movement. If you allow them to exist, if your KGB stops repressing them, if you listen to their ideas which are perfectly sensible, you take away your problem.'

It was a brilliant speech, couched in terms that made perfect sense. For a brief moment, they stared at her, stopped in their tracks, before another indignant chorus arose – the Moscow Group for Trust – who were they? A figment, they did not exist. They had never heard of them. The KGB? They wriggled their shoulders in mock disbelief. Olga tried once more to speak, to stress the efforts that had been made to communicate with the Peace Committee, to state that several letters had been sent by the group. 'We've never received them,' they said, fidgeting and squirming, rapping and tapping and looking anxiously at their boss.

We were getting nowhere.

Olga Medvedkova finished her tea, tapped out her cigarette, rose to her feet and, into the brief moment of astonishment that ensued, spoke a couple of uninterrupted sentences to say that she was very glad to have at last had the opportunity of dialogue, and that as dialogue and understanding were the way forward, she did not wish her presence to prevent a meaningful exchange between the Committee and the women of Greenham, and with dignity intact, left the room.

Who stole the banner of peace?

Oleg Kharkhardin decided we needed to be put in our place, reminded of where we were. His final speech was a museum piece of contemporary bombastic propaganda. For collectors of Soviet-era verbiage, I reproduce as much of it here as memory and my notes of the time will allow.

'We thought you came here to talk about your peace movement. Maybe you should learn something about ours, instead of trying to teach us about it. What need is there for so-called independent groups, when true Soviet peace movement is already involving wide circles of public opinion in discussion of disarmament proposals? Ours is a nationwide movement, a very big movement. Your movement, is not so big. Money given by eighty million Soviet citizens has built this building,' he gestured at the grand surroundings. 'How can the Moscow Group for Trust afford to be independent? Who pays for their activities?

'These are people,' he continued inexorably, 'who are attempting to steal the banner of peace, which rightly belongs to the millions of our peace-loving nation, to our peace champions who daily struggle for peace.'

Unfortunately, this metaphor only served to forcibly remind me again of Lewis Carroll's story, and the question which has perplexed so many succeeding generations of literary critics – who really did steal the plate of tarts? Our systems were saturated with adrenalin, and since one primary effect of this fight-or-flight hormone, so vital for human survival, is the apparent slowing-down of time so that seconds last minutes, the big man's speech seemed to last about an hour and a half. His pudgy fingers rested spread out on the table before him, reinforcing the amphibian-like impression he gave.

At last he seemed to be drawing to a close. He lowered his voice to deliver a final, chilling warning. He intended to be taken seriously. The equation was simple. Because the Trust group claimed independence from the state, they were anti-Soviet – and that was that.

250

'You brought Olga Medvedkova with you. What was the result? Instead of talking about your successful movement for peace, we have had to waste time explaining unpleasant things.' He opened his fingers. 'A person who opposes our society cannot expect any reaction other than that we showed Olga Medvedkova. We lost twenty million lives in the Great Patriotic War. We will never forget this. We sacrificed our lives for the sake of this system, this society. We will not let anyone raise a hand against it. You must realise this when you assess our intentions towards the likes of Olga Medvedkova. In future, if you wish to return here, you will have to choose your company more carefully, or the consequences could be unpleasant.'

The interpreter paused before key words, such as 'unpleasant', giving me 'you'd better be hearing this' looks.

'We find this totally unacceptable,' he concluded, sitting back in his seat, locking his fingers together, looking up the row on his side, and back down at our side.

His words were having the intended effect on our intestines. Nonetheless, Karmen replied. She had to get across just how most people in Britain saw the USSR. It wasn't easy. She leaned forward across the table, and forced herself to look at him. 'I don't think you understand what we're saying to you.'

The interpreter conveyed her words back across the table. The young-men-at-the-end-of-the-table, having had time to recover their self-control, craned forward to hear.

'We realise that you made enormous sacrifices in the last war. But we are trying to prevent another, far worse, war, in which even more of your people could die. We are trying to influence public opinion in our country. We knock on doors and talk to people, we call public meetings, we try to persuade people that they don't need nuclear weapons for defence, and this is what they say. "Yes, we agree with you," they say. "We don't like nuclear weapons either, *but* what about the Russians? Why don't you go there and protest?" You see, they're afraid of you, they see you as their enemies,' here there was a little chorus of tut-tutting as if anybody could have such a naughty, mistaken idea. 'Yes', she

251

went on. 'This is why they support the missiles, and when you persecute the Trust group, it makes all the bad propaganda about your society seem true. If you leave the group alone, you might get some attention paid to your mass movement, to your wish for peace.'

Kharkardin looked at her in stupefaction. How dare she answer him? His deputy, Grigory Lokshin, a small round sallow-faced man who frequently led delegations on visits hosted by Western peace groups, began to reiterate the theme.

'You wish to discuss a larger delegation? Our Soviet leadership reflects the true aspirations and wishes of the Soviet people. A planned programme of visits and introductions could take place through our committees and the committees of local peace champions that might make this clear. But, such a visit cannnot become a circus for imposters, undesirable hooligan elements, to put forward their slanderous views of our society, spreading false notions of "equal responsibility" of imperialist and socialist countries for the Cold War.'

Lokshin had inadvertantly conducted us to the heart of the matter. Both sides denied responsibility for the arms race, and therefore the responsibility for making any new conciliatory moves. Suddenly everybody seemed to be talking at once, an eruption of real discussion in the midst of which Oleg Kharkhardin, who was plainly not the discussing type, stood up and left.

Everyone's shoulders seemed to drop two inches. There was a general outbreak of tepid tea-drinking, chatting and cigarette-offering. 'There's no need for translation,' said someone brightly, 'We all speak English. Now, tell us what your ideas are for a visit'.

We asked for their help and co-operation in devising a visit that would produce an unusually frank, open, warts-and-all view of life in the USSR. Lokshin looked highly dubious, and continued to make long speeches culminating with more ritual denunciations of the Trust group. He said the visit would have to be officially organised, or it might be a 'flop' – thus revealing that he saw no value in it beyond that of propaganda for Soviet state. The rest of them seemed intrigued.

When we told them we had been doing this already – chatting to people at random wherever we could, on the trains and buses, in the parks, they leaned forward, listening intently. We told them the kind of things we had been hearing. Which were not so different to the kind of things people said in the West.

The subject under discussion was not really a visit that would test how far they were prepared to allow open personal contacts to take place. It was lies and secrets, and the part played by them in the creation of the Cold War. A concept that, five years later, would become a buzz-word of the Gorbachev administration, *glasnost* – transparency – sat in the middle of the table like a new puppy, wagging its tail.

Which was crippling their society more – the pressure from the US to keep up with an absurd level of military expenditure, or the repression of independent thought, discussion and initiative resulting from their fearful response to the US? Was not the state security apparatus, originally conceived to protect a new society against the real threat of foreign invasion by military force or intrigue, now the main problem with this society? Did not its exaggeration of a perceived threat, whether from its own citizens or from a hostile, but essentially conservative West, give rise to the answering fears of those western populations? What purpose was served by the repression?

'You have a lot of good things in this society. Take away the KGB,' we said, airily, 'and in fifty years time you could have a wonderful country, a country that people would want to migrate into, not out of.' This time, nobody tried to pretend they hadn't heard of the KGB.

We stood up to go. We had been talking for two hours after Kharkhardin had left. Hands were shaken. The two from the US-Canada institute didn't just shake our hands, they nearly pulled our arms free from their sockets. So did the interpreter with the genial moustache.

'That was the most interesting meeting I have ever had,' he said, with feeling.

What had we done?

The apple cart

We had got them to do something new, something that broke their rules. That's all. Despite all the warnings we had received in Britain about not doing anything to cause offence to these officials, we had shown that speaking our minds, with sometimes brutal frankness, standing up for the truth in the face of a deep-seated culture of lies and denial, would not result in official contact being severed. They needed us, the Western peace movement, to produce a general pressure for disarmament. Our biggest achievement was simple: nobody had walked out or shown us the door when they realised the identity of Olga. Even Kharkhardin had sat at the same table – his table – with a member of an officially despised, officially non-existent, group of upstart 'hooligans' who dared to make suggestions to the Soviet State concerning its conduct of the arms race. Because Olga had been there, a small number of people close to the top of the Soviet hierarchy had been obliged to do something genuinely new. In the place where novelty could only happen in secret, something unprecedented had happened, in public.

Outside the building, Olga and Masha were waiting for us. Once we were well away and walking along a street, we could talk openly.

'I have been to the Lubyanka to ask them where have they put my husband, when they arrested him and held him for two weeks while the Scandinavian women were here, and that really scared me,' said Olga, 'but that did not scare me as much as being in there this afternoon. You could show your emotion, but me, I could not. But I was shaking, like you.'

Olga described for Masha's benefit the gut-curdling image of Kharkhardin, lording it over the rest of them and the terrified reactions to the revelation of her identity. The alleged theft of the 'banner of peace' caused particular merriment, as did the description of internationally recognised academics such as the Medvedkovs as 'hooligans'. But beneath the relieved laughter, all sorts of demons were stirring to life, ready to start prowling round our minds. Because the meeting had taken place in Kharkhardin's personal office, he would be likely to react as if he had received a very personal insult. There would be no doubt that he would seek revenge, but what form this might take, or when it would happen, was entirely unpredictable.

If saying, 'Goodbye, see you later,' had been problematic before, now it would be even more fraught with uncertainty. They had to return home to reassure their families and we had arranged to meet Richard, the *Times* correspondent.

Richard was walking up and down in a little park, looking cool and dapper as before.

'How'd the meeting go?' he asked casually, scanning the trees out of habit. When we told him we took Olga with us, he stopped, turned round, took off his sunglasses and looked at us.

'You did what?' He was reacting with gratifying disbelief. 'How did she get in? They'd never let that happen! They can't!'

We assured him they could, and had.

'Hey,' he was suddenly jovial – he looked at us intently. 'Are you hungry?' We nodded dumbly. 'Like you've never been so hungry before ever in your whole life?' We nodded again.

'All right – the only place we can get an edible meal is probably your hotel,' he said. 'This needs some talking. We'll call in at the Tass news agency on the way, you can see how the Western peace movement is reported over here, just for your interest.'

Suddenly, the Trust Group was a news story, one that wouldn't fit the story told by Tass.

Chapter 23

The red flag shivers, and so do we

In Valery Gdyak, physicist, Trust group member's Moscow flat, on the warm evening of May 24th, 1983 people were arriving for an exercise in trust. We were to tell them the truth about Greenham Common, and Olga was to tell the group about the Peace Committee meeting. More and more people crowded in, filling the floor-space.

Greenham Common – the truth
no one would believe

Olga and Yuri were delighted with the way the meeting had gone, but because of the presence of bugs, they could only convey the news of the meeting that afternoon, in whispers. This at once created an atmosphere of intrigue and suspicion, making these Russian peaceniks more nervous than usual, and more than ever inclined to go into secretive huddles.

With Jean translating amidst a chaos of questions, we started recounting the story of the march and the start of the Peace-camp. Those who were meeting us for the first time looked dubious. They were used to reports of the British peace movement churned out by the Tass Soviet news agency, such as we had been shown by Richard, with low-key, spontaneous, often zany little events being described as 'mass rallies in all major cities by workers demanding an end to imperialist aggression, and removal of American missiles'. Why on earth would anyone in the West, such as the Greenham Women, want to spend their time demonstrating unconditional support for the USSR, unless they were being paid by the USSR State Security Services to do so?

'This sounds like nothing like what we are shown on our television,' said one. 'Aha!' said another, as if they had caught us out on a telling point of detail that would show our whole story to be a sham – and Greenham Common would be revealed, after all, as a KGB invention – 'You say you gave out a leaflet. But how could you get a leaflet, one you had written yourselves, printed? This is impossible, no?'

'Easy,' we said, 'we had borrowed some money and anyway it's not expensive – we found a printer from the phone book,' (here we diverted to explain how the *Yellow Pages* worked for businesses) 'took what we'd written to him, told him how many we wanted, and—er—he printed them.'

'See?' Olga was saying. 'This is what I've been telling you! And what's more, over there, you can give out leaflets in the street, and you don't get arrested either!' They shook their heads. They were not easily convinced. Jean was becoming exasperated. 'It's time you people showed some trust in us!' She was suddenly shouting in Russian at a wispy young man in a red Snoopy baseball cap who was demanding whether we knew about 'the repressions'.

Karmen and I went out on to the balcony. A police car had driven by as we had arrived. We fully expected the meeting to be invaded and broken up by thugs at any moment. Richard had arrived with us, to tape record the meeting, but had had to leave after an hour, taking with him his magic umbrella of Western journalistic cover.

The people we had already met, like Yuri and Olga and Volodya, seemed calm, but we could hear the rest of them shouting and arguing. The fright and uncertainty seemed to be tearing them to pieces. We had discussed the likely outcomes with Richard, who was not only showing a sudden interest in the Trust group, but also a concern for our safety which was as unnerving as it was reassuring. He was intrigued, and wanted to share the story with other correspondents. More people would then get to hear of the Trust group, and this could help protect them, by creating an ozone layer of awareness above them. But if 'the story' was reported as Greenham Women making fools of the Peace Committee, not only would this scupper our chances of getting any further cooperation out of them for the kind of visit we intended, but it could also make 'unpleasant things' a far more likely outcome for the group.

'We've got to stress the positive, that she wasn't thrown out, that we carried on round the table talking, make it sound like they were all very reasonable. No mention of their appalling behaviour, shouting her down.'

'So we lie, basically,' concluded Karmen. 'To try to soften whatever happens to them.' She gestured into the crowded room, where heated arguments were still in full swing.

We leant over the balcony and looked out over the now dark, shadowy park where we had sat that morning, and beyond it at the city of grand buildings and empty shops, of crowds of people trudging through the dandelions, at the city decorated with slogans, banners and air-brushed photos of portly middle-aged men looking like men-in-charge the world over, a quiet city sinking into a thick amethyst twilight. We had insulted someone in power; we had been issued with a chilling warning. We had no idea what might now happen. Kharkhardin, according to the group, was effectively the boss of the Peace Committee. He was a known 'hard-liner', in the KGB. Our impression of having sat opposite somebody who could send innocent people to their deaths for the crime of having opinions was accurate.

'Half of these people probably still don't believe any of what we're saying is true. It's not surprising – they haven't a clue what it's like to live anywhere other than in this sort of place. I'm not surprised it's driving them nuts. We've only been here a week and it's driving me nuts,' said Karmen.

Then we went back into the room. We went over everything we had said, explaining how groups like the local peace groups worked, the minor laws, such as obstruction, which we broke and the laws we didn't need to, because we had over the years won for ourselves, as a people, the right to demonstrate our views in public places and in public ways. How we wrote letters to the papers, which sometimes got printed and sometimes didn't. How some papers only printed things giving a certain viewpoint, reflecting that of the owner. We were describing the nitty-gritties of a democratic, free-market, capitalist, society. 'How easy it must be,' said someone, 'to tell people about nuclear war and its effects. If you want to work for peace, you really have no problems.'

We told them about how some women had been prosecuted for invading the base or damaging it, and had been given prison sentences of several weeks, or in some cases, months.

'When you go to prison, it is for weeks. When someone goes to prison here, it is for years.'

They began to think we inhabited some kind of earthly paradise, when your needs could be satisfied by a simple trip to a corner shop, or a once-weekly visit to a supermarket, thus leaving you surely with huge amounts of leisure time. Where you could campaign about issues which troubled you without fear of arrest, injury or death; where you could join any number of political parties or even form your own...

What we really could not explain so easily, was why, when anybody could get hold of information and give it out, we had resorted to marching to Greenham in the first place. Why it was, with a choice of parties, so many people chose not to bother to vote. Why people often ignored information, freely available, that might show them the truth. Why people who protested were often viewed with suspicion. Why people, with such a cornucopia of pleasures to choose from, had so little time to enjoy them. What it was like to live in a place where money had real value – and lack of money meant something too, so that if they spent their time hunting goods, we spent our time hunting money. But at least, by the end of a long evening, they really did believe that those improbable images of women demonstrating were all for real.

They all came outside to see us off. We hugged, shook hands, and got into the taxi, waving until they disappeared from sight. We knew we wouldn't ever see them again, all together like that.

The red flag

As our taxi rounded the corner past the yawning crevasse of Red Square, we glimpsed a large orange full moon, hanging low in the sky. 'Let's be tourists,' said Karmen, as we attempted to introduce a sense of order into our minds by tidying our hotel room. We strolled around taking in the guitar-strumming, apparently normal, crowds – even at this hour queuing to see the embalmed body of the long-dead leader, under the huge wall atop which all those leaders had watched all those parades of tanks, missiles, and before that regiments, detachments of this, detachments of that. Here in this place, the patriotic march-past, the endless march-past of people grouped into collectives behaving identically, had reached its apogee and created what must surely be the world's most boring art-form, reducing human variety to competitive norms. The very word 'march' carries with it the taint of such regimentation. Perhaps banners, too, were a bad idea, merely encouraging theft. Grim, how grim it was, how serious, how seriously and agonisingly grim, and cold, and hard, and cruel. If we women were ever to really have influence, power, would we do that? Would we choose the military parade as our way of glorifying our achievements? Perhaps we wouldn't even have anything anyone could recognise as 'achievements'.

We stared in fascinated horror as a detachment of great-coated soldiers goose-stepped past the row of rigid, neatly trimmed fir trees below that tall blank wall, behind which lay the body of Uncle Lenin (Uncle Joe had been removed by Kruschev) whose achievements for mankind I had read all about in the *Daily Worker* 'Children's Corner'. The red flag on top of the Kremlin shivered like a crinkled poppy petal in a wind we couldn't feel below.

Thursday, May 26th, our last full day in the city of the world's largest book-shop and the world's biggest ballet, would be a day combining all the elements of fear, farce and coincidence we had come to recognise as the signature of this particular Moscow experience.

The day started well enough. We had slept well. Jean arrived to join us for breakfast. Then, returning from a trip to the bathroom, which boasted more pipework than the Pompidou centre, I noticed the door to the room next to ours was half open. Glancing in I beheld two men, one holding open a large briefcase, which seemed to be full of wires, and the sort of tackle that comes under the general title of 'electronics'. Then they saw me standing there with my mouth hanging open, and slammed the door shut. Shortly afterwards, we went downstairs and Karmen returned to our room to collect a jumper. She reappeared in the lobby white-faced, giggled nervously, and reported that two very large, very fat men were sitting on inadequately-sized chairs, either side of the door to our room.

'They were completely, totally expressionless, like sphinxes. I said "Hi," and they didn't flicker an eyelid. I had to walk between them to open the door. I didn't bother to lock it,' she said, 'There didn't seem much point.'

Obviously Kharkhardin had gone straight out of the previous day's meeting to a telephone where words something along these lines had been said, 'Look, boys, I want to know where these women go, who they see, what they say, what they've brought with them in their luggage. I want to know when they fart, OK? And you can be as obvious about it as you like – no need for discretion in this case.'

Richard had arranged for us to meet some other correspondents over lunch at his flat. We were more than ready for food that hadn't been preserved in vinegar and some nice calm, sensible discussion, which, likewise, hadn't been pickled in terror and conjecture. But first their editors wanted us to have a photo taken against the backdrop of Red Square, 'because it looks like Russia.' We felt quite affectionate towards the *Times* man. His cool urbanity and sceptical detachment from events was a welcome relief from the passions and panics of the Russians, and we valued his insights. The Moscow posting was an unenviably dreary affair, entailing attendance at endless meetings and official functions where the world's experts in extended and repeated bombast delivered themselves, free from rude curtailment by criticism of any sort, of their absurd claims. Our fools-rush-in approach had provided a welcome diversion. Furthermore, he was about to become a father for the first time, of twins. He confessed to being completely ignorant about babies and how to approach them, and to feeling apprehensive. Karmen and I were able to give him our highly biased beginners' crash course in first-time parenthood; Module One: theory. We role-played nappy changing, burping, putting a small piece of cloth, what the Welsh call a *clwt* (known the world over in myriad languages as a rag) over your shoulder to catch the inevitable gobbets of sick and dribble. Babies – it wasn't a topic he could discuss in diplomatic circles, and he was dying to talk about it. We had an excellent symbiotic relationship.

We were still carrying with us the 'Natasha's toast' poster, showing the pink Greenham march banner with its green tree of life and its CND-symbol roots. On the other side it now sported many signatures. Some were from the 'peace champions' of the Women's Committee, all the Trust group people of course had signed up to Natasha's high-minded sentiments, while an increasing number came from people we had simply approached at random. On the bridge over the Moskva river, which Colin had photographed whilst under construction in 1937, we continued to invite passersby to sign our poster. A couple of young women were so keen to do so that they practically tore the pens out of our hands, and happily posed for photos with us afterwards. As far as they were concerned, there were no risks involved at all in setting one's signature to something spontaneous and independent, and nothing suspicious about being approached by friendly foreigners. Older people often looked over their shoulders and carefully made sure no one else was looking, before speaking to us in low voices, but the younger people already seemed to be migrants from a future whose only sign of arrival was their own behaviour. Then we started to walk back over Red Square, beneath the precipice of the high, dark red wall of the Kremlin.

Suddenly our way was barred by a line of uniformed police. We had arrived at the Spassky gate, a medieval-looking tower forming the main entrance into the complex of buildings from which the USSR, its European satellite states, and its global interests, were run. Shortly the huge gates opened and the police kept a wide passage open along rising ground into the high arch, through which could be glimpsed white walls, cobalt blue sky, and a patch of gold onion dome. Odd, I thought, how Russian architecture was so clearly based on the nation's favorite vegetables – two soldiers stood at attention either side of the arch. The crowd had become suddenly dense, and suddenly tense, silent, packed tight behind white lines on the road. We had arrived first, so we were in the front, with the best view of whatever was about to happen. Then, one after the other, huge black stretch cars, bigger than anything we'd seen so far, with curtained back windows and smoky glass, swept at speed out of the arch and across our vision and away over the square.

Some held several people, some two, some just one person. They were all men. They stared from behind their blackened glass at the crowd and everyone stared at them, but no one waved. The uniformed chauffeurs drove straight and fast across the cobbled square, with what seemed like reckless disregard for passing pedestrians, and disappeared into the far corner. My stomach was churning and I was tingling all over. Who were these people – to be precise, these men? They didn't look like a visiting delegation. There were no black faces, no Asian faces. From what you could see through the smoky grey glass, they looked Russian. Were they really who I was beginning to think they were – who else could they be? In a daze I unrolled our poster and held it up. A policeman whistled at me and waved his baton, but by then the occupants of the final posse had craned to look as they passed. These men had just left a meeting, and I had a prickly feeling that I knew what at least one of the topics under discussion had been.

Flowers for Felix

Richard had provided us with a driver, hoping to inject some reliability into our movements. The car took us past Dzerzhinsky Square, past the great black statue where the day before our taxi had broken down, in front of the infamous KGB headquarters. We gasped in surprise. There on the black plinth of the statue, lay an enormous, ostentatious wreath of white lilies, red carnations and red roses, backed by swathes of pine branches. It was gigantic, as high as a man. Was this significant? Was it the birthday, or the anniversary of the death of the founder of the Cheka, forerunner of the KGB? Or was somebody just overcome by affection for the dead state terrorist, whose statue had such symbolic value that in a mere ten year's time, it would be the first to be toppled from this self-same plinth? The taxis that plied their trade outside hotels were all reputed to be driven by informers, and we had remarked more than once on Felix's unadorned state, his lack of flowers – was somebody trying to tell us something, or were we by now the victims of our own paranoid delusions, seeing connections in mere coincidence?

The interior of Richard's Moscow flat was decorated in a cool, white, Habitat-style fashion. We sat at a medium-sized table and began to tuck into an excellent meal, whose ingredients had arrived not many hours earlier on a plane. A civilised, relaxed and sensible conversation began to flow. We began to feel almost normal. Then with a crash, a sound as of a pneumatic drill being wielded in the next-door flat shattered our fragile idyll. The large round white Japanese paper lampshade, the *pièce de résistance* of the room, fell to the floor with an ignominious flop, a sound that was seen but not of course heard.

'What the hell's that? It sounds like a pneumatic drill,' we yelled across the table.

'It is a pneumatic drill,' Richard shouted back. 'They say they're having to redo the plumbing. What they're probably doing is renewing the bugging system,' he screamed.

'Who were those guys leaving the Kremlin in those big cars an hour ago?' we cried.

'That was the Politburo — they meet every Thursday morning,' bawled the quietly-spoken, clean-cut *Observer* correspondent.

'We thought that's what they were,' we boomed back.

'They would probably have discussed your meeting yesterday — it would have been recorded. They'll have listened to the tape — there's not a lot happens here that has shock value,' he continued through a loud-hailer improvised from a rolled-up newspaper. 'Nothing ever changes. They're completely cocooned, cut off from reality.'

'So they won't even know about the—' the noise had stopped, 'economy, the shortages, the feeling that everything's on its last legs, and people only manage because of the black market?'

The cacophony began again.

'No,' they roared. 'Who's going to risk telling them? As far as they're concerned, all the plans are being fulfilled.'

'And they wouldn't have heard of the Trust group?'

'They will now — after your meeting, because it's public. Reaction in the West — they're sensitive to that — they'll have to decide how to deal with them.'

The glasses and crockery were vibrating, the chairs shaking.

'They'll want to crack down, just get rid of them, but there's this thing, Western public opinion, they don't understand it, but they think it matters, or it could matter — who knows?'

Hair-line cracks began to appear in the ceiling. After an hour, it stopped.

Cake

We had arranged to make a second visit to the Women's

Committee, who were waiting, all four of them, visibly terrified, in the lobby of their building. Their relief that we had not arrived with a 'hooligan' in tow was evident. They seemed extremely friendly and wanted to discuss details of our planned visit with a bigger group. They had even, as a genuine gesture of goodwill, baked us a cake – their cake was a soft sponge in the style of Delia Smith, betraying their privileged access to baking powder, unlike the Trust group's 'peace picnic' cake which was unrisen, like a large pancake. Then Ksenia Proskurnikova seemed to be building herself up to something. 'Frankly,' she began, her chin wobbled and the blonde interpreters's eyes began to swivel. She got no further and collapsed into wittering on in code about things that unite us and don't divide us.

Later, when we were back in Britain, we exchanged letters about the visit. In the spirit of openness, we sent them a copy of the report of the Peace Committee meeting that appeared in the *END Journal*, a publication which would have been considered 'anti-Soviet'. Ksenia's letters were typed, on numbered sheets of wafer-thin poor quality paper. On a separate, unnumbered sheet, someone had used a different typewriter to request that we please send a copy of the *Journal* itself. Even the Women's Committee was hungry for new ideas.

Cake is a good tranquilliser for people in nerve-wracking situations, but you need an awful lot of it, in regular doses. Our nervousness, despite all the cake, was growing. The doorstops had disappeared from outside our hotel room, and everything looked exactly the same as we had left it, but when the *Daily Telegraph* man picked us up in his car, he immediately said, looking in his mirror, 'You do realise you have a tail? I've been here years, and this is the first time it's happened to me.' He seemed amused that the Greenham Women whom he had presumed would be stooges, conveyed by a fleet of official vehicles, should instead be followed around by the KGB. His wife had also thoughtfully baked us a cake (using imported baking powder, since you ask, as we did). Meanwhile her husband the correspondent asked silly questions.

'I have to ask you this, because my editor will want me to – have you asked for permission to camp outside an SS20 site?'

Fear

There were men talking into radios outside the hotel, and more of them talking to the reception-bouffant-woman, so that we felt surrounded and very vulnerable. Brodsky, nominally employed as a cardiac surgeon, still had a working phone but several efforts to contact him earlier had failed to get a response. By early evening we decided to try to find out what had happened. It seemed probable, on past performance, that in response to our stormy meeting with the Peace Committee, all the Trust group people we had met had been placed under some sort of detention.

We decided to enlist Richard's help, hoping we could leave Karmen at the end of a reliable phone while Jean and I set off to find Brodsky and the Medvedkovs and put our fears to rest. Instead, we had a nerve-wracking evening of mounting anxiety. As we took the lift down in our hotel, a huge whale of a man got in with us. When we went in the nearest phone booth to phone Richard, he squeezed himself into that as well. We shouted at him and he disappeared. We arranged to meet Richard outside the Hotel Ukraine, a classic heap of Stalinist gothic architecture. We set off in a taxi with three cars full of leather-jackets in tow, all of whom got out with us outside the Hotel Ukraine and then stood ten metres away in the bushes, fiddling with their radios and cool shades, as if directed by Quentin Tarantino. Doing our best to ignore them, leaving Karmen at Richard's flat, Jean and I tried first Brodsky's flat and then the Medvedkov's. We found no response, but had the distinct feeling we were being watched in both places. Sick with fear, both for them and for ourselves, we felt convinced that they had been arrested, and could well be undergoing interrogation in a police cell. We knew that anything – a broken lift cable, a body falling from the 18th floor, a vicious beating in a stairwell – could be explained as an "accident" and never be disproved.

But we were calmed by the taxi-driver, who to our relief had waited for us outside the Medvedkov's block, for taxis were hard to come by out in the suburbs.

The driver began talking about the jumper his wife had knitted for him, then about his kids, then about the people we'd been trying to visit. He could see they were people in trouble, because he could see the KGB outside the flats. Jean told him who they were, and what the trouble was. We talked all about it. 'This is wonderful, driving round, talking with you guys,' Jean translated Russian into American. 'I work for peace too, but quietly,' he made a wavy, under-the-table sort of movement with his hand. 'The city looks beautiful tonight, doesn't it?'

We went to Richard's flat, where he poured us a large drink each.

Flowers for Richard

We had to leave at midday to catch our plane. We got up very early, rushed over to the Medvedkov's by metro, rang the doorbell, and still there was no reply. Not bothering to try any other addresses, we returned to pack our bags. I was all for not leaving until we at least knew what had happened to them.

'What if we just sat outside the door and said we're not catching the plane until we know they're safe? They don't want us here in their country – they'd have to do something.'

Karmen insisted we couldn't push it, couldn't take further risks with the authorities.

'Look, that would be doing the same as the politicians – having stand-offs, confrontations. They're not the only people that matter, there's other people – we have to keep going, keep the channels open.'

Nor, she pointed out, could we risk bringing retribution on ourselves. If the Medvedkovs insisted they weren't martyr material, nor were we. We couldn't jeopardise the September visit.

'Bugger the September visit! We can't let them get away with just arresting them all!'

We yelled at each other in the breakfast room of the Metropole and stomped out in separate directions, Jean and I to make a last-minute visit to give another book to another ecologist Jean had met while a student, Karmen to stay and await news. We worried that we would be followed, but our tails seemed to have disappeared.

The man we met, in a street drenched in the smell of roses, was, like Sasha in Leningrad, one of countless numbers of quiet, well-educated dissidents who made information-gathering and dissemination their main hobby. He knew the Medvedkovs but was wary about the path of openness they had chosen.

'There is a soft layer to this society, a very pleasant layer, even,' he said in quiet, carefully worded English. 'And there is a hard layer. You have come fairly close to this layer. And then there is in-between. I exist in-between.' He wanted us, if we were able to return, to argue, with the Party committees we would inevitably meet, for scientists like him to have access to international scientific journals. Highly educated, highly qualified scientists like him couldn't discuss reform or demand access to any international database of scientific information without putting themselves in danger of the wrong kind of attentions. So they were reduced to asking Westerners to argue for these things for them.

We jumped on the bus to return. Outside the Metropole I spotted a queue for carnations. Richard had said he'd meet us in the morning. It occurred to me that he had really been a mate, a good friend, and without him and his flat and his good sense, we would have gone to pieces a lot sooner. Meeting the ecologist had calmed me down. I began to see things from Karmen's point of view. There were other people to consider, other things going on, all moving in the same direction. The Trust group were responsible for themselves – if they had indeed all been arrested, there was little we could do about it, here.

Flowers in the USSR were not so highly-bred as they were already becoming in the West, and smelly things like sweet peas, roses, and carnations still had their old-fashioned, heart-stirring scents. I bought a big bunch of pink carnations for Richard and went through the door of the ground-floor restaurant. At the same moment, Karmen entered from the door at the opposite end, carrying a big bunch of yellow carnations. We met somewhere in the middle. 'I've been thinking. You're right,' we each chorused to the other, 'and I've bought some flowers to say thank you to Richard.'

Various correspondents, including Richard, were sitting in the lobby. They had spent the morning with the Medvedkovs, who had been out the night before with all our other friends in the group, celebrating the Peace Committee meeting, at the Gdyak's flat, which, stupidly, we hadn't tried on our evening of frustrated visiting. The famously rare, hard-to-reach, Dolgoprudniki group of scientists, with whom we had tried to rendezvous at the Mayakovski statue a week earlier, had been there at the party too. They had turned up to meet us at the rendezvous they said, but late of course – they, like us, had wrongly assumed KGB interference. The journalists no longer thought the Trust group were a bit dodgy. Now, it seems, they had credibility at least with the much-reviled Western press. Of course the Western press also traditionally thought people like us, and especially women like us, were dodgy too, but now we too had credibility, even people to carry our bags.

Goodbye USSR

Brodsky was at the airport wearing a very sexy white denim jacket, no doubt a gift from a grateful patient (or, as today's National Health Service would have it, 'client') who had been snatched from the jaws of death. He watched sadly as several men in shiny brown suits unceremoniously shoved the other passengers out of our queue for customs, and worked their way through our bags, which by now contained huge amounts of written material, typed and hand-written, official and unofficial, posters, addresses, books,

270

notebooks, diaries. We pointed at our watches as the time for the plane to leave came and went. They shrugged their shoulders, and continued trying to decipher our hand-written scrawls. They were looking for what used to be called '*samizdat*', writings by individual Soviet citizens, anything from a one-page letter to a full-length novel, anything which might not reflect the State's view of itself. With increasing desperation, they flicked through huge, turgid official reports given to us by the Committees, any one of which could have concealed an unofficial document, the scraps of thin, carbon copies of type-written sheets which traditionally conveyed the unspeakable truths of the twentieth century's greatest social experiment. But unfortunately we had no *Dr. Zhivago* or *Gulag Archepelago* cunningly stowed away. One of them seized on a scrap of paper from Karmen's bag on which the Medvedkov's address was written.

'He's a well-known Soviet citizen,' she said, 'you've got his address already.' Behind the barrier, the Reuters man translated the joke for Brodsky, who began to laugh. We decided to give the men in suits the last of our Women for Life on Earth posters, to brighten up their office. Jean translated this for them, 'Here you are – a gift for the KGB, something to make your office beautiful and to always remind you of us!' The customs man, who had been sidelined by the secret police, giggled behind his hand. The recipient of the poster rolled and unrolled it, puzzled.

Then the *kaygaybayniki* suddenly gave up, began to laugh, threw their hands up in the air, and with unmistakeable gestures indicted that we were very welcome to leave the Soviet Union, the world's first socialist state, now entering its final phase of mature, fully-developed, actually-existing Communism.

We ran across the tarmac to where the plane had been kept waiting. 'So you're the reason for the delay,' said an English accent straight from the Henley Regatta. 'What on earth have you been up to?'

Chapter 24

The bleak midwinter

Things would get a lot worse before they got better.

The date for deployment of 'Cruise' at Greenham, November 1983, grew closer. The Peace-camp became hugely popular, and sprouted off-shoot camps at all the gates around the base. The preparations for the housing of the huge missile transporters, and the building of the concrete bunkers for the warheads, continued but were dogged at every turn by women who would sit in the road, blocking deliveries, lie in the trenches cut for the new sewage piping, or simply cut the fence and attempt to hold events alternative to the launching of nuclear warheads, such as tea-parties, or egg-and-spoon races, inside the base. Many went to prison as a result of these invasions of the base, and Newbury magistrates court began to be a regular scene of anger, passion and hilarity, both inside and out, as women came in their hundreds to support their arrested friends.

Wimmin, womyn, women

Many of the women becoming involved either were to begin with, or became, lesbian, which has provided an interesting discussion topic for women's studies courses at university ever since. The emphasis inevitably began to shift away from opposing 'Cruise', and towards the idea that what mattered was to create a space where women, by living together, proclaimed female values. When CND, in the autumn of 1983, wanted to hold a demonstration, which would have involved perhaps a half million people, or more, at Greenham, the majority of women actually living at the Peace-camp refused to countenance this, as it wouldn't be women-only. We – by 'we' I mean people actively involved in the peace movement – became bitterly divided over this issue, and the rights and wrongs of women-only protests seemed to overshadow the gathering pace of the arms race, which for some of the women now permanently at Greenham, had evidently dwindled in importance.

Karmen and I were on the 'wrong' side, as were some of the other 'originals', in supporting the idea of a mixed demonstration. We didn't see that anybody could own demonstration rights over a patch of land, and besides, it was only for one day and the women's camp would continue anyway. Perhaps we would always be on the 'wrong' side, since the biggest thing we had in common was our mistrust and dislike of orthodoxies, whether new or old, establishment or alternative. With apparently sensible people descending to serious discussion over the spelling of the word 'women' – should it be 'wimmin', 'womyn' or 'wombyn'? – the peace movement had become a cantankerous place to be.

Our Soviet trip, and our Peace Committee action with the Moscow Group for Trust, was not well received in established British peace circles. The CND committee that dealt with USSR relations was most disapproving when we naïvely went to see them, which was hardly surprising since it was packed with pro-Soviet sympathisers. We had not realised the extent to which the conventionally organised peace movement was prepared to take the side of the hawks who dominated the policy of the USSR. Included in this were Helen John and some of the women at the Peace-camp who also disagreed with our action, and wrote to the Soviet Women's Committee to say so, emphasising that we didn't represent the Greenham Women. However, nobody could have represented the Greenham Women, since it wasn't a representative organisation. This was Greenham's main strength.

The weakness of the peace movement remained its identification, by extension, with the USSR. The public had re-elected Mrs Thatcher in the wake of the Falklands war, and she seemed more popular and more confident than ever. The alternative thinkers' movement felt big when we were a quarter of a million in Hyde Park, but in reality we were a minority, quite a small minority at that. The Labour party was declaring itself in favour of unilateral disarmament, but it could safely declare itself in favour of anything it liked, since it was clearly unelectable. Its socialist principles had degenerated into slogan thinking that shied away from serious examination of time-honoured assumptions.

Yet the network of support for the Peace-camp had become so large and strong that when, on October 31st, a quietly dis-organised fence-cutting action took place, thousands of women took the police completely by surprise. Apparelled as witches as befitted the occasion, we gathered quietly at various points around the perimeter and fortified ourselves in the normal manner, with tea, cocoa, cake and biscuits, emerging at dusk to assault the fence The permanent police presence, clad in the new wonder-material, Goretex, was already large, but not large enough to prevent us cutting and pulling down several miles of the fence. The army quickly repaired the fence which came to look more like a piece of macrame than anything designed to keep mass murder in and protest out, but it became hard to see how, once the missiles and their huge transporters arrived, they could be deployed on exercises with the smooth efficiency envisaged by NATO planners.

The cancelled visit

The Moscow Group for Trust had a good summer. They had found themselves a breathing space. Publicity and discussions resulting from our visit, and a general heightened interest in the whole business of East-West relations, meant that more people from the

US and Europe felt emboldened to go and see them. Protected by an almost constant Western presence, the Russians became far more confident. The Trust group were able to hold seminars, give out leaflets, spread information about the likely effects of a nuclear war, and increase the number of signatories to the 'Appeal to Governments and Peoples', while the KGB seemed to hold back from interference. Visitors returned to tell their friends and talk to peace groups, and a network of supporters slowly began to build up in Britain, Europe and the US. It was a network which would soon prove vital.

Karmen, Jean and myself planned our follow-up visit, recruited thirty women by the usual hit-and-miss, word-of-mouth method, raised money for the fares and drew up, with the assistance of the Soviet Trades Union Congress, a complicated itinerary to take place in September 1983, as planned and discussed during our May visit. Then with no warning, twenty-four hours before our flight, the visit was cancelled by the Soviet authorities.

All the visa applications had, however, been granted – except for mine. Ironically, in 1983 Helen John was likewise refused an application to visit the US.

This sudden cancellation was a tremendous blow, because the amount of work we had put into organising, fundraising, dealing with questions and suspicions about the group (including the charge that they were 'Western-oriented intellectuals' and not 'ordinary citizens' like the Peace Committee) and finding enough fluent Russian-speakers to make real communication possible, had been colossal. The women who had volunteered themselves for this exercise in East-West relations were characteristically undeterred. Like water flowing round a rock, they split up into small groups and visited the following year.

Meantime, I wanted to get in touch with the Trust group to explain why we had not arrived in September as promised. Getting support for the group in Britain was uphill work. I personally knew of no other people who could convey a message, nor of any at that moment who were planning visits. Their phones remained cut off, letters were out of the question, Western newspaper correspondents couldn't run the risks of acting as go-betweens. The only way to find out what was happening with them was for someone to go there and see them.

Olga's arrest

In November, 1983 my partner Barry travelled to Moscow with two others. One of his companions was a Russian-speaking academic keen to meet with suspected liberal-minded members of the Communist Party of the USSR. He was searching for signs of hope, but East-West relations seemed to be approaching breaking-point. The 'Cruise' missiles had just arrived by cargo plane at Greenham Common.

A mood of despair began to overtake the peace movement. Huge demonstrations in Britain, the US and Europe, and the unprecedented, high-profile disruptive actions at Greenham appeared to have had little effect on the inexorable process of 'nuclear weapons modernisation'. The Geneva talks on arms reduction were stalled, as ever, with each side off-loading the responsibility for taking any kind of radical initiatives on to the other. The 'Cruise' and 'Pershing' missiles for Europe were meant to preserve the 'balance' which was keeping the Cold War cold. They were the response to the Soviet SS20s that had been stationed in European Russia. The proposal on the table was 'Zero Option' – a US proposal which basically said, 'You get rid of the SS20s and we won't deploy "Cruise" and "Pershing" in Europe'. November 1983 was the deadline for Zero Option. Nobody had ever believed it anyway.

On November 23rd 1983, Soviet fighter jets shot down a Korean airliner which had strayed into Soviet airspace, killing all on board. The Soviets at first denied everything, then lied in bits. The only conclusion the Western strategists and politicians could draw was that they were crazier and more unpredictable than ever. At one point, Reagan's advisers really thought they might launch a nuclear war over the incident, believing themselves about to be under attack.

By late November 1983, the period of relaxation towards the Moscow Group for Trust ended abruptly with the start of the trial of Oleg Radzinski. Radzinski was the young man whose bearded face had stared out from the torn poster we had found amidst the rubble of Brodsky's old flat on our first evening in Moscow. He had been kept in the Lefortovo prison since then, a reminder to everyone of their possible fate, and considerable pressure had been put on both him and his family, who disowned his peace-dissident activities. When he was finally put on trial in Moscow, his supporters tried to attend court but were detained in a police station.

One of those supporters was Olga Medvedkova. However, the day of Radzinski's trial coincided with the last day of Barry's visit. On their last morning in Moscow, Barry and his companions decided to pay a final visit to the Medvedkovs. With barely an hour before they had to catch their flight home, they found Yuri in the flat, scarcely able to hold back his tears. He had just been given news of Olga's arrest on the clearly trumped-up charge of assaulting a policeman. Shortly before this, she had attempted with several others to deliver a letter to Mrs Thatcher, via the British Embassy, protesting at the arrest and imprisonment of Greenham Women.

That same November afternoon, as soon as he landed, my indefatigable partner telephoned me from Heathrow with the news of Olga's arrest, and thanks to organisations such as END and the network built up under the loose umbrella of 'UK Trust-builders', with a few phone calls we were able to generate a swift response. Just how good that response was, was described by none other than Oleg Kharkhardin to a visiting Quaker delegation some months later!

'Within hours of the arrest of Olga Medvedkova,' he told them when they duly raised the taboo subject, 'my telephone was ringing and telegrams were arriving on the desk of the First Secretary of the Supreme Soviet, comrade Andropov himself. What further proof do you need of the hand of the CIA at work?

It is the only explanation! How else could the news of the arrest on a criminal charge of one of this worthless, unrepresentative handful of swindlers have reached the West so quickly? How else could such replies have been coordinated?'

Who would have believed the improbable truth? That yet again, it was not manipulation by oversized organisations staggering beneath the weight of generous government funding that produced swift action undertaken with cool efficiency, but a mere coincidental stroke of luck – in the words of the poet Bob Dylan, a 'simple twist of fate'. That, and the genuinely good-hearted actions of all the people who sent the telegrams and made the protesting phone calls. They responded in such numbers that one could have been forgiven for thinking they were being 'coordinated' or in other words directed, when like all the real movements, they weren't. They simply directed themselves to take action.

It was the deep midwinter between the years of 1983 and 1984, and everything seemed to hang in the balance, suddenly. This dual world, this Tweedledum and Tweedledee, called the Cold War, seemed to be teetering, featherlight. Such precarious instability gives disproportionately grave weight and significance to the acts of individuals.

Perhaps it is only at times such as these – when enormous forces are finely balanced, when the outcome is completely unpredictable – that ordinary powerless people can make a difference. The arrest of Olga indicated a hardening of Soviet attitudes, and with the arrival of 'Cruise' the arms race shifted into a higher gear – its highest, and (but we were not to know that at the time) final, gear

Woman + potato

Everything is forgotten now so quickly, and I too have forgotten what it was like not to know the outcome of the Cold War, not to know that we were not heading into a runaway nuclear war. There were only two possible outcomes, you see: (1) eventually, by accident or paranoia or design, a release of some, or many, or all, of the vast array of warheads now facing each other across Europe. Or (2) there was a negotiated major reduction involving one side being prepared to climb down, lose face, and become vulnerable. Protracted negotiations had shown option (2) to be an impossibility, which left option (1) as the fall-back likeliest outcome. Why, you may ask, did option (3), a continuation of deterrence, a 'modernised' version, not apply? This was because option (3) was in constant and increasing danger of sliding into option (1).

But for the time being, option (3) applied. The 'Cruise' vehicles soon began their regular trips around the leafy lanes of southern Britain. In fact, their exercise schedules were predictable: they trundled down the main roads towards the military bases on Salisbury plain, where their drivers could practise driving them around, pointing them skywards and so on. Soon they began to be intercepted by women – one convoy being brought to a complete halt for several hours by a woman who cunningly placed a potato in the exhaust pipe of the leading truck. The next time you find yourself short of something or somebody to toast or celebrate, may I suggest you raise your glasses to the unknown woman who invented the potato method of stopping a convoy carrying nuclear weapons. And the next time you find yourself thinking that protestors such as her were somehow on the fringe of things, well-meaning but misguided, and wrongly dressed to have been of any importance in the overall scheme of things, I suggest you spend a quiet ten minutes thinking carefully about a nuclear bomb going off on a town or city say, twenty miles from you, and perhaps consider the effects of a bomb dropped by our government on people somewhere else. Then do mental follow-up visits at five-year intervals. Don't forget – don't ever, ever forget what radiation does to the unborn, either.

Those 'Cruise' movements were now being watched by nervous Soviets, who had no way of telling the difference between an exercise and the real thing.

The response within the USSR to the deployment of 'Cruise' and 'Pershing' was to step up its anti-American propaganda to near-hysterical proportions, giving the impression to the hapless average Soviet citizen that unprovoked Armageddon really was about to be unleashed upon them. With distrust at such levels, with the responses so jumpy, who could guarantee it was not? Meantime, the response on the ground was to move forward the deployment of the SS20s into Czechoslovakia and East Germany, thus providing the hawks in the Pentagon with the pretext for Armageddon, and for their own rhetoric of threat-response.

The interception of 'Cruise' missiles grew into 'Cruisewatch', an efficiently dis-coordinated system of blocking roads with female bodies, using CB radio to plot the movements of the convoys. Their progress became slow and, from the military point of view, frustrating. Still, decision-makers who claimed to be sensible pretended that a realistic threat of all-out nuclear war was the only reasonable way to defend Britain against a supposed threat that half an hour spent examining the Soviet realities could have convinced them was non-existent.

The protests on Olga's behalf grew, the ripples spreading wider and wider. Radzinski was sentenced to two years' in a Siberian prison-camp but Olga's trial was postponed to January and she was allowed home on bail.

Her arrest was the Soviets' final, considered response to her daring to attend the meeting with us. Her fate came to seem more and more bound up with the whole direction taken by the USSR. If the state had hoped to deal with the Trust group quickly and quietly, at least they were wrong there. Correspondents from all the main Western newspapers thronged the court for Olga's first appearance. Intense attention was being focused on the outcome of her trial, by Kremlin-watchers both amateur and professional, for whatever happened to her, was coming to be seen as a litmus test for the state of play between hawks and doves within the highest levels of the USSR. The amount of Western attention, and likely response, now ensured that the decision about Olga could only be taken at the top level.

Walking in the woods in the deep midwinter

On December 12th, the anniversary of Embrace the Base, even more thousands of women – they estimated afterwards fifty thousand – turned up. This time, the women at the camp decreed noise, expressing anger and outrage. I went up, with the few women who had now become old friends, the night before, and we held a silent vigil in the night-time woods. Since we had become Greenham heretics, there were members of the opposite sex also there with us. Silence can be strangely powerful, more so than noise. It was very cold, by our standards at least, a few degrees below freezing. We stood there in our circle in the dark woods for a long hour, experiencing all the oddness one does in circumstances such as those, feeling nothing like you think you are meant to feel, trying to dismiss thoughts such as, did I switch the lights off in the car? And then, perhaps I should just allow the thought 'Did I switch off the lights?' to have its space – perhaps it really is the thing I should be thinking. Into all this, other anxieties start to interpose, such as, how do we know when we've stood here for an hour? No one's going to be the first to look at their watch, and, will anyone notice if I shuffle my feet to keep warm? Then like a tiny firefly, an optimistic little feeling winged its way in past all the petty and huge anxieties, and the awareness of cold feet and frozen fingers. The sudden little feeling carried with it this message: that you wouldn't notice it for a while, yet, but something had happened to reverse the whole flow of events. Somewhere in the world, perhaps everywhere in a way that was sub-atomically tiny, sometime in the dead of that winter, the tide had imperceptibly turned.

Later on I went for a walkabout in the woods, which were full of women sitting around camp-fires, drinking tea and cocoa and alcohol and talking and singing. This was what made Greenham so brilliantly different and creative: it was outdoors, which put it right back to primitive, time-tested basics. For a half million years, humans have warmed their spirits with their stories, and with music, around a fire at night. Only in the last fifty or so years, have the fires gone out all over the Western, developed world, to be replaced by centrally heated rooms and televisions. I was walking round, and hearing languages I couldn't understand. There were women there from all over Europe, especially from the Netherlands. Then I stumbled across some American accents. I asked how they had come – had they come especially? Oh yes, they said – they had chartered a plane. I was awestruck – a plane.

The beauty of the winter woods, the fungal smell of the dead leaves, the sharp smell of woodsmoke, the sound of the singing rising and falling, the pinpricks of candle light far off and the yellow light of flickering flames on faces and branches and trunks – I was spell-bound. We had needed so much faith in ourselves to set off on that march, and so many times we had felt ridiculous and I had doubted my own instincts. Like a high spring tide, these women brought with them a huge renewal of all the optimistic energy with which we had set out.

Sometime that December, the two chief negotiators, for the US and the USSR, at the permanently stalled Geneva arms negotiations, also went for a walk in the winter woods. They too must have fallen under a spell, for they found themselves (they were, on this unusual occasion, alone together) in complete agreement on a programme for the implementation of a step-by-step, verfiable, nuclear arms reduction. Somehow, they had found a way to really talk to each other, to develop trust, and so to take the crucial first step. It didn't happen of course, because their governments couldn't agree, but the thought had occurred. As if to kill the new thought before it could grow any bigger, the rhetoric of threats grew even louder from the Cold War governments.

Chapter 25

January, 1984, Greenham Common

By the new year of 1984 I was waking up in the middle of every night. We felt so powerless to help Olga – all we could do was keep up the pressure. I felt that I was going to have to speak to whoever I could find at the Peace-camp to get them to listen to me, to tell them the story and explain why I felt it was so desperately important to show support for Olga. A measure of our desperation was the fact that Karmen and I had contacted an organisation which gave support to Jewish prisoners in the Soviet prison camps, in the *Gulag*, to gain some insight into the likely conditions she would face. 'Harsh' would not be a word that could adequately describe what we were told of those conditions, in eye-witness accounts smuggled out of the country by their network. Things had changed little since Stalinist days. Just as in the Nazi concentration camps, violent criminals were put in charge of 'intellectuals' and political prisoners, food was inadequate, punishments cruel, and the hard labour in intense winter cold could be relied upon to kill off those whose voices the state wished to silence. We began to consider the possibility of travelling, illegally under Soviet law, to wherever she would be sent. We did not know whether we could muster the courage to do that.

Feeling very apprehensive, on a cold, drizzly day in early January I drove round the Newbury roundabout with my stomach churning, dreading the reception I would receive after all the flying accusations over the men-women-wimmin demo business. I knew I would be regarded with suspicion by possibly the majority of the women there. I was alone, I had no idea whether I would even know anyone there. To make matters worse, I had stopped overnight with Marjorie Lewis in Cardiff on the way down, and had caught an infection in the throat that had reduced my voice to a barely audible whisper.

But, again, my plans were upset, for which I was soon to be very grateful. First of all, I ran into Helen, who fell upon my car with the ravenousness that greeted the arrival of any road-worthy car at Greenham, and asked me to give a lift to some German women who wished to view 'silo corner'. This was the stretch of fence, which had been endlessly cut and repaired, closest to where the missiles were actually kept. It was near the Green Gate, the entrance to the base that was concealed in the most gorgeous woods of all. Here the women who wanted to live free from publicity and free from the annoying public with their irritating questions, and their irritating habit of handing over money, wood and food, hung out, polishing their spirituality. Reluctantly, because night was approaching and I just wanted to put up my tent in some obscure corner somewhere, I agreed to Helen's request. A short while later, a young soldier on patrol on the inside of the fence had been sufficiently provoked by Helen's well-honed sarcasm to summon the military police to our side.

'Is it Mrs John, again?' they enquired, world-weary.

'No,' he replied, and then he pointed to me, identifying me as 'that little one there in the middle,' and told them that I had cut the fence with wire-cutters, and requested that I be arrested. I was seized under the armpits and hauled off, to protests from Helen and squeaks from me, this being the only sound I was capable at the time of producing. Processing me on a completely fabricated charge of criminal damage took many hours, and it was after midnight by the time the police drove me out of the base and deposited me at the Yellow Gate camp fire, where I was warmly greeted – I had become a victim of injustice.

They were all convinced I had been picked on because of my

role as instigator of this business, but my hours under police questioning made it quite clear that I had just been singled out at random. I had even been asked 'What's a normal sort of woman like you doing getting mixed up with this lot?' A question that I did not answer truthfully, more out of weariness than cunning. Interestingly, the WPC who had been assigned to me confided that she agreed with the aims of the Peace-camp, and that the fact of it being a women's action had made her think about a lot of things.

Later as I lay in my sleeping bag in the well-appointed 'bender' I had been allocated, feeling safe from the sleet thrumming on the plastic roof, my toes warmed by a hot water bottle and enjoying the luxury of reading by candlelight, I could only marvel at my good fortune, and give profound thanks to that little soldier who had made my job so much easier. By a wonderful irony, I had been made the recipient of a trumped-up charge just as I was trying to muster support for a Russian woman who had also been falsely charged. I felt extraordinarily privileged.

It was a dynamic time at the Peace-camp, with constant comings and goings, but attitudes were also beginning to congeal. The question of lesbians and heterosexuals was beginning to dominate discussion, both in the media and around the various fires. A lot of the more daring 'Actions' were now undertaken by big groups of very confident young and young-ish lesbians, who had huge fun and didn't give a damn what anyone thought of them or their behaviour. I couldn't help noticing, however, that it was the two oldest women, Jane Dennett and her friend Sarah Hipperson, who would be up long before anyone else in the morning, walking around filling black bin bags with all the rubbish from the previous day's activities and visitors. As it was just after Christmas, there was a lot of rubbish, in particular the half-dismembered carcasses of turkeys donated by well-wishers to a mainly vegetarian Peace-camp. The two of them acted a bit like mothers to the other women, who were mostly much younger. At other gates there were different groups and every day there were women arriving who didn't look like what had become a kind of Greenham stereotype, but Yellow Gate was generally the one the media went to, and hence was the origin of whatever image went out to the public.

One woman in particular had a reputation as the most 'hard-line' of the anti-men tendency. She was American, and with her near-shaven head, militaristic style of dressing, an emaciated body and an expression of intense severity, she seemed to embody everything scary the public had come to stick in between the two words 'Greenham' and 'women'.

A few weeks prior to this visit I had accompanied a coachful of supporters from my local area to the Peace-camp. It was a day-trip, and for many of these devout rural Welsh chapel-goers it was a way of showing appreciation of the Peace-camp women and their gratitude for what they were doing. There were a handful of men with us, for these were deeply traditional communities where many people went out together as couples, or not at all. On our arrival, as the elderly husbands appeared alongside the elderly wives with their food offerings, we were greeted with shouted abuse from a number of women, the rudest and loudest being this strange American. I felt deeply ashamed of the arrogant attitudes so ignorantly displayed. Without local supporters like these people, who spoke up for the women, sent them money and food, and supported them in all sorts of ways, the Peace-camp wouldn't have been there.

I've often wondered about her identity since, as it seemed there was little known about her or where she had come from. Certainly by this time the women were a major security worry to the Americans, and seemed to be able to get through any amount of razor wire. The US must have wanted at least to know what they were likely to get up to next. If I wanted to minimise the influence of the Greenham protest with the public, and maybe find out a few things about what was being planned, I would put just such a woman in there to shout at the male well-wishers turning up, and the reporters, and to be very visible as the hatchet-faced enforcer of a kind of gold-standard of 'militant' feminism which could be guaranteed to alienate 99 per cent of people. On the other hand, her massively off-putting, ridiculously aggressive style was one which was increasingly shared by quite a few of the other women at the camp. So perhaps no outside manipulation was needed to create the image that to this day causes many people to be more frightened than they are inspired by the words 'Greenham Women'.

When it rained, sleeted or snowed we retreated, a few of us, to Jane's Bedford van and told stories. I told them about our trip to Russia and about Olga, and the stories from the beginning. Jane and Sarah had both been at the camp many months, and they told the stories of the times I had missed – how all the lights had fused and gone out at the moment of the first planned invasion of the base, how Sarah had spray-painted the 'Blackbird' – the first Stealth bomber – at the Greenham air show, how Rebecca had said, 'It's all right, don't be afraid, we won't hurt you,' to a US soldier carrying a gun as he entered, terrified, the room of the watchtower she and two others had occupied... The stories were many, and they are told by those who took part in other books, in other places, as they should be, because they are part of a saga which belonged to its time, and won't happen again.

Being at Greenham was so much simpler a life than trying to wrestle with all the conflicting priorities of my life at home in Wales. You didn't necessarily have to blockade a gate or get into the base to make your protest and cause inconvenience – the bottom line was simply to be there. All I had to do was keep warm, which meant collecting firewood, putting the black kettle on, washing up maybe once a day – or not, if I didn't fancy it – stringing the odd sentence or two together for the odd journalist, walking round the fence through the woods, adding to the many decorations on the chain-link, having conversations with interesting women from many different walks of life, as that rather charming phrase goes. I returned home feeling I had had a holiday. This, mind you, was in the cushy days before daily evictions and bender-destruction began.

Two trials

'You're nothing but a pack of cards!'
Lewis Carroll, *Alice in Wonderland*

As Olga's trial date drew closer, Sarah and some of the other women went up to London and asked for a meeting with the First Secretary to the Ambassador in the Soviet Embassy. Once inside, they enforced an hour's silence on the man, having told him what they thought of his country's actions with regards to the Moscow Group for Trust. Sarah, a Scottish ex-magistrate sternly put her finger to her lips every time he tried to speak. Unsure of how to respond to the situation, the hapless diplomat was reduced to having to read the Trust group's proposal, the 'Appeal to Governments and Peoples of East and West', which he had at first refused even to look at. Outside about a hundred more people were demonstrating with placards. Many more sent messages supporting Olga to the Embassy and to Moscow.

Her trial was postponed again, to February. The date arrived, the protests continued, an avalanche of letters, phone calls, telegrams, and sporadic demonstrations and pickets outside the Russian embassy. The trial was postponed yet again. *They were hesitating.* They didn't know what to do. That meant the hard-liners and the reformers were arguing in those Thursday morning meetings in the Kremlin.

Olga was finally tried on March 23rd 1984, found guilty, and given a two-year sentence to a corrective hard labour prison-camp. Then gasps from the scribbling correspondents went round the court as the judge suspended the sentence, in view, it was stated, of her condition. She was pregnant. It wasn't an acquittal, but it was a climb-down. It was a tiny tremor, a crack in the ice-sheet. Someone in power, it seemed, inside that extraordinary place, the old USSR, had been influenced by Western public opinion, and their view had prevailed.

In March 1984 Andropov died. He was succeeded by a very elderly Politburo member who appeared to be very nearly dead himself, Victor Chernenko. He would last a year of hesitancy, as the USSR teetered on the brink of change.

Both Olga and I faced trumped-up charges, by a state whose loyal servants thought nothing of lying if it helped suppress awkward voices. There the resemblance ended. Olga's trial held significant potential for tragedy, and for hope, both personal and political. Mine, like most of the proceedings against peace activists, was an insignificant, merry farce. She faced the possibility of a long prison sentence. I would be fined, or serve two weeks in prison if I didn't pay. I would be surrounded by friendly supporters. Only journalists would be able to witness her court appearance – any of her supporters who tried to enter would be arrested.

In due course I was sent a summons to appear in Newbury Magistrates' Court to answer the charges of criminal damage by cutting the fence and trespass by entering the base, these arising from my arrest in January. The charges were based on the soldier telling lies, but I knew it would be hard to prove it.

With the help of a friend, I conducted my own defence. Mine was just one among many hundreds of cases being heard, and the court in this little market town was sitting just about every day all through 1984, hearing cases of obstruction, breach of the peace, trespass, criminal damage and so on. The many supporters who gathered there daily, packing the small court-room and spilling out onto the steps outside, made it a kind of annexe of the Peace-camp, with singing, dancing, chanting, flag-waving, and the day of my appearance was just like any other. The court was packed to bursting, mostly with young women, who by then had no idea of the part I had played in bringing them there, although Helen and some of the older ones had turned up.

The soldier wore his uniform and told his lies in an unconfident mumble. Worst of all, he was a young lad from a Welsh regiment. The level of unemployment in the valleys of south Wales made the army an attractive option for young men at the time. When my turn came to ask questions, I asked him first of all whether he had a clear memory of that particular afternoon and whether he had had a good, clear view of me and my alleged activities.

My poor soldier trotted like an obedient lamb into the little pen I had provided for him, answering – I've no idea why – my question: 'With which hand did you see me cut the fence?' with the words, 'You used your right hand only.'

When I held up my thumb-less right hand as evidence, there were gasps followed by waves of laughter and the shouts of the magistrates threatening to clear the court. The case was dismissed. I felt genuinely sorry for the lad, who, perhaps instructed by his superiors to pick on someone to make an example of, had had the misfortune to pick on the one woman out of many thousands, physically incapable of performing the action of which she was accused.

Candles

I felt as if the real threat had receded, but had scant evidence to support this gut feeling. The peace movement in the West seemed to have run itself out (with hindsight, I can see clearly that that's exactly what had happened). But ideas don't respect frontiers. Rebellion in various forms was afoot in eastern Europe. Poland had been in revolt against its orthodox Communist leadership since August 1980. The popular movement for real, not sham, workers' rights was growing. In Hungary and Czechoslovakia, East Germany, Lithuania, Estonia, there were movements of people demanding democracy, wanting change. Like the Trust group, they were asserting their right to 'normal' direct contacts with human beings from the 'other side'. And they were supported in the West by the same growing numbers of people who had stood up for the Trust group. Their Communist regimes were reacting in time-honoured fashion, meting out imprisonments and repression, murder. But this time, it wasn't working.

Strangely, the motifs and methods of protest popularised by the Western Peace movement began to reappear in these growing eastern European movements against Soviet control. People did not, on the whole, don balaclavas and hurl paving-stones, scream, shout, or chant standardised, orchestrated slogans. Instead, they held hands, forming vast human daisy chains across or along frontiers and around buildings. They sat down with thermos flasks and food and just stayed in city squares for days. They sang and danced in great circles. They blocked gates and entrances to buildings with their bodies. The candle was the universal symbol of hope, of the truth that may be constantly assaulted but can never be destroyed. Ten years after the start of the Peace-camp, people in Moscow would surround the Lubyanka, the terrifying KGB headquarters. There they would stand, hand in hand with their feebly flickering candles, each one symbolising a life pointlessly destroyed.

On March 10th 1985 Victor Chernenko died. He was succeeded by a man with a strawberry birth-mark on his forehead, a complete unknown from within the Politburo, Mikhail Gorbachev.

A corner turned

With the release of Olga, I felt a corner was turned, even though repression continued during the early days of Gorbachev. Volodya Brodsky was arrested in July 1985. He was charged with 'hooliganism'. The occasion of his arrest was his attempt, with some Dutch activists, to hold an exhibition about civil disobedience actions in the US. Held in prison until November, he was finally given a sentence of three years in prison-camp. Physicians the world over protested strongly on his behalf but he was not released for two years, finally being given permission to emigrate to Israel. At the time of his sentence, as if to bear out Yuri Medvedkov's belief that one goes East, one goes West, the Gdyak family were given exit visas to the United States. In 1986 they were joined by the Medvedkovs. I met Brodsky in London, on his way to a new life in Israel. He had a beautiful young wife, and they had a baby. I often wonder what attitude they have to the Israeli government and to the Palestinians. Eventually, most of the original Trust group members left the USSR for Israel or the US. However, what happened to them, in a sense, no longer mattered, because their work had been successsful. Their idea was now being put into practice by the new head of their own state, never mind that they remain to this day largely unknown and unsung.

Chapter 26

How the Cold War ended

The truth is, I can't remember. I can only remember the bits I have already told you about. It was as though, one minute we were seriously worried that our lives might end with a billowing of mushroom clouds, or a slow death by radiation poisoning, and the next we had forgotten about the whole thing, indeed were embarassed by it – 'Oh that? Well, I never really thought they would do anything so stupid.'

The man who drove a combine harvester

If we want to scrape up a flicker of curiosity about how the nuclear arms race ended, and somehow that seems a near-impossible intellectual feat – perhaps because it is as far from today's Western preoccupations with D-list celebrities and asylum-seekers as you can get – we might as well turn to the man who took the initiative to end it, Mikhail Gorbachev. There are plenty of views on the reasons why the Cold War ended. According to some, it was the West what won it, end of story. But there is no serious dispute about where the impetus for change came from – and that it came from the least expected quarter, from within the USSR.

Russia could no longer afford to go on crippling itself in its efforts to keep up with the West, so the argument goes. These 'modernised' nuclear weapons in Europe, 'Cruise' and 'Pershing', were all part of a clever strategy, one enormous bluff designed to produce just exactly this outcome – Russia would have to throw in the towel, at least so those who like to play this kind of game with our world have said.

It's perfectly true that the USSR could ill afford the drain on a centralised economy of a huge military-industrial complex. But it took an individual, a thinking person, to recognise that and to have the courage to realise the changes that would have to be made.

Right from the start Gorbachev was intent on making big, serious, real changes. He had nice eyes, too, behind which those who met him could discern a real person, not another automaton. He was a trust-builder, a disarmer, a thinker and a true internationalist, who clearly saw the absurdity of the arms race, the stalemate resulting from each side blaming the other, and the fact that 'security' could not be achieved by military means, by one nation at the expense of another. 'Security' had to be collective. This meant a new approach to arms control and to what was going on inside the Soviet Union.

Shortly before he was elected to the leadership he came to Britain and met Mrs Thatcher. His overriding concern was the arms race. From his account of that dinner he obviously found it refreshing to talk to someone who, although with diametrically opposed opinions, expressed herself clearly and forcefully and did not deal in formulaic speeches. Impulsively, he tore up his notes on arms control, and she, he observed, put hers back into her famous handbag. Instead of reiterating the 'positions' pre-agreed in endless rounds of consultations, they just talked about it off the top of their individual heads. Oh, it's not earth-shattering stuff. He took out a little home-made diagram, of the sort we peaceniks were always producing and rather like the one we showed the Soviet Women's Committee, depicting the size of the world's nuclear arsenals as a thousand squares, and tried to get across to her the awesome absurdity of the globally destructive power of nuclear overkill. 'Each little square,' he told her, 'suffices to eradicate all life on earth. Consequently, the available nuclear arsenals have a capacity to wipe out all life a thousand times.'

At last! I'm thinking, reading this a hefty wodge of years later. Someone in power who actually realises this!

Mrs Thatcher didn't really get it, and would never really see beyond the idea that deterrence kept the peace. Nonetheless, he described her response as 'eloquent, emotional and sincere', and the conversation 'a turning point towards a major political dialogue between our countries.'

She would go on to describe him as 'a man with whom we can do business'.

For his next trick, he stuns the British parliamentary MPs in a meeting. They began with the usual list of Soviet acts of aggression – such as sticking SS20s into European Russia, the treaty violations, and so on, but he said he wanted to get off the old merry-go-round and have another kind of conversation. 'I too,' he said 'could start making an inventory of all the actions against the Soviet Union and against the establishment of normal relations. But what good would it do?'

In his speech, he stressed the need for 'new political thinking', described the Cold War as 'an abnormal form of international relations, fraught with military risks', emphasised that 'nuclear war has no winners' and concluded, 'whatever is dividing us, we live on the same planet and Europe is our common home – a home, not a theatre of military operations.'

Gorbachev could not have indicated more clearly to the Cold War addicts, both in his own camp and that of the West, his intention were he to have the opportunity (he wasn't yet in power, remember), to drag them kicking and screaming out of the stalemate and into real arms reductions. Not only the things he was saying, but his whole approach was exactly what the Trust group was asking for. He was building a real dialogue. Within the USSR, he was clearly the candidate who represented change.

As Chernenko lay in his coffin, the Politburo had to decide who should succeed him – another worn-out representative of the status quo, or the obvious man who would take risks? Gromyko, who had been waving at the march-pasts from atop that Kremlin wall longer than anybody else, rather fancied his time had come round. By tradition, whoever chaired the funeral arrangments committee, would also go on to become the future General Secretary (the bizarrely bureaucratic title by which the leader was known). As they dithered about who should do this job, someone called Grishin spoke up:

'Why the hesitation about the chairman? Everything is clear. Let's appoint Mikhail Sergeyevitch.'

Good old Grishin, I say.

Characteristically, though, Mikhail Sergeyevitich didn't take that as *fait accompli*. It went to a plenum, a meeting of all the representatives of the party throughout the USSR at which he made another of his speeches. This time, he talked about *glasnost*, openness, transparency, for the first time. In this society built on secrets, it was a powerful coded message. He said he wanted to 'stop and not continue the arms race'. As he said himself, this was nothing new. But to these statements 'there was a different tone – peace and an invitation to dialogue were in the air.' There was overwhelming and genuine support for his candidature.

What made Gorbachev so different? How had he developed his ideas? Why didn't he just want a quiet comfortable life? He was from an ordinary farming background, and his dad sounds like a sensible decent sort of bloke. At fifteen, young Mikhail was driving the combine harvester. He was practical, and he knew about seasons, growing, planting, harvesting, and how bureaucrats can really screw things up for farmers and peasants just trying to grow food. But what I think really made him different was that he talked to and listened to his wife, Raisa, who was as clever as he was.

Together, they had a little island of trust. It is impossible to exaggerate the significance of this. People informed in Soviet Russia. The poet Mandelstam spoke his poem about Stalin aloud (it was not written down) to no more than a dozen of his closest, most trusted friends, only to find it on the interrogator's desk when he was shortly thereafter arrested, to be sent to his death in a Siberian labour camp. This was the place where Raisa and Mikhail were brought up. This was their context, their background.

The Gorbachevs met as students, they shared a kind of seriousness, a genuine humanitarian concern that socialism should work for people, and they talked in confidence together all their lives thereafter until her death, so much is clear from what he has said. Tellingly, he describes in his memoir how on the night of March 10th 1985, as the Politburo met to discuss who would succeed Chernenko, he and Raisa walked round the garden, talking, and how they always talked outside.

'From the very beginning of our life in Moscow we never carried on serious conversations in the apartment, or at the dacha, one never knew...'

In a speech to the United Nations shortly after he came to power, Gorbachev said that it was people in the peace movement who had made him think seriously about the arms race, had made him realise the urgency and the need for fresh thinking. He and Raisa would have been well aware that the Peace-camp was not a KGB film-set, that it really did exist, and they must have wondered what motivated such a strange protest.

Did Gorbachev know about the Trust group...?

A strange anecdote told me by John Cox confirmed my feelings that news of our disruptive Peace Committee meeting had reached the Politburo. In early 1985, as Chernenko lay dying, a visiting delegation from the British Communist Party was received by a relatively unknown Politiburo member, Mikhail Gorbachev. He surprised them by his apparent familiarity with such new-fangled notions as EuroCommunism, singling out an article John Cox had written himself for criticism, since it proposed the concept of equal responsibility for the arms race.

Gorbachev himself would base his actions upon this view, but at this point he was evidently keen to display a degree of orthodoxy reassuring to his Politburo colleagues. Going on to discuss other recent acts deemed 'unhelpful to our mutual cause of peace and disarmament' he surprised them even more by describing the provocative behaviour of someone called Ann Pettitt who had visited with a Greenham 'delegation' and had brought an uninvited person into an official meeting. He suggested to the astonished delegation that they should keep these peace movement comrades under better disciplinary control. The weird assumption – perhaps not so weird, since it also seemed to be shared by much of our right-wing press – was that the British Communist Party controlled, in a democratic-centralist fashion, the huge sprawling networks of the peace movement, including the Greenham Common Peace-camp. They shook their heads. 'We've never heard of her – we've no idea who she is,' they replied truthfully – which is, to my mind, just as it should be.

In his memoir, Gorbachev describes the deployment of the SS20s as an 'unforgivable adventure'. He ploughs on with his determination to get disarmament moving and in the autumn of 1985 there is a summit with President Reagan in Geneva, the site of the endless deadlocked talks. The sticking-point is 'Star Wars', SDI, Reagan's plan for a kind of space-based laser shield which would finally guarantee, once and for all, that America could not be attacked. It was an idea based on complete fantasy, but Reagan would agree to all sorts of things so long as he could keep his Star Wars plans. The Russians, quite rightly, pointed out that giving one country – the US – the right to have the whole of outer space under its military control was not a wise idea. Nor was the idea of starting an arms race in outer space. That wasn't what Gorbachev was after, he really meant it when he said he wanted to stop the arms race and make really big reductions. Replacing one arms race with another was not what he had in mind.

So yet again, talks got nowhere. Only this time, 'the human factor' as he put it, 'had quietly come into action... we both sensed that we must maintain contact and try to avoid a break.' After sitting and tallking by an open fire, the two leaders agreed to meet again, soon.

Such were the hopes hanging on these meetings, that neither side wanted to the talks to appear a failure, to have produced nothing. The old let-out of blaming the other side was wearing thin. The peace movement had turned into a general world-wide atmospheric pressure. A joint statement was produced to satisfy the cravings of billions for some sort of common sense, to the effect that 'nuclear war cannot be won and must never be fought', and that 'neither party shall seek military superiority'. It says something for the pathetic state of international affairs of the time that this banal statement of the glaringly obvious is described by Gorbachev as 'a truly historic document'. Other softening measures were announced, air traffic between the two countries, humanitarian exchanges, 'contacts between our young people'.

Then, the hawks in the US administration appeared to throw all their toys out of the pram. They attacked Libya, a Soviet client state, carried out a nuclear test right on the deadline of a treaty banning such tests, and Reagan began talking about the 'Evil Empire' all over again.

In the summer of 1986 Reagan sent Gorbachev a letter suggesting a continuation of the dialogue begun at Geneva, but Gorbachev decided he wanted to move faster, and instead proposed a summit in Iceland.

The dropped prompt cards – Reykjavik 1986

They met in Reykjavik on October 10th 1986. Gorbachev's memoir describes how he tried to see the situation from Reagan's point of view. He knew that the Americans considered the Soviet desire to make big cuts in weaponry genuine – because of economic pressure – and so he knew Reagan would be bringing with him a 'big basket', a willingness to meet those cuts. He did not know that Reagan still regarded 'Star Wars' as non-negotiable. There was by no means universal support inside the USSR for the Gorbachev plan for radical cuts in nuclear arsenals. Many of the traditional thinkers in the military were unhappy indeed at these proposals.

It must have been frustrating for Gorbachev, although he was well used to dealing with powerful elderly men who were already showing signs of mental senility. At their first one-to-one meeting, Reagan dropped his prompt cards, and then shuffled through them trying to find the right response to what Gorbachev was saying. But since the conversation he was trying to have wasn't the one the US advisers to their president had scripted for him, the right answers weren't there anyway. At some point in the subsequent meetings, both sides agreed to 50 per cent cuts in big long-range missiles, long-range aircraft, and nuclear submarines. Talks were to begin on the 'Zero Option', the American proposal to dismantle all the missiles stationed in Europe – that is, the SS20s, 'Cruise' and 'Pershing'.

It all looked hunky-dory, but Reagan refused to drop SDI, or even accept a ten-year moratorium on testing for it. So Reykjavik was a failure – these were terms the Russians could simply not accept. Why then does everybody who can remember anything about this time remember it as a big success, a milestone on the road to disarmament – well, the partial disarmament we're living with, anyway?

Because Gorbachev said so, that's why. He decided, on the spur of the moment, to describe it – what in reality was yet another blocked, failed attempt to reach agreement – as a 'breakthrough'. He arrived as dusk was falling in a roomful of a thousand journalists from around the world, all tensely waiting for the outcome of this meeting. Reagan had already gone to catch his plane home.

'When I came into the room, the merciless, often cynical, cheeky journalists stood up in silence. I sensed the anxiety in the air. I suddenly felt emotional, even shaken. These people standing in front of me seemed to represent mankind waiting for its fate to be decided.'

He could have denounced the Americans for their intransigence in refusing to negotiate over their plans for anti-missile technology in space. Most of the world would have sympathised. But, as he writes, 'had we not reached an agreement both on strategic and intermediate-range missiles? Was it not an entirely new situation, and should it be sacrificed for a momentary propaganda advantage?'

Any other Soviet leader, past or present, real or fictitious, would have gone for the propaganda advantage, for the truth was they hadn't reached agreement, but that wasn't their fault. The propaganda war was the true war they were fighting, that was the old world they knew and lived in and to which they belonged. That was what was different about Gorbachev. He said that when he said to his audience, 'In spite of all its drama, Reykjavik is not a failure – it is a breakthrough, which allows us for the first time to look over the horizon' they stood up and applauded. One of the journalists present described seeing Raisa, at the back of the room, watching her husband with tears flowing down her face.

How Newbury got its common back (and a few other places their independence)

In a sense, whatever events followed were mere technicalities. Eventually, the agreements were signed, the objections about SDI were overcome, by agreeing to shelve it for the time being. Gorbachev kept on talking, meeting American writers and artists in Issy-kul with a back view of the Himalayas, meeting Reagan again in America, having frank discussions with about-to-be president Bush, meeting Mrs Thatcher in London, Moscow and Brize Norton, where she suddenly says a most un-Thatcherish thing and remarks that in speaking of first-strike and second-strike weaponry, she is using 'outdated language'. He created trust, he showed a willingness to embark on real dialogue – and he found reciprocation, in the American Foreign Secretary Schultz, in Margaret Thatcher, despite her clinging to her comfort-blanket of deterrence theory, even in Reagan, certainly in Bush Senior.

On the 8th December 1987 the INF treaty was signed, and the process of removal of 'Cruise', 'Pershing' and the SS20s began.

When the Polish, East German, Lithuanian and Estonian people demanded an end to Soviet rule, he did not send in the tanks. For all this, he paid a high price. He still believed, naïvely, that Soviet Communism was capable of reform, and could survive in some form. But it had gone beyond that point a long time earlier.

In July 1991, the Strategic Arms Reduction Treaty was signed, a scant three weeks before the attempted coup to remove Gorbachev from power. The Soviet old guard could take no more 'new thinking' and what they saw as 'concessions to the West'. It was Yeltsin who saved the day, but the state fell apart and became prey to the various bandits in whose hands it largely remains to this day. Gorbachev, looking old, tired and shaken, in his cardigan, survived but would soon be forgotten as history rushed on past him, his compatriots almost knocking him over, the man who led the world out of the arms race, in their headlong rush to get to the shops.

He was a wise and honest leader, astonishingly undervalued by a people who had perhaps become incapable of judging truth of any kind. Poor Gorbachev – he wanted the Soviet people to think, and to act independently and, released from their chains of fear, responsibly. Instead, they behaved like teenagers who have just left home. Appalled at the sight of a nation apparently drinking itself to death, his puritanical streak caused him to react like a foolish parent, and he tried to ban vodka. How they scoffed! 'Lemonade Joe' they called him. His demand for *'glasnost'* – openness, truthfulness – was not exactly greeted with dancing in the street, either.

When he first came to power, he visted factories, touring the country, wanting to see for himself the real state of affairs, not the propaganda state of affairs. 'How are things here at tractor factory no. 57?' he'd enquire.

'Oh, we are overfulfilling our targets, a token member of the workforce would reply, his line manager standing close by. 'No, but how are things really?' the General Secretary of the USSR would persist. They would look at him in incomprehension. Had they dared, they, like the Peace Committee lady, I'm sure they would have blurted out, 'Are you mad?'

When at Party meetings they began to praise his achievements before he even had any, he told them politely to cut the usual clap-trap. It wasn't needed any longer. He wasn't motivated by some messianic religious belief or by any religious belief. He was, I think, an idealist, one who actually believed in that same vision of a fair and just and rationally ordered society that had inspired Colin, my dad, and so many of his generation.

If he had faults as a leader it was probably his naïvety. He seemed to believe the Soviet system could achieve the efficiency and flexibility of capitalism, whilst somehow remaining a centralised, command economy. It was like assuming you could order people to start thinking for themselves. Had he been more ruthless, more of a traditional Soviet leader, he might have prevented the drunkard Yeltsin from making a fool of him in public and seizing power, to preside over the final demise of the red flag.

Now the US reigns alone, waging its impossible war on 'global terrorism' like a child playing blind man's buff. Patriotism blocks the mouths of critics almost as efficiently as fear did in the old USSR, and a nation eating itself to death believes its way of life is the best for everyone, and any means are justified to ensure the delivery of that enlightenment to a world where most people still don't own a car or a television or a telephone, but do still grow some food and sit down to eat it together.

Chapter 27

The dance – Tourcoing, October 1944

But wait a minute! (I told you this wasn't going to be a straightforward journey...)

We have left our two chief protagonists stranded, he chasing a retreating German army across Normandy, she in celebration of the battle of Stalingrad. The outcome of the war is still undecided. We could yet be in for that thousand-year Reich, with blonde women breeding blonde babies to rule the world. We know it all, now, swelled with hindsight. It wasn't obvious then, but hope began again in wartime Europe sometime in January or February 1943.

You can't dictate atmosphere or celebration – parties that go-with-a-bang often do so despite or even because of, an absence of state-of-the-celebratory-art preparations and facilities.

In October 1944, Tourcoing, a textile-manufacturing town in Northern France, held a fraternisation party in a shabby, run-down wooden hall in the Rue de la Croix Rouge, a five-minute walk from Solange's house in the Rue de Renaix. Flags, red white and blue, British and French, the stars and stripes also, draped the wooden sides of the hall. The band was the town band, silver and brass, and they played, not the marching tunes they had been ordered to produce by the Germans, but the new music of the day: swing. The women had been all day at their hair. Wine corks had done duty as curlers, and all wore those big bouncy waves.

The soldiers wore their uniforms, for the good reason that

they had no other clothes. Among them was Colin. Four days after the D-Day landings, his hour had come. The Germans had destroyed the road signs as they retreated across Normandy and the British needed to be able to ask directions from the local people. Colin found himself thus in the front line of the advance across France. Via a stint in a concrete pillbox at the back of the huge windy beach of the town of Calais, Colin had been finally quartered in the town of Tourcoing.

The soldiers lined the sides of the room. Solange was with Raymonde and Fernande, whose fiancé Arsene, a strong man with a huge barrel chest, played the trumpet in the band – the big, jazzy band. As the evening progressed, the bolder of the Englishmen went up to girls and asked them to dance. But many of the servicemen remained drinking at the tables and not moving from their seats, immobilised by shyness.

'He looks nice,' said Raymonde, pointing out a slim man with blue eyes and a slightly hooked nose, older-looking than the other soldiers in their early 20s. 'He's shy, he hasn't asked anyone all evening.'

Step forward, my future-mother, into this little pool of limelight I have created: the equivalent of one human memory, for what other life do the dead have but in our memories, and how else can we remember but in telling our stories as best we can. Step into the middle, cross the room, oh my stick-thin girl, brown from your bike-rides this summer of the German army's retreat, in your white socks and sandals, you who have already risked your life to save another, smile your wide smile, speak to him...

'Vous voulez dancer?'

'Je suis desolé, merci, mais, je ne sais pas dancer.'

He speaks French! She is not deterred. She smiles again. My God she is beautiful, despite having a near-black tooth right in the middle of her upper mouth. (Dentistry in occupied Europe was a problematic affair.) She offers to teach him to dance.

'Alors, je peux vous montrer.'

And so, my mother met my father, thus creating the possibility that I would get born.

Because, of course, without this detour, without this meeting I might never have taken that momentous decision, might never have walked to Greenham…

Encounter with the old woman
with the shopping bag

The last time I spent time at Greenham Common was in the autumn of 1984. There were hundreds of women camping around the place or coming for the day. It was meant to be 'two weeks of actions', but I, like many of us, was too scared to clamber across all the dense razor wire into the base, so most of my time was spent walking on my own or with a friend round the fence, sketching or talking through the mesh to the soldiers on the inside. That was the thing about being at Greenham – you didn't really have to do anything except be there, to feel you were making a difference. It was magically simple.

I found the sight of the fence itself fascinating. I would be enthralled by its visual drama, by its giddy plunges and twisting perspectives, by its transparency allowing the two worlds glimpses of each other, above all by its poignant embroidery – from the inside, metal clips where the freshly-shaven, youthful soldiery joined severed parts; from the outside, multi-coloured wool, paper, flowers, ferns and grasses where the women wove their insubstantial materials into the words and symbols whose message travelled round the world.

The wire mesh lent itself to these traditional female arts of stitching and weaving, and in places it became a continuous, dense multi-coloured patchwork. It was the older women who often did the weavings: they liked to be busy. There was a delightful irony here, for as 'liberated' women we disdained these cosy crafts, these emblems of conformist domesticity. But here they were to become something else, producing a military enraged by cross-stitch that impeded their view, driven to hysteria by embroidery, policemen utterly stumped by women who had knitted themselves together with ordinary, fuddy-duddy wool.

The fence had been pulled down and reinstated so many times it had assumed a more feminine shape, a wavy appearance. In fact, it had begun to look ridiculous.

I was traipsing round the fence with a friend on a blustery autumn day when we came across her, at an isolated, lonely spot on the perimeter, deep in the woodland of oak and birch, a very frail old lady with a kind, wrinkled face. She came tottering down beside the fence, leaning on a wooden walking-stick. We were a long way, perhaps a mile or more, from any road. Even so, someone – someone's mother, sister, daughter – had dragged heavy wooden pallets to lay across the muddy steep gullies to make the going easier, but after all the rain, these were treacherously slippery and almost as difficult to negotiate as the ankle-deep, sticky mud.

The old lady seemed undeterred by all this. She was amazed when I asked her if I could draw her picture. 'Is it because I look so awful?' she said, humorously, speaking with a slight middle-European accent that pronounced 'awful' like 'offal'. From the deep lines round her mouth and eyes, I guessed her to be in her eighties. Had she come to this country forty-four years earlier as a refugee from Nazi-occupied Europe? I think it likely, almost certain. In which case, she probably had family who had been murdered. She wore a whitish, rather shabby raincoat and a black scarf on her head and carried a black plastic shopping bag such as I remember my French grandmother – Memère – always carrying. A small black furled umbrella poked out of the bag. Her dumpy appearance was accentuated by the short black wellie boots, and the way her feet pointed outwards in the awkward, arthritic way of the elderly. I know all these details because I still have the drawing I did, and because she has stayed in my mind. I asked her how she had come. She replied simply, 'I came here on my own.' My friend Barbara and I looked at each other. We couldn't speak.

We walked on and when we looked back for a last glimpse of the old woman, we could see her coming on slowly down the fence, while on the other side, as if summoned to adopt poses of maximum contrast to her steadfast but feeble gait, four US soldiers in peaked caps appeared silhouetted on the horizon. Unaware of her presence in the muddy trough below, on the other side of the saggy, feminised fence crested with rolls of razor wire, they stood with their hands on their hips and their legs akimbo, looking bold, confident, and arrogant.

Because of the shared strength of spirit by which she was inspired to go to that place, despite all the physical difficulties, whereas they were merely paid to obey orders to be there, the old lady and what she stood for would in the end prevail.

In 1992, the removal of 'Cruise' missiles from Greenham Common began.

For several years, the women who had made the Peace-camp their permanent home had campaigned for the base to be returned as common land to the citizens of Newbury. Eventually part of it was and the fence was removed, so I read in the papers, by the mayor and others from the town. Another part of it, near where the old main gate camp was, became a 'Business Park' – a contradiction in terms if I ever heard one. The stone circle and memorial to Helen Thomas, a Peace-camp woman from Wales, who was killed by a military vehicle on the road here, are beside the entrance to the Business Park. The environs of Newbury are a lot less leafy and more built-up, now. Bitterly opposed bypasses ring the town, which like many such red-brick southern English market towns, seems a place under siege by roads and their accompanying 'developments'. Newbury has long since ceased to be 'Newbury, as in Greenham Common'.

Postscript

Thunder and lightning

There is no inevitability about history. Big forces build up like thunderclouds. But where and how and when those energies will be released depends on chance and individuals making decisions.

This is why ordinary people can and do make a difference. It is important to try to know what is going on when terrible things are happening, even when you can do nothing to stop it. Go and see the train with the hands sticking out of it, don't walk away. Be a witness.

The Cold War, and the arms race it spawned, were avoidable and largely the result of decisions made by a few highly paranoid and irrational individuals. The blindness of 'patriotism', in both West and East, built a monstrous military edifice distorting the economies of both the US and the USSR, on the basis of pure absurdity: a game of bluff played with the threat of global destruction. Eventually it would topple, in one direction or another. In my view, it is thanks to the millions of people in the western world for whom protest was a relatively easy option, and to a brave few in the East for whom it wasn't, that the arms race ended with a whimper (the end of the USSR) and not with a bang (the end of the world as we know it).

We are left, still, with the problem of what to do about the nuclear weapons, the only real weapons of mass destruction. They, the weapons and the technology needed to make them, still threaten us, and it is still the case that the majority of people deciding on our behalf to hang on to these relics of a bygone age are woolly-minded male politicians unable to reach a sensible agreement about how to get rid of them. If reading this makes you feel angry then all these days indoors writing this book instead of getting on with my garden will not have been wasted.

We, the women who marched to Greenham and the thousands who followed, who stayed there or went there, succeeded in our aim: we shoved the arms race to the top of the agendas of those in power, and kept it there until someone who could did something about it. We did this, despite the scorn that greeted us from the media and the powers-that-be – not because we were good at campaigning, but because we were bad at it; not because we went about things in a professional way, but because we were amateurs; not because we were clever, but because we were naïve. We wanted to stop the nuclear arms race, which was then the greatest threat to the human race and indeed to all life, and we thought marching down a road a long way would be enough to start people talking and thinking. When it wasn't, we had to do more.

Unfortunately for those who would seek the formula, nothing we did can be reproduced. But fortunately, the spirit in which we did it is infinitely fertile. An effective response to the present threat we humans have devised for our very habitat itself, our planet, will have to be new. As such, all I can say is that it too will appear amateurish, apparently naïve, and coming from the most unexpected of places, will at first be beneath notice.

Meantime, if you can, grow vegetables.